Unlikely Champions:
A Miracle in Williamsport

CHRISTOPHER GALLO

Copyright © 2014 Christopher Gallo

All rights reserved.

ISBN: 1500461970

ISBN-13: 978-1500461973

DEDICATION

To my wife and best friend, Debbie, and our children, Jennifer, Chris and Jessica, thank you for joining me on so many trips to Shea Stadium and Fenway Park, as I followed my passion for the game.

CREDITS

Cover design
Jennifer Gallo-McPhatter, *Jennifer Lynn Photography*
www.JenniferLynnPhotographyCT.com

Cover photo
Bridgeport Post-Telegram, ©Hearst Conn. Media Group, (from left) Chris Kelly, David Galla, Chris Fasano, Todd Halky, Cody Lee, Dan Brown

Book design
Jennifer Gallo-McPhatter, *Jennifer Lynn Photography*
Chris Poston | CAP Graphics | chris_poston@hotmail.com

"*Little League Baseball*", "*Little League Baseball, Inc.*", and "*LL*" are registered trademarks of Little League Baseball, Inc., Williamsport, PA 17701, and are used here for identification purposes only.

TABLE OF CONTENTS

Foreword by Chris Berman 1
Introduction 3

1 Selecting the team from Trumbull's all-stars 11
2 Trumbull's road to Williamsport begins in Bridgeport 26
3 …and continues through the heart of Connecticut 35
4 Teams from the East gather in Bristol 42
5 An easy opening win against Vermont 48
6 Biting nails against New Hampshire 53
7 The Electric Company shows up against Cherry Hill 57
8 A day of destiny with Brandywine 67
9 Going where no team from Trumbull has gone before 77
10 "Hello Mr. Galla. Your assignment, should you choose to accept it, is…to win" 86
11 Golden gloves quiet the Davenport bats 92
12 Two favorites face off 102
13 The "dart pitch" silences San Pedro's bats 111
14 The US champions prepare to face a dynasty 124
15 Championship Saturday 129
16 The championship game 139
17 The winning reaction 157
18 Our champions return home 167
19 …and we celebrate them 179
20 Go West, young men – throwing out the World Series' first pitch 189

21 Remembering the experience and sharing life lessons learned	200
22 A few final reflections	219
Photo Gallery	224
Epilogue 1 – The Next 25 Years - Where Are They Now?	235
Epilogue 2 – The End of the Taiwan Dynasty	256
Epilogue 3 – Congratulatory Letters	262
Epilogue 4 – The Sports Writing Community Celebrates the Victors	270
Appendix	*279*
Acknowledgements	*281*
About the author	*285*

FOREWORD BY CHRIS BERMAN

I remember how much pride there was in the State of Connecticut and really all of New England when Trumbull won the Little League World Series in 1989. It certainly doesn't happen often – Connecticut representing the US in the Little League title game.

I remember watching these youngsters running around the field in their forest green jerseys, celebrating. The joy you saw on their faces is a reminder to everyone that the Little League World Series is still pure. It's fun. It's competition. It's baseball. It's America. Everything was right with it, and I was proud to be from Connecticut.

To have these youngsters, their coaches and their parents put it all together to wave the flag for our country was very cool.

Of course, just like most everyone else of my generation, I played Little League baseball. Our team wasn't very good...we were a long way from ever getting a chance to play in the Little League World Series, but we had fun playing.

We were an expansion team, the Rye Town Eagles (Rye, New York). Just as happens today with expansion teams in professional sports, our coaches didn't get too many of the better players. So when we had our first practices, I knew we weren't very good. I'm not saying we were the '62 New York Mets, but we certainly were not the '61 Yankees either.

I played first base, was a pretty good fielder, but didn't hit well for my size. But...it was *fun*!

I remember when we won a few games against some of the better teams; there was a real sense of accomplishment. It wasn't really important that we won every game or every tournament. Little League baseball is really all about having fun, first and foremost, competing second, but really understanding what teamwork is, and having a good relationship with your coaches.

Sure, when we won a few games, it was like we had won the World Series.

My best memory wasn't about anything I did, a home run or anything like that. We were playing one of the better teams that had beaten us often. Our pitcher that day, a little lefty, 10 years old, pitched his heart out, but the score remained tied going into the bottom of the sixth inning. It had been a well-played, tight contest...very intense. Everyone was on their toes. It was WOW! *What a game*!

Finally, we scored a run in the sixth to win it. We all ran out of the dugout like you see major leaguers do, mobbing the guy who had scored.

CHRISTOPHER GALLO

Then afterwards, we went out and got ice cream.
It was pure baseball; it was great. All these years later I still remember it as special.
I was, and still am, a San Francisco Giants fan; in fact, our whole neighborhood rooted for the Giants. We all loved Willie Mays, but being a first baseman, Willie "Stretch" McCovey was my guy.
At 12 years old, you don't realize how good you have to be to play professional baseball or even college sports. But we were always playing some kind of ball game when we were kids. So, over time, playing so much baseball helped me, maybe subliminally, fall in love with the game. And watching sports all the time, I just loved sports in general.
By the time I got to Brown University, I was a pretty smart fan watching a baseball game. I think playing Little League helped me understand the nuances of the game, maybe not all of them, but, for example, I knew when there was a fast guy on second with one out and the ball was hit to me, how to play it. I was intrigued when I was at a game. Baseball was fun to watch. So, while at Brown, one of my life goals became to be an announcer for the San Francisco Giants.
Now, I never got that job, though I had a chance at it once, but that's another story. I was at ESPN at the time, and wasn't going to leave. So, when ESPN got baseball, one of the highlights of my 35-year career at ESPN was doing baseball games every week; 30 games a year.
I know this all didn't happen because of Little League, but playing Little League certainly stoked the flames a little. Some of my fondest memories were doing games in the middle of the summer, like the Padres at Candlestick Park against the Giants. It's 5 to 1 in the middle of the sixth, but I was having a ball.
I've been fortunate enough to broadcast the Home Run Derby now for 20 years. It's a simple contest, really pure – just hit the ball over the fence. Who doesn't remember as a kid wanting to hit it over the fence? It's every kid's dream. I just love how simple and pure the Home Run Derby is, just like Little League baseball.

Chris Berman
July 31, 2014

INTRODUCTION

"Do you believe in miracles? YES!!"

That famous line, uttered during the 1980 Winter Olympics by ABC sports announcer Al Michaels, described the emotional final seconds of the US Hockey Team's stunning 3-2 victory over the Soviet Union en route to winning the Gold Medal.

The **Oxford English Dictionary** defines *"miracle"* as "a surprising and welcome event that is not explicable by natural or scientific laws and is therefore considered to be the work of a divine agency." It's also the title of the 2004 movie telling the story of a remarkable event dubbed the *"Miracle on Ice."*

Trumbull National's unlikely 5-2 victory over the titans from Taiwan in the 1989 Little League World Series, though not a *"Miracle on Ice,"* still, even a quarter-century later, evokes memories of a Little League upset like no other. Similar to its hockey counterparts, the Trumbull National team won the hearts of American sports fans by stunning the mighty Taiwanese to win the Little League World Series.

Teams from Taiwan ruled as Little League champions for the previous three years, crushing their US opponents by scores of 12-0, 21-1, and 10-0. Taiwan won 13 times in those last 20 years, while no team from Connecticut had made it to the Little League title game since 1965, before Taiwan ever entered the tournament.

The Taiwan kids could hit, they could field, and they could run.
Hard, gracefully, and fast.
The Fundamentals.
And, they could pitch.

As Trumbull National's Manager Tom Galla put it, "You're crazy to think you can win it all. When you think about the things that could happen, it's a minor miracle that we did. Somebody up there has to *want* you to win."

A beautiful, late summer afternoon graced Williamsport, Pennsylvania. The boys of summer from Trumbull, Connecticut, have outwitted and outplayed the team with the dynasty to uphold, the key play arriving in the top of the fifth inning of the six-inning, winner-take-all Little

League World Series championship game that held a national television audience captive at their television screens.

With Trumbull clinging to a now-tenuous 4-1 lead, Taipei's best hitter, Chien-Chih Lee, stepped to the plate with the bases loaded and only one out. He smashed a line drive off the left-field wall, usually more than enough to score the runners from both third and second base. Trumbull leftfielder Danny McGrath, an Australian native just learning to play this American game, had other thoughts, grabbing Lee's shot and uncorking a one-hop strike to catcher Cody Lee, nipping runner Chieh-Hao Lai in his attempt to score from second. The play proved so close that ABC television analyst Jim Palmer questioned whether the Trumbull catcher actually made the tag in time.

Trumbull intentionally walked the next batter to once again load the bases, this time for Chih-Hao Hsu, who slapped a hard bouncer to Jason Hairston at third. The Trumbull third baseman juggled the ball momentarily but grasped control and stepped on third, barely beating Chien-Chih Lee to the bag for the third out. What could have resulted in a disastrous inning for the Trumbull youngsters ended up with their returning to the bench with a 4-2 lead. Taiwan had not trailed this late in a title game in Williamsport since their 6-0 loss to Kirkland, Washington in 1982.

Trumbull carried a 5-2 lead into the sixth inning, thanks to Ken Martin's fifth-inning lead-off blast deep over the left field fence. Chris Drury closed it out in the sixth, the final out recorded as a long fly to the warning track in left field that settled into Dan McGrath's glove. McGrath leapt in joy, arms raised in triumph, and the home crowd responded with a resplendent roar of delight. The Trumbull dugout emptied, teammates piling upon one another, burying Chris Drury on the mound of joy. The celebration began...

By all accounts, the kids from Trumbull should not have made the championship game, much less won the title, a fact that Palmer and play-by-play announcer Al Trautwig repeatedly pointed out during the proceedings by tagging the US representatives "heavy underdogs." In making these predictions, the sportscasters had history on their side, as the US had not brought home the prestigious Little League championship trophy since 1983. No team from the East Region had won since 1975, and no team from Connecticut had won the title since Windsor Locks in 1965.

But as the game unfolded, Palmer changed his tune: "Trumbull doesn't know it's not supposed to win," he observed at one point. *The New York Times'* Jack Curry said, "They wore their underdog label like a charm."

What the Trumbull team and its crafty manager *did* know is that if you're good enough to get there, you're good enough to win. In a one-game, winner-take-all scenario, anything can happen.

This book celebrates the 25th anniversary of a magical summer that captivated a nation, a state, a small suburban community, and the entire

UNLIKELY CHAMPIONS: A MIRACLE IN WILLIAMSPORT

Little League world. Indeed, Trumbull National's historic, if unexpected, victorious season forever changed the lives of everyone involved. Together, we will follow the team's journey to victory in Williamsport with analyses of key games, key plays and key moments, all through the eyes of the players and their coaches.

But playing flawless baseball – an unimagined possibility for a 12-year-old boy – alone is not enough to win the Little League World Series. As in any sport, the team had to catch a few breaks along the way, and Trumbull surely caught their share.

The late A. Bartlett Giamatti, former president of the National League and commissioner of major league baseball in 1989, worshipped the sport and the field upon which its players pitched, hit, caught, and threw the horsehide. When rumors first surfaced in the late 1970's that he might become president of Yale University, located just 20 miles to the east of the sleepy town of Trumbull, the media quoted Giamatti as saying, "The only thing I ever wanted to be president of was the American League."

In an essay entitled "The Green Fields of the Mind," published in his collected works *"From a Great and Glorious Game: Baseball Writings of A. Bartlett Giamatti"* [© 1998 by A. Bartlett Giamatti], Giamatti, who served as Commissioner of Baseball, poignantly described the game as follows...

> It breaks your heart. It is designed to break your heart. The game begins in spring when everything else begins again and it blossoms in the summer, filling afternoons and evenings, and then as soon as the chill rains come, it stops and leaves you to face the fall alone. You count on it, you rely on it to buffer the passage of time, to keep the memory of sunshine and high skies alive, and then, just when the days are all twilight, when you need it most, it stops.

Each spring, millions of 10-to-12-year-old boys and girls put on their uniforms, grab their leather gloves and bats, and "PLAY BALL!" just as thousands of older athletes take the field from legion teams to the minor leagues to the major leagues. And similar to their big-league diamond heroes, every Little Leaguer has dreams of his or her own, sometimes more realistic dreams... maybe to be president, or to become a teacher, a lawyer, a soldier, a school-bus driver, perhaps a firefighter. But as the snow melts on Little League diamonds, those dreams transform into winning the Little League World Series.

Baseball, the national pastime, attracts passionate fans, fanatics who study the game, play in fantasy leagues, collect bubble-gum cards, purchase autographed balls, bats, photos, and other mementoes on eBay or at a local baseball card show, get to games early to watch batting practice, and, with gloves at the ready, maybe snag a ball that comes their way. When the game ends, the kids go home only to hide under their bedcovers with a radio to catch a late-night game that has traveled into extra innings...

When their own leagues start up, thousands crowd Little League diamonds throughout the world, whether empty lots in the heart of a city or a cow pasture in the country. The early games may just draw their parents, siblings, and grandparents. But then the crowds grow as the teams start winning: first in the local all-star contests, and then in state and regional competitions... until before they know it, they're playing in Howard J. Lamade Stadium in South Williamsport, Pennsylvania before 40,000 American-flag-waving fans chanting, "U-S-A! U-S-A!"

Since 1953, they've also played this game before the millions watching on television, first on CBS, then as part of ABC's Wide World of Sports, and more recently on ESPN, which covers all the regional tournaments.

But even before television, the Little League tournament, which started in 1947, proved a national treasure. In the first decade of the tournament, only US teams competed to determine the World Series champion. Then, in 1957, Little League officials decided to go global by adding four teams from outside the United States. The decision made an immediate impact, with the team from Monterrey, Mexico winning the title that very year. Moreover, the Mexicans' pitcher, Angel Macias, threw a perfect game in the championship game, a 4-0 victory over La Mesa, California, the only such piece of perfection ever crafted in Little League World Series history.

In the years following tournament expansion, the US lost its dominance to foreign competitors. For example, as previously cited, prior to the 1989 game against Trumbull, Taiwan had won the title three summers running, outscoring their US opponents 43-to-1 in the championship games.

Was it any surprise that the world regarded the Trumbull team as a heavy underdog? Why would 1989 prove any different than recent history? Based on their success, experts and fans alike generally agreed that players from Taiwan could hit the ball farther, run faster, field better, and dominate on the mound.

Pressure weighed heavily upon the team from Connecticut to restore some level of national pride to the country that created the game of baseball and founded Little League. In 1989, on that sunny, late-August afternoon, then, **it all came down to Trumbull against the World**, a challenge the team accepted with skill, determination, and the passion to become "**Unlikely Champions.**"

That Trumbull team of champions comprised accomplished, likeable kids who, against all odds, played out the dreams of every Little Leaguer, from the time they first set foot onto their neighborhood diamond to winning the Little League World Series. Each youngster has his own inspirational story, each took a different path to adulthood, and each has led a distinguished, remarkable life, traceable to their experience with that memorable Trumbull Little League bunch of boys.

But without the passion, selflessness, and courage of the men who led them -- Manager Tom Galla, by day an insurance salesman, by night a supreme motivator and baseball strategist who knew how to get the best out of his team, and his staff -- those boys might not have achieved such glory. The challenge of those adults? To get a group of 11- and 12-year-olds to buy into the "team" concept, to cope with the pressures and challenges of facing the best in the world... and to handle the victories with humility... *and* pride. The adults also had to remind their players that, after and above all, this was a time to have fun.

The story of the Trumbull National All-Star team's championship quest opened in July 1989 with Tom Galla coaching his 12-year-old son Dave's Little League team, the Mets. Then the League's Board of Directors asked Galla, Bob Zullo, a Trumbull roofing contractor, and Ed Wheeler, a retired Bridgeport policeman, both also coaching in the Trumbull National Little League, to get a team of the best 11- and 12-year-olds ready to compete in the post-season tournament.

Tom Galla and his staff had but two weeks to shape this group of youngsters for their first game and the coming rigors of the next six weeks of competition, leading up to the World Series championship game on August 26th.

It's a good story that Tom Galla still enjoys telling to anyone interested in listening. Reality, however, proved a bit different.

As Galla recounted, "I keep telling everyone we put this team together on July 1st and we played our first game on July 15th, which gave us two weeks, but, in fairness, we knew who they were and, for the most part, they knew each other."

The boys had played against each other since they started playing Little League baseball. Some attended school together, not strangers, but not necessarily friends.

The boys played the game with varying skills, varying egos, and varying goals. They themselves knew who among them played the best, an important element because the kids chose 10 of the All-Stars, with the coaches filling the final four spots of the original roster plus two alternates.

Galla continued, "I had coached these kids the two years before in the All-Stars. When they were 10, I coached them and we won a tournament in Shelton. Most of them played on the All-Star teams for a number of years so they knew each other well, and I knew them well."

Ed Wheeler remembered that tournament in Shelton. "They dominated as 10-year-old kids, so we knew what they could do. We worked with them for two years to get them ready, and not just in the summer but every Saturday during the winter in the gym. I expected we could go all the way with these kids."

Around the world, nearly 7,000 other all-star teams got ready to go after the same prize: the Little League World Series championship. And each coach told his team the same thing that Tom Galla told his players on July 5th, the first day of practice for the Trumbull National All-Stars: "We can win this thing. We will be going to Williamsport -- there is no doubt that we will be there."

They knew they had something special. But did Galla really believe his own words? If you ask Tom, he would state emphatically, "Absolutely!"

Galla's home contains boxes full of news clippings, each recording various stages in his team's journey to the championship. But one set of clippings – those recording the District 2 tournament, the first on that journey – seemed meager in contrast to the rest. It remained at this early stage, that, even Galla held doubts about where the road would end, "I didn't think we would really go as far as we eventually did. No one knew," he will reply quietly when asked about it. Of course, no one could have imagined they would end the season as champions of the Little League world.

But for the team to succeed, the players themselves had to buy into Galla's optimism. At this stage, many unanswered questions remained – questions that would ultimately determine the team's fate.

But before anyone could answer any of those questions, Galla and Zullo had to assemble a team. Of course, baseball skills would prove primary but the intangibles would ultimately determine champions -- the ability to focus, handle pressure, and remain motivated, among others. Most importantly, the coaches had to select players who truly believed they individually possessed the goods to go all the way. Self-confidence? Key.

Throughout the championship drive, different patterns of interactions between players and coaches evolved, as did relationships among the players themselves.

Each player knew that, at their age, "next year" didn't exist. They held one shot at the title – the summer 1989.

Ultimately, while I wrote this book to tell the story of this extraordinary group of 12-year-olds and the adults who helped them become "Unlikely Champions," I also endeavored to relate how their experiences during that magical summer of 1989 changed their lives forever and how they learned that if they worked hard and believed in themselves, they could achieve the seemingly impossible...a lesson we could all learn.

And remember this: Although winning the Little League World Series had a tremendous impact on their lives, so did it change the lives of their families, their coaches, and their community for many years to come.

After becoming Little League World Series Champions, how could life ever be the same?

Go ahead, talk to anyone from Trumbull who knows their story and they say it will forever be remembered as one of the most important ever in the history of Trumbull, and if not, then at least the last 50 years. It was so

UNLIKELY CHAMPIONS: A MIRACLE IN WILLIAMSPORT

magical an event that it ranks as one of America's best sports stories, as well, right up there with the "Miracle on Ice."

Then in 2012 as part of its 200th anniversary, *The New Haven Register* ran a series of stories in the Sports Section called "200 at 200" in which it shared "200 stories about the most fascinating sports people, places and events to grace these pages," including one story entitled, *"Trumbull National captures Little League World Series crown."*

So, as Tom Galla starts off his version of "The 1989 Little League World Series Champions Story" that he wrote for the Trumbull Historical Society, "Now that you know the final results, let me take you on the trip of a lifetime" or what pitching ace Andy Paul described as "a perfect storm of fun."

CHRISTOPHER GALLO

CHAPTER ONE

SELECTING THE TEAM FROM TRUMBULL'S ALL-STARS

Unless you hail from Trumbull, Connecticut, or root for the Red Sox, 1989 was not a year to remember in the history of baseball. In fact, it "...may have been the most depressing year in baseball history since 1919..." [*Baseball: An Illustrated History* by Geoffrey C. Ward and Ken Burns].

In 1989, several notable but forgettable events rocked the world of Major League Baseball, the biggest involving all-time hits leader Pete Rose. On August 24, Commissioner Bart Giamatti banned Rose from baseball for gambling on baseball as a player and as manager. Rose, a shoe-in first vote pick for the Hall of Fame, maintained his innocence and refused to admit he had violated baseball's Number One Rule. Eight days after banning Rose, Giamatti, an unabashed fan of the game, suffered a fatal heart attack.

What made 1989 so special for Red Sox fans was not their 83-79 record and third place finish in the American League East, nor was it that their roster included two future Hall of Famers – Jim Rice and Wade Boggs. The magic involved Carl Yastrzemski, the first Little League graduate to gain admission into Cooperstown. "Yaz", the first of many former Little Leaguers to enter the Hall of Fame, and Little League both got their start in 1939.

Early February in New England saw snow piled up everywhere and even more precipitation in the forecast. Opening day for the Major Leagues in April seemed so far away...and so did opening day for Little League. But signs of both approached. Pitchers and catchers would report to Major League spring training camps in Florida and Arizona in only another week. And a public service announcement on the local radio station informed listeners that sign-ups for Trumbull Little League's annual tryouts will be held, with practice to follow soon thereafter. The same routine occurred in Little Leagues everywhere. Opening Day was fast approaching.

And so, as Little League Baseball celebrated its 50th anniversary, 1.9 million boys and girls in 6,840 leagues in 33 countries began the quest to be crowned World Champions in this most special year for the organization. It would take more than 12,250 games to determine who would wear the crown.

In 1989, Trumbull Little League had grown to include two leagues: the National and the American, each comprising five teams with 12 players on each team at the "major" level. The league also included teams in the "minor" divisions focused on providing younger players with the nurturing and learning experience they would need in order to move up to play at the "major" level.

Trumbull Little League added a softball program in 1986 to teach girls how to play softball in a competitive environment. Then, in 1989, the town formed a Challenger Division to enable boys and girls with physical and mental challenges to share the joy of playing baseball.

Among the three programs, 800 boys and girls participated with the benefit of more than 100 volunteer parent/coaches during 1989.

No matter how good a team they assembled each year, the Trumbull All-Stars could never seem to make it past the teams from Fairfield in the Districts or Stamford in the States. Until 1989, no team from Trumbull had won more than one game at the State Tournament level, let alone advanced to Bristol or Williamsport.

The regular season

In order to ensure a level field of competition during the regular season, Trumbull Little League puts its teams together with the coaches selecting players from a pool of players not previously assigned to a team. Not everyone follows that practice…

Jason Hairston, who coaches baseball in Virginia, said the competition is not always fair. "Here in Virginia, I see so many stacked teams; teams that have all the talent," he said. "It's not a lot of fun if you're playing one of those teams. What I thought was great about how Trumbull Little League was set up was that we always had a fair competition during the regular season, because none of the teams was stacked with all the best players."

Tom Galla had coached the Mets since his son David reached his tenth birthday. "I was like a million other fathers who coached their son. The Mets had finished last the prior year so I got the first pick. Guess who I took? Chris Drury. My son Dave was automatically on the team. We also got Danny McGrath, who was a good pitcher. We ended up winning the season. We won three years in a row. We were winning just about all the time and I'm trying to get all the different players into games. So one game we were really blowing somebody out and I decided to take out all my best players. So I pulled Chris. Well, you would have thought I just broke his arm. That's just how competitive he was. I said, 'Chris, take it easy.' I wanted to give some of the other kids some innings."

Tom Galla's assistant coach on the Mets that summer, Ray Baldwin, recalled what it was like coaching Chris Drury. "Having Chris on the team was like having another coach. Even as a nine-year-old, people identified Chris as a future star. His maturity level and work ethic were good. There was no fooling around for Chris Drury. He was intuitive, and seemed more mature than the other kids, even at that age. He knew the right thing to do, almost all the time. There was very little coaching we needed to do for Chris; he was that good."

Andy Paul remembered facing the Tom Galla-coached Mets. "I loathed playing against his team, the Mets, during the regular season because he always had the best players and always found a way to win. I played on the Phillies with Ken Martin under Coach John Heher, who was a great coach and a great man."

"I miss him," Andy continued, "Coach Heher collapsed and died of a heart attack refereeing a basketball game in 2000 or 2001. There were some really great Phillies-Mets games that season, with me facing Chris on the mound several times, plus lots of other talented players on each team; but they always got the best of us."

The selection process

In 1989, no official rules existed specifying how to select the players for an all-star team to represent a league in the annual Little League tournament, nor were there rules about who should coach the All-Star team. In many leagues, the All-Star team manager is someone who's been coaching for 25 years, and may or may not have a kid playing on the team. As Tom Galla described it, "Trumbull was never set up that way. Trumbull always worked with a current father coaching the team."

Also, in most leagues, the coaches as a group selected the players for the team, but this could create hard feelings among the players not chosen but who thought they qualified. As Tom Galla put it, "The problem with that is, you know, you do me a favor and I'll help you get your kid on the team, that sort of stuff."

So, in 1988, John DelVecchio, who had served as president of the Trumbull Little League Board of Directors since 1983, proposed that the players also have a say in the process. In an experiment, the players received the opportunity to vote for their choice of players. While the coaches still held the final say, the kids did pretty well, and the next season the process changed.

The coaches still put together their list of players, but the players on each team get to vote for the top 10. The all-star coaches complete the 16-

player rosters with the final six selections including two alternates. As assistant coach Bob Zullo quipped to *The Trumbull Times* reporter Bill Bloxsom, "This encourages the boys to make friends. If they get on each other too hard it might cost them a vote."

Tom Galla remembered the selection process, "In 1988, we did it that way and it ended up being identical to what the coaches selected. So in 1989 we did it again and we used it."

"At the time, everybody told me this wouldn't work," recalled John DelVecchio. "Looking back, I think it worked pretty well. I put the ballots together and then met with each team to explain the process to the kids. I told the kids to vote for the best players, not their buddies. No one would know who they voted for because they did not put their names on the ballot."

During the regular season, the boys had faced each other several times, with the Tom Galla-coached Mets finishing in first place. They had played on the following teams:

    Mets – Chris Drury, David Galla and Dan McGrath
    Phillies – Ken Martin, Andy Paul and Harlen Marks
    Cardinals – Todd Halky, Matt Sewell, Cody Lee and Chris Fasano
    Giants – Danny Brown, Matt Basztura and Paul Coniglio
    Pirates – Jason Hairston and Chris Kelly

Eventually, when Matt Sewell got hurt in August, alternate Chris Fasano made the roster, a reward for his hard work and attendance at every practice.

Tom Galla remembers several of the boys made All-Stars as 11-year olds when he coached in 1988. "There was Drury, Basztura, Martin, Paul, Galla, and I want to say Hairston, and maybe Brown."

"These kids began playing together when they were nine and 10. They played against each other in the regular season." So, the selection process that John DelVecchio had implemented worked well, because the boys knew the best players among them.

Todd Halky remembered playing with most of the other guys on the 1989 All-Star squad for several years with some success. So, when he made the All-Star team in 1989, he knew the team was pretty good. But, he had no expectations about what they could do or where they might go. Todd simply considered playing baseball just "a fun thing to do with your friends," and the tournament just a chance to "play more baseball. It wasn't like if we didn't win, then well, we hadn't have been successful. We were just playing baseball."

Todd continued, "We got along well with each other, never had any real problems as a team. But Cody and I were always at each other even though we were best friends. It was just being competitive. We always had each other's back."

Jason Hairston remembered, "It all started the year before. I think the All-Star team the year before [1988] was even better essentially on paper [even though it didn't win]. But what it did was give so many people an idea of where we could go, what we would accomplish the next year [1989]. And that winter, we did a lot of work. We started doing workouts in the fall that went all through the winter."

Dan Brown "...wanted to play on the All-Stars because that's what I did as a kid, I played baseball. I played all kinds of sports. I played baseball, football, basketball, tennis, soccer. Anytime I could play in an organized league, I did. I always played with these same guys since I was nine. So, I expected to be on that team. I wasn't the hitter some of those other guys were, but I always expected to be on the team."

"It was definitely the coaches and the town's [Little League] program that developed a core group of players who were fundamentally sound," Brown explained. "We were serious about it and knew it was more fun to win when you played. Some of us gave up summer vacations to play baseball."

"I was pretty excited to be chosen for All-Stars," recalled Dan McGrath, "as I was unhappy I had missed out a year earlier. It just meant playing ball into the summer with friends and hopefully traveling. I didn't think about the Little League World Series at all...well, about when we reached regionals I did. I just wanted to play more baseball... I hated to sit around and do nothing; playing more games at a higher level was very interesting to me."

"When I was chosen for the All-Star team," Cody Lee said, "I thought it was the best thing that would ever happen to me. Todd Halky and Chris Fasano were teammates. I knew most of the other players that made All-Stars pretty well, except for Harlen Marks and Dan McGrath. After spending all this time together, we're all pretty good friends."

Each player considered it a big moment to represent Trumbull.

Selecting the coaching staff

After the team returned from Williamsport, Bill Bloxsom of *The Trumbull Times* put it well when he described why Tom Galla appeared "the perfect man for the job": "It was [his] caring, the ability to see through the glare of the lights, to the reality of the situation that made Galla the perfect man for the job of guiding this group of players to the top of the Little League baseball world."

"The league's board selected the coaches and I was on the board, which certainly helped," said Tom Galla. "I wanted to coach this team. I felt that I knew the kids and I knew the game pretty well. So I made it clear to the board that I wanted the team."

John DelVecchio said the other league coaches also had a say in selecting the All-Star coach. "There were only five teams so there weren't that many guys to choose from, but Tom was a good baseball man, as were

Bob and Ed. Also, you have to choose someone who has the time and ability to devote to the team, with practices every morning and evening. How many people can take that kind of time away from their jobs?"

In addition to Tom Galla, members of the Trumbull Little League Board of Directors included John DelVecchio (president), Tony Autuori, Ray Baldwin, Carl Charles, Joe Desabia, Betty Halky, George Hairston, John Heher, Matt Kenosh, Hank Rydecki, Nancy Sparks, Wayne Stokes, Doug Waterbury, and Bill Woods.

"Tom knew his baseball, for sure, and had a good grasp of the game and a good grasp of talent," noted Ray Baldwin, who had coached the Mets with Tom for several seasons. "He had the ability to put people in the right spots and at the right time. He had some tough decisions to make once the team was formed about who would play. He had 14 kids on the roster but only nine could play at any given time. Obviously, parents want to see their kids play, and the difference in the talents among the kids was not great. So, this created situations where somebody wasn't going to be happy about how much playing time they were getting."

Tom Galla once again asked Bob Zullo to serve as his assistant. They had coached the All-Star team in 1988, which lost in the District to Stratford and "...a kid named John Paola, a big lefty, who threw the ball hard and beat us."

Bob Zullo, a roofer, proved "the tough guy who's not really tough," according to Ed Wheeler. "He loves the kids."

Ed Wheeler, a carpenter, pitched batting practice, serving as the team's pitching coach, and he worked effectively during the summer to teach both Chris Drury and Andy Paul "all the junk" he could, such as the "dart pitch" and knuckleballs and sidearm deliveries. Later, the "dart pitch" would mark the turning point against a talented California team in the US finals.

"Where he got that from, I have no idea," said Galla. But Wheeler quite happily related how he came up with the dart pitch. "The dart pitch was designed not to hurt their arms; they don't break their wrist when it's thrown. It was pretty simple to teach, it's like a circle change-up like the pros throw. You can't put much on the pitch because you're not holding it tight. I just figured it out pitching batting practice to the kids."

Andy Paul described the "dart pitch" as "delivered by pinching the sides of the ball and sliding it through your fingers in the delivery like you were throwing a dart. I used it sparingly to keep hitters off balance so as to not automatically have batters think I was throwing a fastball every time. However, once those home runs happened in the San Pedro game I used the dart pitch as my primary pitch, and my fastball as the changeup."

Baldwin also recalled when Ed Wheeler began working with Chris and Andy Paul on the dart pitch. "The work that Ed Wheeler did with them, teaching both the dart pitch, was great. First, it was a good pitch because there was no strain on the arm like a curve ball, and second, when you're facing the caliber of team you were facing in Williamsport, you're not going to fool them with a fastball. Chris was just the right kid to be taught that pitch. Ultimately, so was Andy Paul, although he was a little reluctant because he thought he could continue to throw the fastball, but that didn't prove out in the California game. Finally he realized he was going to have to adapt a different pitching strategy."

From Galla's viewpoint, Zullo held great baseball knowledge, particularly as a hitting instructor.

"In my mind the thing that made [Zullo] so invaluable was his experience and his instincts to always do the right thing, to plan it out ahead of time," Galla related. "I was more of an impulsive kind of guy, fly by the seat of my pants. He wouldn't let that happen. He wouldn't let me make a bad decision," Galla maintained. "I wanted to take pitchers out earlier to save them for future games, kind of like what Westport did this year (2013) and he said, 'No, no, we don't do that, we win today and then worry about what we are going to do tomorrow.' That was Bob."

Ed Wheeler's special talents as an assistant included being the team's "pressure relief valve." "He was good with the kids. He was the guy who would console them. I always felt like I was the tough guy," Galla commented. "But when I asked my son David about that, he said I wasn't."

In reality, these kids didn't need a "tough guy" coach. They came to the team wanting to play and wanting to learn.

"They responded to what we asked of them, they wanted to be driven, they wanted to be pushed," Tom Galla affirmed. "But Ed was the guy who would console them afterwards; there were some tears throughout the process, and usually it was Ed that handled that."

"We always had pool parties for the kids," Ed Wheeler added. "They called it 'Wheeler World.' We always celebrated here. It was a big part of winning; if the kids can't celebrate winning, then what does it all mean?" The name Wheeler World "…came from one of the kids when he was interviewed after a game. Instead of going to Disney World, he said he was going to Wheeler World."

Ray Baldwin agreed with Tom, "Bob Zullo was another good baseball mind, a good complement to Tom. Tom respected him a great deal. He had his role. And the kids loved Ed Wheeler. Tom was kind of the hard-ass. The three of them were a great combination and each brought value to the success of that team."

"Once we reached the States, Ed Wheeler couldn't sit on the bench or in the dugout with us," said Tom Galla. "Still, the three of us would talk, preparing for the next game as soon as one game ended. Our conversations were like, 'So who do you think we should start tomorrow?' We talked about things like that. When we went to the Regionals and Williamsport, Bob and I were together 24 hours a day. We only saw Ed at practice, so some of that discussion between the three of us went away."

Getting the team ready
From Day One, Manager Tom Galla knew his team possessed potential. "Obviously, I knew we had a good team," Galla remembered.
But we hear plenty of stories about baseball players having "potential" that never pan out. Just look at the list of Major League first round draft picks who never became stars, let alone make it to "The Show." Let's just say, it's a long list.
There are no sure things in baseball. Even a team with top-to-bottom talent can have a bad game and get knocked out of a single-elimination tournament. And then one must factor in luck. So if you asked Tom Galla how he thought his team would do, he probably felt nervous, not willing to commit too much of anything about the team's chances.
Looking at his pitchers, Tom said, "Chris Drury and Andy Paul were our top-line starters. But we also were counting on Matt Basztura and Matt Sewell" to pitch in when needed. "We had confidence in their ability," Galla continued. Not only could they pitch, they "…had a good assortment of pitches. But most of all, they were poised individuals. They don't get rattled."
Tom Galla and his staff immediately start working to form these boys into a cohesive unit. Practice began on July 5th, with their first game scheduled for July 15th. That's not a lot of time to get a group of 12-year-olds ready for the biggest challenge of their young lives; one they wanted to win, just like every other kid playing.
Tom Galla organized the practices just as he had learned in college, a rigorous practice schedule with an emphasis on batting, fielding, and game situations; the fundamentals that every team must focus upon until reactions become second-nature. Double sessions were common every day until the tournament started, and often for non-game days.
"Everything I did, I did from memory from my college days," Galla remembered. Besides batting practice, the team practiced "situation baseball," such as rundowns, cutoffs, runners on first and third, the double-steal, and others. Tom remembered the team as "…beautifully prepared."
Andy Paul remembered how hard they worked that summer. "Practice and more practice. You wouldn't think a team that loaded [with talent] would practice as much as we did. It would be easy to rest on our reputation and early success, but we put in a lot of time working on the fundamentals at Unity Park [Trumbull Little League's home field], hours of infield practice. We really honed our skills at Unity leading up to the championship run."
The coaches set a tone that carried throughout the playoffs: on the field, they were all business; off the field, they tried to create a relaxed atmosphere so that the kids could relieve their tensions and participate in the

activities of a normal summer vacation. So the coaches frequently scheduled pool parties, movies, and watermelon and popsicles after practice for the whole team as well as the parents and the coaches themselves.

When it came to ground rules for the team, Galla made it simple – baseball was to be their top priority for the summer, which meant no family vacations and no missing practice.

Later, when Jason Hairston showed up late one afternoon, Galla added another one – don't be late if you wanted to stay on the team. Danny Brown had a similar experience, when he was "…late to one of the early practices. I was given an ultimatum by Mr. Galla, 'You can either come on time or not come anymore.' I think I was playing tennis and had lost track of time. I knew he wasn't kidding around."

"Yeah, I kind of gave everybody an ultimatum," Galla admitted, "saying, if you're going to be part of this team, you have to be committed 100 percent. You can't miss anything including practice. Kenny and his family went to Cape Cod every year, so Kenny made the decision to come back. It was a good decision on his part. Jason Hairston played a lot of soccer, and he wanted to continue to play soccer. I said, 'You can continue to play soccer as long as it doesn't interfere with anything we're doing.' Everybody made their own decision. There were a few kids who got left behind because they decided they had other things to do. Luckily for us it was none of the stars. There were a couple of unhappy people who made the wrong decision."

David Galla remembered being "drilled every day to make the routine plays and not try to make the spectacular play. That's a Bob Zullo-ism. That's what he told us every day. That stuck with me then, it stuck with me through high school, through college, and after college, and I teach my kids that now. You're not going to get very far if you can't make the routine play."

Ed Wheeler knew "These kids were good athletes, so we really worked on our defense at each practice. We had infield-outfield every practice for a good half hour or hour, so the kids knew what they were doing when they got the ball. They knew how to field it and where to throw it. One of our main jobs was to get them to just play ball, and keep them level-headed, and not think they were better than everybody else. You can't play as good as you can play if you're thinking that. We wanted them to fear the other team and work hard every game."

After the first week of practice, Tom Galla sat his team down and asked them if they knew why he had worked them so hard, been so tough. "They didn't answer," Galla said. "So I told them we wanted to go to Williamsport and win a world championship. That raised a few eyebrows; then we went back to work."

Andy Paul remembered that "John Heher was probably the first person to actually talk about the fact that we could make it to Williamsport.

He took me to the Eastern Regional tournament the summer before [1988] to give me a sense of what could be and I spent a lot of time practicing with him before the All-Stars, even during the winter inside in the gym. One of my favorite pictures from that summer is Coach Heher high-fiving me after a win at the Eastern Regionals that was in the newspaper. Although he wasn't a designated All-Star coach, he was along for the ride and was instrumental in Trumbull's rise as a Little League town."

From the first day of practice until their season ended, 52 days later, they would spend every day together, either practicing, usually twice per day, or playing games. During the District and State tournaments they would go home each night with their families. But once they reached the Regional tournament in Bristol, they would be a family. They would eat, live, play, and sleep as a family, pretty much a 24/7 commitment until the tournament ended.

In one sense, it's like going to camp, where they would occasionally reconnect with their real families, and in another, it's an early-life lesson of the nomadic life that often occurs once you go to college or play professional sports.

The impact on their families and friends proved tough as well. Everyone would need to adapt to something none of them had likely experienced, a life on the road, a life with a schedule that they didn't control. They put family vacations on hold until… Well, no one wanted to talk about that. Their rigorous schedule meant practice twice per day nearly every day until…the summer ended, either in tears or victory.

The kids would feel plenty of pressure. Or would the adults feel the pressure more? Twelve-year olds can be resilient; especially when made to think what they are doing is fun, distracted from the real pressure of the situation at hand. Let the adults feel the pressure. Let the adults take the pressure off the kids.

Tom also wasn't afraid to ask for help during practice, such as when he asked Bernie Martinelli, who had coached the Trumbull All-Star team a few years earlier, to come talk to the kids.

"I was always looking for help, and he was a good baseball guy," Galla said. "This was early on, maybe during the States, and you never know what sinks in with the kids," he commented. "Usually at that age, you always had the feeling that they were listening and absorbing, and appreciated what you said to them, but you never really knew."

And as with all Little League teams, a few parents will always help out on an informal basis, perhaps throwing batting practice (BP) or doing other things that need doing. Andy Paul's dad, Ken, remembers tossing lots of BP that summer. "I may have thrown a hundred thousand baseballs for batting practice that summer."

Without the support of the Trumbull Little League Board of Directors, led by President John DelVecchio, who took care of so many administrative details, and John Heher, Little League District 2 Administrator, Tom Galla and his assistants might not have had the focus and the countless hours necessary to ready the boys for the challenges ahead.

Later, when the team returned from Williamsport, John DelVecchio provided the leadership that would keep everyone grounded when requests poured in for the countless endorsements and participation in events everywhere and anywhere. As Ken Paul put it, "These volunteers provided the necessary infrastructure to react to everything as the team won. It happened so fast; it was such a whirlwind. They had to be prepared for so many things."

"Certainly, they were very talented kids, and yes, we worked them very hard," Tom Galla affirmed. "We stressed defense as much as we stressed offense. We didn't make many errors in the big games. I think our defense really carried us in the game against Taiwan. But we never stressed making the spectacular play; we stressed making the routine play...

"As an example, our shortstop Danny Brown was a good athlete, a solid player, not a spectacular player, not a flashy player, but he made all the plays. Jason Hairston, on the other hand, made the spectacular plays; there was something special there."

As the team's shortstop, Danny Brown loved "having that big target, Kenny, at first. It really helped our defense. And when Chris was catching, I thought our team defense was great."

Setting expectations
Todd Halky doesn't recall having any great expectations as the All-Star workouts began. But he knew he was still playing baseball, and that's what mattered. He had never really played any other sports, never had the desire to play anything but baseball.

"I don't think any of us had any expectations," said Jason Hairston. "That's why I felt it was surreal when we won. I know our parents had some idea what was at stake, and certainly Mr. Galla had expectations right away. He wrote it on his folder." Hairston remembered one day after practice, Tom Galla sat everyone down and told them that "This team was destined to be there [in Williamsport]."

Hairston remembers the hard work.

"We did two-a-days at the age of 11 and 12 years old. People don't understand the level of commitment we had at that young age. I think we all expected to work hard, play hard. We weren't forced to do it. We loved to do it. We were kids who enjoyed playing baseball. It's what we did during the summer. As we moved along through each tournament, we were just playing baseball. It probably wasn't until we got to Williamsport, that's when we knew we were doing something different. Certainly, after losing in the Districts the year before, I'm not sure we had any expectations."

"We enjoyed every win," Dan McGrath recalled, "but I wasn't

cognizant of what would lie ahead, having no real experience beyond Little League. I didn't have a base to judge the wins on. All I knew was that we were doing better than previous teams [from Trumbull]."

When Tom Galla became his All-Star team coach, Andy Paul's view of him changed. "I kind of feared him as an opposing player because he was authoritative. But my perception of Coach Galla changed when he was my coach for All Stars – I loved him, I respected him and always listened to what he had to say. He commanded attention and demanded the best out of us... very regimented and a great motivator. The kind of coach you wished every young man had a chance to play for and learn from."

Watching Tom in the dugout during several of the televised games, viewers could see that he wore his nervousness on his uniform's sleeve. In fact, several sports writers indeed described Tom Galla as "nervous" in stories they wrote leading up to the Little League World Series.

"Sure I was nervous, I was always nervous. I didn't want to lose." Galla said. Did Galla feel a higher level of responsibility because of what stood at stake for these kids? It certainly translated into a great deal of responsibility leading a group of 12-year-olds playing with so much at stake, whether they realized it or not...

"I think it's just my nature," Galla responded. "I knew that at any time, we could get beat. We had some real close games. We got beat by Park City in the Districts, 2-0. We ended up beating Manchester 1-0. Just one break either way and we could have lost the game and that would have been the end of it. I was relaxed when we were winning 15-to-2, but otherwise I was nervous. I didn't want to lose."

Tom continued, "I didn't want to go home crying like I did when I was a kid playing Little League baseball. I had it in my mind that someday I would be the starting catcher for the New York Yankees, and if we didn't win a game I would go home crying because we lost the game even if it wasn't my fault...talk about competitive."

"Little League [officials] kept preparing us to lose, telling us how proud we should be of our accomplishments," Tom remembers. "Then when we got to Williamsport, they told us how the team from the East is always the worst team. And I said, 'Oh, thanks for telling me that.'"

So, from Day One, he talked to the kids about the hard work it would take for the team to get to Williamsport. They didn't want to lose either, though they may not have had the same reasons in their minds as Tom did in his.

The amazing aspect of this story is that these 12-year-old-kids – 6th and 7th graders, not high school seniors – possessed the maturity to understand that nobody hits a home run every time they get up and nobody pitches a perfect game each time they take the mound.

UNLIKELY CHAMPIONS: A MIRACLE IN WILLIAMSPORT

Tom Galla agreed, "You're right, sometimes you have a bad game. When you are 12, you have to learn how to deal with that stuff. Twelve-year-old kids think in a totally different light."

Tom Galla explained. "A good example is when we pulled Andy Paul out of the [championship] game [after he struck out twice]; the weight of the world was off his shoulders. He was better a moment later. It was nice to see and we knew we couldn't put him back in there. It was just too much. Andy gave his heart and his soul in the California game [two days earlier], and there just wasn't enough time for him to bounce back."

Tom's son David explained what these 12-year-old boys thought at the time.

> I vaguely remember my dad talking to us about going to Williamsport. I had no expectations when the team was put together. I remember as we progressed through the tournaments being surprised that there was another tournament to go to after that. We obviously kept winning.
>
> So it was, ok, we played in the Districts and beat Bridgeport. What are we going to do now? Hey, we're going to play in Forestville, Connecticut. Where's that? The States are different because we were traveling to different places to play different teams. When we got to go to the Eastern Regionals, we were told it was going to be a lot of fun because we were going to be living together in one place with our friends. And it *was* fun.
>
> The coaches did a good job shielding us from the fact that there was an end goal. There was never any pressure. There was the hope for improvement. There was the expectation of winning baseball games. We felt we put a pretty good team on the field and all we wanted to do was go out and hit the ball hard, make all the plays, not kick it around. That's what we were looking to do. It was fun because our parents came; they were in the stands.
>
> I think that the older you get the more pressure you put on yourself to be successful, maybe you heighten the level of expectation. Unfortunately, I think that is what is happening now with Little League. It's no fault of the kids; it's a TV thing. They go out, they have to perform well; they do the pre-game interviews, the post-game interviews. We didn't really have any of that. When we won our games, we went home and went swimming or delivered newspapers. It was just different. And it's not the fault of

Little League. It's just the way it is.

Each and every player agreed that he loved playing for Tom Galla. Todd Halky: "Coach Galla was a phenomenal coach. He knew baseball, was a baseball guy, and had played at a high level. And he didn't treat us like children, he treated us like men. He expected a lot from us. He put us together, knew how to get the most out of each one of us at the right time, and he worked us like dogs. Without that we would have been a bunch of soft kids and never would have won anything. I loved playing ball that summer."

Jason Hairston: "Mr. Galla was disciplined, hard on us, but, also, he was fair. I remember one time, when he was questioning my effort during one of the District games, I was very frustrated. But we talked about it and after that we were fine."

Dan Brown: "He was great. He's an intense guy, always fair and nice, and he made you serious about baseball. But we also had fun doing things off the field that summer. [Coach Galla] was the kind of guy who always knew how to teach you the fundamental things about the game. He certainly treated everyone with respect. Being a player himself, he approached the game in the right way, preaching to us to not to try to do too much, play good defense. We all enjoyed playing for him. He also knew the game was more fun when you played it well. He always believed in us and brought intensity and energy to us."

David Galla holds a slightly different perspective, obviously, as Tom Galla performed double duty with David as parent *and* coach.

"Playing for my dad was great. He was a great dad and a great coach. He worked us hard. Sure, he was tougher on me, because he wanted me to be better than he was, just like I want my kids to be better than I was.

"Playing for my dad was no different than playing for anyone else. My dad certainly had his on-field intensity. After the game, if I had a bad game he told me why I had a bad game, but he also tried to pick me up if I was down or lessen the enthusiasm if I had a pretty good game. You know you are only as good as your last at-bat. He wanted me to be consistent and play with a high level of intensity without going overboard."

Matt Sewell "Always thought of Tom as a really good coach. When I got to play for him, I thought he was a fantastic coach. He always wanted us to play to our expectations."

Dan McGrath remembered Tom Galla "Being hard but fair. My memory is fuzzy about all the details but he demanded respect, earned our respect, and was well prepared. Coach Galla punished me pretty hard one day for lipping off to a parent helper. He made me run a few laps for not showing the respect this gentleman deserved. That event stays with me even now and it is that level of respect I demand from the guys and kids I now coach. Funny how something simple like that can have an impact."

"He also had two great helpers," McGrath noted. "Eddie was our pitching coach, showed us some stuff and had a great love for the game. Big Bobbie Z, I admired, as he was a great helper, guide and very personable…"

CHAPTER TWO

TRUMBULL'S ROAD TO WILLIAMSPORT BEGINS IN BRIDGEPORT

To advance to the Little League World Series, Trumbull National had to win three tournaments – the District (a double-elimination contest), the State (also a double-elimination contest), and the Eastern Regional.

Trumbull National participated in the District 2 tournament, played at Artman's Field, located on the campus of Blackham School in Bridgeport's North End, about four miles from Trumbull National's home field in Unity Park. Trees line the left and right field sidelines, with all seating beyond the outfield fence -- not quite the norm for the typical Little League field.

The seating included four sections of bleachers, and a dozen or so picnic tables, along with impromptu seating beneath several large shade trees. On a brilliant Sunday afternoon in July, the temperature approached a humid 90 degrees as the umpire called "Play Ball!" to launch the 2011 District 2 championship game.

With no bleacher seats behind the dugouts, the kids stood far from the cheering and the watchful eyes of their families and friends who have come to watch the game. The 2010 District 2 champions, Fairfield American, who made it to the 2010 Little League World Series in Williamsport, faced their cross-town rival, Fairfield National. Fairfield American had ended Fairfield National's six-game winning streak the previous afternoon to force today's winner-take-all District 2 title contest.

The crowd of maybe 400 people, mostly families and friends, sounded like 2,000, never stopping their chants of each batter's name as he steps to the plate, and acknowledging every good play by someone on "their" team. Horns tooted every time a runner scored or a ball flew over the eight-foot fence for a home run. The crowd was into the game. Those were their kids out there, living their Little League dream of playing baseball and ...a bus ride to Bristol and then Williamsport, for more games.

After five innings and two hours, Fairfield National stormed back from a 10-3 deficit to grasp an 11-10 lead, aided by several misplays by Fairfield American. The way it played so far, as in most Little League games, no lead is safe.

The crowd buzzed: "How many runs would American need to score in their half of the sixth to hold off an expected additional rally by National in the bottom of the sixth?"

Everyone knew that a one-run lead would not suffice.

Nearly one hour later, American has scored 16 runs and taken a 26-11 lead. National need only muster 15 runs in their final at-bat.

Fairfield American's last pitcher of the day, all-around athlete and team leader, Sean Gutierrez, shut down National. American moved on, collecting one more win on the road to Williamsport; one step closer to returning to the Little League World Series.

Fairfield National would not play in Williamsport that year; let their summer vacations begin. [Author's note: Fairfield American's road to Williamsport ended in Bristol with a loss to Rhode Island in the New England Regional semi-finals. In 2012, Fairfield American returned to Williamsport, winning two games in the loser's bracket before falling to the West Regional champions, Petaluma, California, for a second time.]

The 1989 double elimination Connecticut District 2 tournament ran from July 15th through August 3rd at Blackham School Field in Bridgeport. What did the coaches expect as the District 2 tournament opened?

If you asked Tom Galla, he had told the players from Day One and every day since that they would make the trip to Williamsport and the Little League World Series. Of course, he kept that to himself, as did the coaches of the other 6,830 teams getting ready to play.

As the tournament began, Galla and his staff held no expectations, nor did the kids or their parents. Sure, they had some pretty good players, but doesn't every all-star team have pretty good players? Sure they had a goal of going to Williamsport, but doesn't every team think they can...go...all...the...way?

As 12-year-olds, the kids really didn't understand what they faced. To a 12-year-old, baseball is simply a game. It's something you do in the spring and summer. It's supposed to be fun. Sure, everyone wants to win, but what's this stuff about pressure and focus and making plays and execution all about? When can we go swimming?

Apparently, no one held great expectations at the start.

Why? If you browse the newspaper clippings collected by Tom Galla since 1989, you'll see his files overflow with column inches of newsprint from every tournament, *except* the District 2 tournament. In fact, his District 2 clippings are almost non-existent.

When asked why, Tom responded, "You don't think I really believed all that stuff about going to Williamsport, do you? I'm sure glad the players never figured that out."

Regardless of their personal expectations, the players could rest assured of one fact – one team from the East would go to Williamsport, but one of the other eight teams there would return home as champions. But, at this point, anything was possible...though not necessarily probable... or even likely.

Mike Riccio, manager of Trumbull National's first draw of the tournament, the Stratford National Little League, considered his all-stars pretty good.

"We had a nice team, a good, solid team, but we looked like Pee-Wee's compared to some of the Trumbull kids. They were physically a lot bigger than us. That just adds credence to how good the Trumbull kids were. Their pitcher, Andy Paul, was really on his game that day. Some of our kids were afraid to face him."

Trumbull opened with an overwhelming 23-0 win over Stratford National Little League on Saturday, July 15th, painted by Andy Paul's perfect game, in which he struck out 13 of the 18 batters he faced. Trumbull's bats also sprang to life as they raked 24 hits, including Andy Paul's self-supporting two home runs and another from first baseman Ken Martin. Trumbull jumped out to a quick 5-0 in the first, led 10-0 after three, and finished by scoring 11 runs in the fifth as 16 batters came to the plate.

Andy Paul and Matt Sewell led the 24-hit attack with three hits apiece, followed by Chris Drury, Jason Hairston, Cody Lee, Danny Brown, and Ken Martin with two hits apiece. Basztura and Lee each drove in four runs, followed by Matt Sewell's three RBI's. Paul Coniglio, Jason Hairston, and Ken Martin each drove two runners home.

Tom Galla remembered the opener against Stratford National. "Andy is pitching a perfect game and we have a huge lead, so I said to Bob [Zullo] that I want to take Andy out. What are we wasting him for? Let's save him," and Bob answered, 'He's got a perfect game going.' I didn't even know he had a perfect game going. So we left him in.

"I knew Andy had pitched a great game, and I knew we had hit the ball really well, but I didn't feel like we were going to win the Little League World Series. I realized that either we were much better than the other teams, or maybe we had caught a team that was very weak. As it turned out, we were very strong."

Stratford National's Mike Riccio, who owns a sports memorabilia business, remembers talking to his son Mike Jr. about the game.

"Yeah, all I remember is they were a lot bigger than us. It was like we were playing the St. Joseph High School varsity baseball team that day."

UNLIKELY CHAMPIONS: A MIRACLE IN WILLIAMSPORT

His teammate, Mike McPadden, echoed those sentiments when he called Andy Paul's fastball "just unhittable." [Author's note: Today, Mike McPadden is a police officer in Shelton, Connecticut.]

Two nights later, on July 17th, Trumbull Nationals' high-octane offense continued with 11 hits in support of Chris Drury's 12-strikeout, five-hit pitching in a 15-3 victory against Stratford American Little League. Drury quickly fronted the Nationals to a 1-0 lead leading off the bottom of the first with a home run. Trumbull added three more runs in the first, keyed by run-scoring hits by Andy Paul and Todd Halky, before Stratford retired them.

Stratford American grabbed one back in the top of the second on two hit batters, a walk, and an RBI single by Jeff McNiff, then scored two more in the top of the third on a two-run blast by Greg Duch, closing the gap to 4-3.

And that's as close as they got, as Trumbull stormed back with five runs in the third inning, increasing its lead to 9-3. Todd Halky's bases-clearing double proved the big blow of the inning. The offense added two runs in the fourth on Ken Martin's two-run homer, and another four in the fifth on Martin's second round-tripper, a three-run shot, and a solo home run by Andy Paul.

Todd Halky, Matt Basztura, Drury, Martin, and Paul supported Trumbull's four-home-run attack with their respective multi-hit games. Martin led the collection of RBIs with five, followed by Halky with four, and Andy Paul with three. Chris Drury walked three in picking up his first tournament win, while Matt Sewell closed it out with a scoreless sixth inning, striking out three.

Trumbull's offensive outburst continued against its next opponent, tournament host team North End East (Bridgeport) Little League, on Saturday, July 22nd, in a 19-1 win highlighted by a 13-run fourth inning that put the game away. Andy Paul picked up his second win of the tournament, striking out eight, while walking none and allowing just five hits.

Once again, the bats roared, with three hits each from Chris Drury, Martin, and Cody Lee, while Ken Martin smacked his fourth home run of the tournament, having homered in each of the first three games. Matt Basztura, Dan McGrath, and Chris Kelly each contributed to the 19-hit attack with two apiece. Ken Martin led in RBIs with three, followed by Chris Drury, David Galla, Matt Basztura, Jason Hairston, and Cody Lee with two apiece.

With the win over North End East, Trumbull National advanced to the winner's bracket semi-finals on Tuesday, July 25th, against Fairfield American. In prior years, this marked the spot where Trumbull often faltered.

This game began as a real pitchers' duel, as neither team scored in the first two innings of play. Fairfield's Dan Kenney held Trumbull scoreless through two, the first time that happened in their four games. Trumbull National's prolific offense had previously produced early and often, scoring 15 runs in the first two frames of their first three games.

Drury carried his shutout through the top of the third, not allowing a hit. Trumbull's brief offensive slump finally broke when Drury led off the bottom of the third with a home run, his second hit of the game. After the Fairfield pitcher hit David Galla, Ken Martin walked, and Andy Paul whacked a three-run homer for a 4-0 lead.

Fairfield American finally scored a run in the fourth on two hits before Drury snuffed the rally with three strikeouts. Trumbull doubled up with four more runs in the bottom of the fourth. After Harlen Marks walked, Matt Basztura singled, and Ken Martin's RBI single to left scored Marks. Andy Paul's single to center scored Martin, and Andy Paul crossed the plate on Danny Brown's sacrifice fly. A single to left by Matt Basztura closed out the scoring.

But Fairfield American tallied three runs in the sixth on three hits and two walks to make it interesting, before Matt Basztura took the mound and struck out Fairfield American's number two hitter, Mike Silvestro, with the bases loaded, no less, for the final out and an 8-4 victory.

With Trumbull's fourth win, Drury's record improved to 2-0 as he struck out 11, walked five and allowed five hits. Chris Drury and Andy Paul paced Trumbull's 10-hit offense with two hits apiece. Trumbull would now face Park City American of Bridgeport in the District 2 winner's bracket finals.

One week later, on Tuesday, August 1st, Trumbull suffered their only loss of the entire post-season, when Park City American's fire-balling, right-hander Shawn Whitaker blanked Trumbull National on a two-hitter. Whitaker, who could bring it to the plate at a nearly-unhittable 74-mph, allowed hits to Matt Sewell and Andy Paul, while striking out 10. He survived a lack of control, giving up eight bases-on-balls, by never allowing Trumbull to have more than two base runners in an inning.

Andy Paul matched Whitaker's shutout inning for inning until the sixth, when Park City American scored two runs in the top on just two hits and several Trumbull miscues. Trumbull National sat down quietly in the home sixth though Whitaker issued a leadoff walk to Paul and another to Sewell with two outs. Andy Paul pitched a fine game, striking out seven and walking none, while spreading out seven hits.

After the game, Coach Galla took the kids out to outfield where they sat and talked about the game, and he asked them, "What happened?"

Jason Hairston spoke for the team, "Well, Chris didn't get a hit."

"I was flabbergasted by that comment," said Galla. "So I told them that Chris is not going to get a hit every time. He's not going to lead off every game with a hit. Each and every one of you needs to pick him up, needs to pick each other up. If *he* doesn't get a hit then *you* have to get a hit."

Did the team worry that if Drury couldn't manage a hit, well, then maybe the rest of them simply weren't good enough? This challenge squarely confronted the coaches as they returned to the field two nights later against the same Park City American team that throttled them 48 hours earlier.

"You don't know what works or doesn't work. You do what you think is right. You try to figure out what you think is right. You try to react to different situations. You try to steer them in the right direction. Then you keep your fingers crossed," Tom Galla recalled thinking. "I still say to this day that that was probably the best thing that could happen to us. It brought us right back down to Earth. It got the kids to realize that we had to work hard; we had to go get those runs, because we *could* lose."

Andy Paul, the losing pitcher that day: "I remember it being a battle with a large crowd on hand. I think everybody knew it was the two best teams of the District going head to head. They had a good team. I remember they had some strong and physically imposing athletes. The pitcher that beat us was their ace."

"He was a big guy, who threw real hard," Dan McGrath recollected.

David Galla remembered the loss as well. "We faced a pitcher who was just overpowering. We were probably a little overconfident. We said, maybe we're not that good, maybe we need to come out with a bit more intensity the next time." But, in spite of the loss, McGrath remembered "our coaches being pretty upbeat as we had a game in hand."

Jason Hairston, who committed an error in the loss to Park City American, reflected on the game.

"It was a turning point for us," Hairston observed. "We realized we could be beat and that it wasn't going to be easy, that we needed to fight all the way through. Losing that game was a blessing but the way the coaches handled it just showed their leadership and expertise. They said, you know, we had a championship party planned, and we're going to go to the party and have a good time. We'll come back and play them tomorrow, and go ahead and beat them. And we had another party the next day when we beat Park City for the Districts."

"When we lost that game to Park City," said Tom Galla, "we went to Ed Wheeler's house for a swimming pool party. The parents sulked all night, but the kids, within 10 minutes, had forgotten about the whole thing."

The winner of the next game, a winner-take-all District 2 final, would advance to the State tournament, sending the loser on vacation. Going into that game, the Trumbull kids had to feel the pressure. After all, in the first four games of District 2 play, the team had hit a collective .538 with 10 home runs, yet their offensive attack unexpectedly ground to a halt against Park City American. They missed opportunities – eight free passes offered many scoring chances. But the timely hit never happened. It was the first time that Chris Drury did not lead off the first inning with a hit, and it proved his only hitless game of the post-season.

Looking back, Tom Galla didn't think he would have a difficult time getting the kids ready to face Park City again. "I knew they couldn't wait to get back at Park City American."

Sure enough, two nights later, Chris Drury slammed the door on Park City American, allowing just three hits and two walks while striking out 12 as Trumbull National collected their revenge with a 7-0 victory that advanced them to the Connecticut State tournament.

While Trumbull's offense tallied seven runs on six hits and eight walks, it looked as though they would face another tough game when Chris Drury popped a fly to centerfield to lead off the first. Drury struggled again at the plate, managing just one base hit in four at-bats for the day. However, Dan McGrath got the first inning going with a walk, and, one out later, Ken Martin singled. Andy Paul then stroked the next pitch by Chris Lord over the wall to instantly lift the mood and put Trumbull National up, 3-0. Trumbull batted around, appearing a different team than two nights earlier in its 2-0 loss.

Drury's two-out double off the top of the fence in the third scored Todd Halky and Matt Sewell, who had singled and walked, respectively. After Ken Martin walked to open the fourth, Andy Paul put the icing on the game cake by launching a two-run shot over the fence, his second home run of the game, and sixth of the tournament.

The Trumbull kids would play in the Connecticut State tournament. After winning the District 2 tournament, Coach Galla felt "...pretty excited, pretty happy. Trumbull teams hardly ever won the Districts, so it was a big deal winning."

No team from Trumbull had won a State Little League tournament, so, once again, expectations remained modest. But this team was different...these kids could hit *and* pitch, the keys to success in Little League's post-season tournament.

In the six District 2 games, Trumbull National totally overwhelmed their opponents. They hit a combined .450 while their opponents managed a collective .185; outhitting their opponents 72 to 25; scoring 72 runs while allowing just 10; collecting 38 walks while only giving up only 10; fanning 66 opposing batters while only striking out 26 times themselves; and, finally, they slugged 12 home runs and gave up but one. While the records to determine how this six-game performance matches up against previous District 2 champions do not exist, clearly this team could hit and it could pitch.

Chris Drury, Andy Paul, and Ken Martin made the All-Tournament team, accounting for all 12 home runs while hitting a combined .518, scoring 29 runs themselves and knocking in 34 others. In addition, Paul and Drury pitched 34 and two-thirds of the 36 innings played, notching five victories. Andy Paul drove in 17 runs with his 11 hits (a .579 batting average), including six home runs, and scored nine runs. In pitching three complete games, with a 2-1 record, Paul allowed just three runs on 13 hits, with no bases-on-balls and 28 strike-outs.

Ken Martin accounted for 11 RBI with his eight hits (a .444 batting average), including four home runs, scoring 11 runs. Chris Drury hit .525, slapping two home runs, knocking in six runners, and scoring nine times. On the mound, Drury went 3-0, allowing seven runs, 13 hits, walking nine and striking out 34 batters.

Matt Basztura (nine hits, 10 runs scored, and six RBI), Matt Sewell (six hits, seven runs scored and two RBI), and Todd Halky (six hits, four runs scored, and two RBI) also contributed to the team's strong offensive performance.

After winning the Districts, Tom Galla said, "We had a team in the District tournament that hit more home runs than I ever saw hit by any Little League team. And they were *long* home runs. So I knew we were strong. We were trying to play the games one at a time. To think that we could do what we ultimately did was a stretch. We just kept plugging and things turned out just right."

As the team kept winning, the parents, in particular, grew very superstitious, going so far as to ban Sandy Galla from bringing her camcorder to any more games after she had brought it to the Park City game for the first time, a game the team lost 2-0. And you thought the *kids* were uptight…

Sitting in the stands and watching can be pretty tough on parents. Sandy Galla recalled: "We all thought the Districts were nerve-wracking, but in retrospect, they were a piece of cake. The competition got tougher and the level of anxiety went up to new heights at every level of play. We were so happy to have won in Bridgeport and we were all prepared to accept whatever progress we made towards our main goal – Williamsport and the final game of the World Series. I was amazed how greedy I got as the tournaments flowed by. Each win was going to make me perfectly happy, and yet, after we would win, I only wanted more."

Sandy continued, "Some parents would actually have "mini-strokes" when their kids were involved in critical plays. The stands would visibly gasp during any particularly well-played ball."

Early on, to "ease" their nerves, the parents turned to doing what baseball fans have been known to do forever…do crazy things, superstitious things. As Sandy Galla remembers, "We started sitting in the identical bleacher formation, wearing the same clothes to each game, picking up coins from the ground, and crossing and un-crossing our fingers so many times that we developed blisters. Each group had their own little superstitions. I had a handkerchief that I waved, and it had to be tied into a knot just the right way. You even had to time your bathroom trips. We started getting really fancy in the stands. Simple shouting wasn't enough anymore. We had air-horns, megaphones, home-run/hit hankies, signs proclaiming our allegiances, "K" markers, coordinated clothing and best of all, our "bugle boy" Mr. John Coniglio!"

"I know that Mike Kelly, Chris's father, wore one pair of shorts once we got to Williamsport," Tom Galla remembered. "I also became very superstitious, looking for coins on the ground as a good luck charm. It got to the point where Ed Wheeler began tossing coins on the ground where I would find them. Eventually, I became very lucky winning nearly every coin toss that summer." In the end, every little bit of luck helps, and Tom Galla's luck in winning 14 coin tosses out of 16 to decide the home team probably constituted more than good luck.

Even Little Leaguers understand the benefit of being the home team. As Andy Paul said, "I know we had a ridiculous streak of coin toss wins before each game to determine the home team. I think the baseball gods ruled in our favor all summer. Batting in the bottom of the inning each game can do wonders for a team." Danny Brown called it "divine intervention." Call it whatever you like, but it ultimately helped bring the Little League title to Trumbull.

CHAPTER THREE

…AND CONTINUES THROUGH THE HEART OF CONNECTICUT

For Trumbull National, the double elimination Connecticut Division 1 State Tournament started on Sunday, August 6th, in Forestville (Bristol), Connecticut. After drawing a first-round bye, Trumbull National opened against Forestville Little League, who had defeated North Stamford in its first game draw.

As Trumbull moved into the States, in the stands, the parents felt a new level of apprehension, but also a greater sense of pride. Sure, parents of Trumbull Little Leaguers had seen their offspring make it to the States, but this felt different. The hitting prowess and strong pitching they had witnessed at Blackham School gave rise to thoughts that this team might really be pretty good. As Sandy Galla recalled, "The stands were understandably nervous and the smiles on our faces couldn't hide the fact that we were beside ourselves with worry. 'How was this one's arm?' 'How was so-and-so's batting practice?' 'Did they look good?' We would ask ourselves these questions a thousand times and the answers were always the same, 'They look great!'"

On a crisp, cool afternoon following a charity golf event – the **Bobby Bonds Classic** to benefit New Opportunities, Inc. played at Country Club of Waterbury – Rick O'Brien recalled coaching the Forestville team. "We had some pretty good athletes on our team, and had swept through the Districts against some tough competition, so I was feeling good about our chances in the States. We thought our team that year was pretty good, and we were going places that summer, but Trumbull beat us pretty good in those two games. We had a lot of respect for how good they were and were happy to see them win it all."

O'Brien reminisced: "I loved coaching Little League because of my own Little League experience; Little League was probably the highlight of my baseball career. We lost that year in the District finals. But one of the kids on my team that year was a pitcher, Dave Cichon, who was later drafted into the Majors. He was a stud, a great pitcher, who tossed two no-hitters in the playoffs. After we lost in the tournament that year, I just focused on basketball, but it was such a great experience. So, when I began coaching my son, I remembered how exciting it was for kids from my personal experience. I even remember when I coached the Forestville team in 1989 talking to one of the parents of a good player, convincing them not to go to Disney World that summer so their son could play for our All-Star team. I didn't want him to miss the experience. When I see her today, she stills kids me that I ruined their vacation that year. But, it was a wonderful summer.

"As a coach, it was great to see the kids develop physically over the summer. When we started out in May lots of the kids couldn't hit the ball over the fence, but by the time we got to the All-Stars, they were hitting it over the fence. The growth spurt was something special to see happen."

"After losing to Trumbull, I watched them play in Bristol and then I went to watch them in Williamsport with my sons. It was a great family vacation. At the end of our season, Tom Galla spoke at our end of season banquet, and told our kids, 'You should feel like you're the second best team in the world.' That was terrific. He was great."

Tom Galla "...had seen Forestville play a couple of times before we played them. Forestville gave us a good game. They were a solid team. They remind me a lot of the Brandywine, Delaware team. Both were really good teams without a Kenny Martin, Chris Drury, or Andy Paul. You need the big studs, the big boppers [to be successful]. They didn't seem to have the power that we had. We didn't see anything that made us play them differently, no one we felt we needed to pitch around. They were tough, never giving up, always coming back."

The memory of seeing Forestville's home field for the first time sticks with Galla to this day. A banner from 1976 hung on the backstop that read "Fifth in the World" as Forestville had finished fifth in the Little League World Series. "I was really impressed," Tom said.

In 90-plus-degree heat, Trumbull National only managed six hits and four walks off Forestville's 5-foot-5 hard-throwing righty, Chris Murphy, but it proved enough to beat the scrappy Forestville squad. Trumbull scored the only run it would need in its 4-0 victory over Forestville in the second inning. It began when Matt Sewell worked out a one-out walk. David Galla came in to run for Sewell, and Chris Kelly's perfect sacrifice bunt moved the coach's son to second. Chris Drury then lined a single to left field that scored the speedy Galla.

Matt Basztura led off the next inning with a blast over the centerfield fence to make it 2-0. Ken Martin kept it going with a screaming line drive down the third base line, and moved to second when Andy Paul walked. Two batters later, Matt Sewell's two-out single brought Martin home, fronting Trumbull a 3-0 lead.

Leading off the fourth inning, Chris Drury lined Murphy's first pitch far over the centerfield fence with what appeared a home run. However, the umpire called Drury out for stepping on home plate.

Tom Galla, still livid that the umpire made the call: "Yeah, the umpire was trying to do the right thing," Galla said. "But the umpire made a mistake. He was trying to do the right thing. I don't care if he did step on home plate, look the other way. It was a home run!"

As the fourth inning continued, Trumbull scored its final run on Andy Paul's two-out single to right. Matt Basztura and Ken Martin got things going, working back-to-back, two-out walks before Paul's single brought Basztura home.

Backed by the flawless and spectacular defensive play of Dan McGrath, Chris Kelly, Danny Brown and Ken Martin, the hard-throwing Andy Paul posted his second shutout in four post-season outings, improving his record to 3-1. In tossing his fourth straight complete game, Paul gave up five hits, struck out six, and walked two, his first walks of the post-season.

Two nights later, on Tuesday, August 8th, Trumbull's bats dominated in the State Division 1 semi-final with a 15-hit, five-home-run barrage in a 17-2 win over Hamden. Trumbull batted around in the first and second innings, scoring 15 runs to put the game out of reach, and giving Chris Drury, now 4-0 in the tournament, a chance to rest after tossing three inning of two-hit shutout ball. Matt Basztura closed out the game for Trumbull, allowing just two runs in the final three innings.

Ken Martin jump-started the offense in the first inning with a three-run blast, followed by Andy Paul's solo shot. Drury topped off the first with a grand slam in his second at-bat of the inning that scored Brown, Sewell, and Hairston for a quick 8-0 Trumbull lead.

The onslaught launched in the opening frame continued in the second when Matt Basztura led off with a homer and Ken Martin followed with another blast, his second of the game. A string of five singles and four walks brought home five more runs. With a 15-0 lead, Coach Galla felt comfortable and put every player on the roster into the game. Ken Martin finished the game with three hits and six RBI for the day, while Drury added three more hits and four RBI to his offensive stats. Todd Halky and Andy Paul each contributed a pair of hits and RBI, while Matt Basztura put two runners across.

Now Trumbull waited to see who they would play next.

Once again, Trumbull sat alone at the top of the winner's bracket, and would face one of the three teams remaining in the losers' bracket, who would slug it out over the next few days.

Who will emerge from among Shelton National, Hamden, and Forestville?

Galla guessed "Forestville."

Emerging from the loser's bracket stresses a squad, and particularly the pitching staff. So...while the loser's bracket battle builds, what's the winner's bracket team doing? Play the waiting game...waiting to see who they play, rest their pitching staff and keep their bats at their peak. That's all. If you asked Danny McGrath for his thoughts, he would burst in full Aussie tilt, "Ha!"

The day after the win over Hamden, the team received some bad news when Matt Sewell broke his arm, falling off his bicycle while delivering newspapers. At that point the coaches added alternate Chris Fasano, who had attended every practice from Day One, to the roster. It remains a true tribute to Chris that he participated in every practice, every day, with no guarantee that he would ever play an inning in a game. And it also proved one of the "luck factors" for Trumbull to have someone of Chris's ability to step in for Sewell.

"Losing Matt Sewell was tough," Tom Galla admitted. "He was our starting right fielder, and was hitting well, batting over .400. Though he didn't pitch much, he was our number three pitcher, so more nerves. At that point we really didn't know what the future held. When we got to Bristol and had to play four games in five days, it was a real concern. We just didn't know if we could get through with just two guys. We survived it." Dan McGrath would have to step in should Galla need a relief pitcher. Danny Brown knew Sewell's injury "shortened our pitching staff a bit."

Assistant Coach Ed Wheeler "...wasn't worried when Matt broke his arm, because I knew we had some depth on the team, but I was disappointed for him...more worried about him. He and his brother were very close to me because I had them on my team during the regular season. I felt real bad for him. It would have been nice having a lefty pitcher. I remember bumping into him at Caldor's [Department Store] one night, and he comes walking in with a cast on his arm. I almost died. I said, 'What happened?' He said, 'I fell off my bike delivering papers.' So I bought him a video game. Then I bought him a TV. The other kids said, 'If I break my arm are you going to buy me a TV?' We all laughed."

Trumbull would once again face the very tough team of scrappers from Forestville. After a day of rain, the game moved to Sunday afternoon, August 13th, to the Annex in New Haven.

Galla recalled the previous tough 4-0 win and he worried that Forestville might have Trumbull's number in a second matchup. Galla's intuition told him that at this level, playing a good team a second time presented a tougher challenge than the first. There are no slouches when a state title is at stake. The tension built as game time approached.

Tom Galla: "We knew playing Forestville a second time would be tough. The first game was close. I knew they were good. We were going to have to play our best game again to beat them."

UNLIKELY CHAMPIONS: A MIRACLE IN WILLIAMSPORT

Forestville's Rick O'Brien knew the challenge his kids faced playing Trumbull a second time as well: "Trumbull was pretty strong up the middle and their lineup was really something. If you got by Basztura then you had Martin and Paul."

Jason Hairston agreed that Forestville "...was very good. Those two games we played against Forestville in the State tournament were very tough. We had a lot of respect for them."

After Forestville loaded the bases in the top of the first on two hits and an error by Andy Paul, Galla visited the mound and told his pitcher to "...get mean."

Andy listened, got mean, and struck out the next two batters to kill the early Forestville rally.

In the Trumbull first, Chris Drury crushed the first pitch from starter Bryant Martineau, blasting it out of the park. After singles by Matt Basztura and Ken Martin, Danny Brown slammed a down-the-middle-of-the-plate fastball into the trees in deep left field. Brown's three-run shot, his first of the post-season, made it 4-0.

Singles from Chris Kelly and Jason Hairston kept Trumbull rolling in the second inning. After Drury popped up to the catcher, Dan McGrath walked to load the bases for Ken Martin. Martin then furthered the Trumbull lead to 8-0 with a two-out, grand slam to left-center off relief pitcher Jesse Griffin, his second of the post season.

In the fourth inning, Trumbull moved ahead 10-0 when Ken Martin singled to score Dan McGrath and Cody Lee brought in Martin with another single.

Trumbull's offense lit up Forestville's pitchers for nine hits, including two home runs, with Andy Paul looking as tough and mean as ever, shutting down Forestville's bats on just four hits and one walk through four innings, while striking out four. It almost looked too easy. Before this game started, no one would have guessed that Trumbull would put away Forestville so handily. There is *no* safe lead in Little League baseball. *Never!*

At this point, the Trumbull kids probably felt pretty comfortable. Who knows what they really thought? No one recalled feeling any different than when they owned big leads late in other games. So, it caught them totally off guard when Forestville came to bat in the top of the fifth looking like a different team, mounting a six-run rally off ace starter Andy Paul.

That inning began innocently enough with Andy retiring the Forestville lead-off batter on a grounder to Jason Hairston. But it quickly grew messy as Forestville filled the base paths on three straight singles.

Tension... and then Cameron Brooks, Forestville's number-five batter, swatted a grand slam off Paul to change the score to 10-4.

Mike Guerrier followed with another single, this one to right field. Tom Galla reluctantly pulled Andy Paul in favor of Dan McGrath.

Now Galla perhaps most missed his strong backup, Matt Sewell. McGrath got a quick out on a fielder's choice, but three more hits brought home two more runners for Forestville, who now trailed 10-6. McGrath finally snuffed out the rally when he got Luke Robustelli to fly out to Matt Basztura in center field, stranding two runners.

Drury completed Trumbull's scoring in the home fifth with his second solo home run of the game before McGrath finally silenced Forestville in the sixth to preserve Trumbull's 11-6 win.

After retiring Sean O'Brien on a fly to center, Martineau and Brooks singled off McGrath to apply more pressure on Trumbull. McGrath bore down and struck out Mike Guerrier, and followed by retiring Steve Morin on a pop-up to left field to end it.

With McGrath's help, Andy Paul improved his record to 4-1. "Danny shut them down, luckily," Tom Galla remembered.

Galla called it "...another wake-up call for us. When you win 17-2, you don't get a wake-up call. It just feels so easy. But these little wake-up calls are good for you. It just shows you that you have to keep plugging, score as many runs as you can and play good defense, do all the things you need to do so somebody doesn't sneak back and beat you. You can't lose your focus." You're right, Coach, *no* lead in Little League is safe.

In one of their more exciting games, Forestville out-hit Trumbull by 14 to 12, but the difference proved Trumbull's power, as they launched four round-trippers to Forestville's single offering.

When asked if he worried when Forestville mounted their comeback attack, Andy Paul said, "I don't think we were ever in jeopardy of letting the game slip away, though I might have been in prevent defense pitching mode at the time."

With its three wins over an eight-day period, Trumbull outscored its opponents 32-to-8 for the Connecticut Division 1 State Championship.

Once again, Trumbull's offense dominated their opponents, as they compiled a .418 team batting average versus .275 (on 33 hits versus 22), and scored 32 runs to 8, including a 26-0 margin in the first three innings of the three games. That early scoring advantage solidified the confidence of the Trumbull kids.

Once again, the heart of the batting order, Chris Drury, Andy Paul, and Ken Martin, led an offensive attack compiling a .418 team batting average in the State tournament.

Individually, Chris Drury hit .545 (6-for-11) with seven RBI, five runs scored, and four home runs.

Ken Martin accounted for 11 RBI and six runs scored with his 7-for-8 performance at the plate (a .875 batting average), including three home runs. Andy Paul batted .600 (3-for-5), including two runs scored, one home run, and two RBI.

UNLIKELY CHAMPIONS: A MIRACLE IN WILLIAMSPORT

Also contributing to Trumbull's strong offensive output: Matt Basztura, collecting four hits in nine at-bats (for a .444 average, with two of his hits home runs, driving in three RBI with five runs scored); and Dan McGrath, Jason Hairston, Matt Sewell, and Todd Halky each contributing two hits. Leaders in runs scored comprised McGrath and Danny Brown with three each, and Hairston, Sewell, Brown, Halky and Chris Kelly, with two apiece.

With this win, Trumbull's post season record stood at 8-1. The team accomplished something that Trumbull elders believe has never happened before – they stood as state champions and would now play in Little League's Eastern Regional Tournament. The winner of that tournament would advance to Williamsport and the Little League World Series.

After capturing Trumbull's first state championship, *The Bridgeport Post* quoted Tom Galla: "This group of kids has always been a special group of kids. We always thought that if we could win a state championship, this would be the team that could do it."

"I was very excited and relieved to get past that tournament and felt great satisfaction in representing [Connecticut] in the Eastern Regional Tournament to come," said Andy Paul when recalling the victory.

David Galla reminisced… "After we beat Forestville, we celebrated a little. We were proud of what we had accomplished. But…we wanted to get to the next game. We wanted to see what it was going to be like getting to the Eastern Regionals, to stay up there [in Bristol]. We were interested in being able to sleep in a room with 14 [other] guys, and hang out. It was like summer camp. It was fun. We took it seriously, but it was fun."

CHAPTER FOUR

TEAMS FROM THE EAST GATHER IN BRISTOL

The victory in the Connecticut Division 1 State tournament advanced Trumbull National to the Eastern Regional Tournament in Bristol, Connecticut, where they would compete against 11 other all-star teams from the northeast [New York, New Jersey, Delaware, Connecticut (Division 2), Maine, New Hampshire, Vermont, Rhode Island, Massachusetts, Pennsylvania, and Maryland] in a single elimination tournament, with the winner earning one of the eight spots in the Little League World Series in Williamsport.

Thus, Trumbull's road to Williamsport would run through Bristol, Connecticut. As the car drives, Bristol stands less than an hour drive from Trumbull, but getting there proves pretty tough, in the baseball sense. And making it from Bristol to Williamsport, Pennsylvania, home of the Little League World Series, proves even tougher.

Once you exit Interstate 84 about 15 miles east of Waterbury, you drive north on West Avenue past the ever-expanding campus of ESPN, the self-proclaimed "Worldwide Leader in Sports." The road passes ESPN's numerous buildings and multitude of satellite dishes, all surrounded by high-security fencing, turns east onto Route 6, and after advancing through a business district dominated by strip-mall shopping centers, turns left at the Dunkin' Donuts onto Mix Street, a tree-lined, residential neighborhood. After another two miles, you reach Leon J. Breen Memorial Field at The A. Bartlett Giamatti Little League Training Center, a complex of buildings and ball fields which now hosts the New England and Mid-Atlantic Region Tournaments.

The Eastern Regional Tournament, first held in 1957, originally comprised a four-team, single-elimination event. Initially, the tournament transpired in a variety of East Coast cities, with Staten Island, New York, serving as the tournament host six times.

UNLIKELY CHAMPIONS: A MIRACLE IN WILLIAMSPORT

The tournament eventually expanded to a 12-team format, and after moving to the Town of Newburgh Little League Complex in Newburgh, New York, in 1977, it eventually settled in Bristol in 1987.

Games initially played out at the Edgewood Little League Complex on Breen Field. Little League's plans for development of the full complex of buildings, including dormitories and offices, began to develop in 1989. A few years later, Little League Baseball opened the Giamatti complex.

Since 2001, two teams have advanced from Bristol to the Little League World Series in Williamsport, one representing New England, and the other the Mid-Atlantic Region. This change occurred simultaneously when Little League Baseball expanded the World Series to a 16-team field, thus doubling the number of US entrants at the World Series from four to eight. As a result, East Region state champions were assigned to the New England and Mid-Atlantic regions, with the winners from both competitions advancing to the Little League World Series.

Bristol sits in suburban north-central Connecticut, hosts the headquarters for world-wide sports media behemoth ESPN's central studios, and boasts Lake Compounce, America's oldest functioning amusement park. For many years, Bristol served as the home of the Boston Red Sox Double-A minor league affiliate, and stands as the city where former Red Sox star Fred Lynn made his professional baseball debut in 1973 and met his future teammate and future Hall of Famer Jim Rice. The two would play together for Boston from 1974 to 1980. [Author's note: In 1971, Jim Rice began his professional career in Williamsport, playing for the Red Sox Class A minor league affiliate.]

The Trumbull kids, who arrived in Bristol on Sunday, August 13th, were assigned a classroom in an elementary school next to Breen Field with 16 cots obtained from West Point Military Academy. The very hot and humid weather made the situation uncomfortable, as the rooms did not offer air conditioning.

Tom Galla recalled "...it wasn't too bad. We stayed in a kindergarten room. It had its own bathroom, which was nice. Some of the other rooms didn't. We slept on cots. Believe it or not, the cots were comfortable. It was real hot with temperatures in the mid-90's every day. The only relief from the heat was a large fan. The food was not too good. But the volunteers did a great job. But, you know, there were lots of kids."

"We were lucky because the Forestville folks took good care of us," Tom continued. "There was Jerry Dube and his son Matt who brought Bob and I coffee every morning to get us started. Bud Kilduff, who was president of the Forestville Little League, told us to use their field for practice sessions, which was great. This was why we didn't have to worry about a practice schedule. Most important, we were also assigned a team Aunt and Uncle. We got Rita Strahowski and her son Chris, who was 15 or 16. These willing volunteers were with us 12 hours a day making us feel at home.

"For many of the kids, experiencing their first trip away from home, having someone to help make things feel like home felt nice. Rita took them shopping and ran errands."

Todd Halky thought that "…living in Bristol at the Eastern Regionals was interesting. We stayed in a school with bunk beds, kind of like an army barracks.

"It was also the first time some of us drank beer. We found a stash in a cooler in the closet with some pony bottles. Cody also found a condom that we filled with shaving cream and put into Coach Zullo's bed. We had a lot of downtime in Bristol, so we were always doing things like that. I remember one day we saw Stephen King, whose son was playing for the Maine team, which was pretty cool."

All Dan McGrath remembers about staying in Bristol: "I can tell you we couldn't go swimming or skateboarding!"

Jason Hairston was "…excited when we won the States and knew we were going to the Regional tournament. Being a kid and being away from your family was different, and fun. Being able to do what we did every day, play baseball, hangout with your friends, live in one room and sleep all together in one big room, was fun. Then we would get ready for a game. That was a totally different experience than any of us had gone through before."

Dan Brown held slightly different recollections regarding living conditions in Bristol.

"It was a nightmare. We had to sleep on these uncomfortable cots in an elementary school, with no air conditioning, and though the rooms had these large fans, it was very hard to sleep. It was hot, it was loud, and it was a strange place to be. Also, there wasn't a lot to do, especially since the coaches weren't big on letting us watch the other teams play. But, we weren't too far from home, so our families were usually around and we could go out with them."

Very little time separated the games in Bristol.

Trumbull did not receive a bye and faced a grueling schedule – four games in five days, starting in 48 hours on Tuesday, August 15th.

After their routine twice-a-day practices, the day still held plenty of time for the boys to just hang out with one another. The coaches also offered plenty of distractions to relax the kids, including movies and lots of ice cream. The players never got the chance to watch many of the other games.

The frequent pool parties subsided once they reached Bristol. After Matt Sewell's broken arm, the coaches could not afford to lose anyone else. Still, many hours remained in the days of a bunch of 12-year-olds who couldn't go swimming or skateboarding.

"When we weren't played baseball or practicing," David Galla remembered, "we often played whiffle ball, or just did stupid things like any other 12-year old. We ate junk food that didn't make us fat."

Trumbull hoped to draw a first-round bye, but didn't. Because they would play four games in five days, Coach Galla lamented the loss of Matt Sewell. The team could've really used a third pitcher to backup Drury and Paul.

The coaches scrambled a bit to get their relief pitching lined up. From this point forward, the pressure grew intense. Given the reality of single elimination, pressure stood great in every game. Being short an "arm" amplified that pressure...

All the teams arrived in Bristol, and no one picked Trumbull National as the favorite to advance onto Williamsport, even though they hit and pitched so well to reach the Eastern Regional.

As a team they had hit .439 while holding their opponents to a .225 batting average, and they had out-scored their opponents 104 to 18, backed up by 23 home runs in their nine games.

But no one noticed. Their high-octane offense receives little credit; their pitching prowess, little respect. Immediately, those who "know" brand them underdogs, unlikely to cause any team any concern. Not so the team from Massapequa, New York, who wore the favorite's tag. Ditto for Cherry Hill, New Jersey; expected to travel to Williamsport as well.

It became clear to Trumbull that what they had accomplished to this point carried no impact on what they would face or do in the next game.

That's how it is in sports. Each team is good. Each game is different. Clearly, the competition grew tougher with each game played on the road to Williamsport, and it would take a few upsets and some lucky breaks to keep that road trip alive.

Arriving in Bristol also provided a new experience for the legion of parents who watched every game. Sandy Galla recalled: "The anticipation and excitement of Bristol was something we had not experienced. We had hit the 'big time!' I was sure we could handle the pressure, but we were still very worried that things wouldn't happen quite the way we wanted them to. We still sat in the "right seat', wore the same outfits, said as many prayers as were necessary (even if it took all day!), and worried 'just because it's our job.' We felt a real kinship up there in our splintered perches; as long as we were together, we were fine. We began to believe that if we did the right things and thought the right thoughts we were capable of 'willing' our boys to victory. I will argue to the death, our right to glean some of the credit for our success. Just think what would have happened if one less novena had been said, or one outfit was wrong, or if John Coniglio had forgotten his trumpet, Heaven forbid! It could have been a disaster."

"As we began to spend more time together, we got more comfortable with each other," Sandy continued. "In the meantime, we had the rest of our families to take care of, though most of us had our kids with us when we got a block of rooms at a motel in Southington. While the guys usually watched the kids practice, the rest of us either stayed at the motel with all the kids hanging out together, or every few days we would go home to do some laundry and take care of things that needed to be done at home. We never knew when it would be our last game, but we kept on winning. Our kids ... were having what they called 'The best vacation of my life!' So many friends were around that it was just like a pajama party, sort of 'Party Central.' It was [when we got to Bristol] that friends from Trumbull began joining us at Breen Field to help out in the cheering section."

During pre-tournament festivities, attended by Connecticut Governor William O'Neill for the first time since Little League moved its Eastern Regional tournament to Bristol, ground broke for the new Eastern Regional Center adjacent to Breen Field.

Those attending the ceremony that morning with the Governor comprised Little League, Inc., President Creighton Hale, Bristol Mayor John Leone, and Bristol Fundraising Committee President Bob Fiondella.

Master of Ceremonies Cliff Greer, the public address announcer at the Little League World Series in Williamsport each year, introduced the 12 participating teams, with the only team returning from last year's tournament, Brandywine, Delaware.

With 12 teams in the tournament, four would receive opening-round byes, with their first game on Wednesday, while the other eight teams would faceoff on Tuesday in Round one. This meant that the four Round one winners would play both Tuesday and Wednesday. If you're playing Tuesday and hope to play on Saturday, then you play three straight days, a regimen that taxes any Little League pitching staff. With a 14-man roster, not many options exist. With number three starter Matt Sewell out, Trumbull's options shrank. Andy Paul and Chris Drury would have to shoulder all the pitching duties this week.

The Eastern Regional tournament schedule, as posted:
Tuesday, August 15:
    1 PM – Dubois (Pennsylvania) vs. Westminster (Maryland), Edgewood Field #2
    2 PM – Bangor West Side (Maine) vs. Westfield South (Massachusetts) Breen Field
    4 PM – Swanton (Vermont) vs. Trumbull National (Connecticut - Division 1), Edgewood Field #2
    5 PM – Massapequa International (New York) vs. East Hartford National (Connecticut - Division 2), Breen Field
Wednesday, August 16:
    1 PM – Wilmington Brandywine (Delaware) vs. winner of Maine vs. Massachusetts game, Edgewood Field #2
    2 PM – Woonsocket Fair North (Rhode Island) vs. winner of Maryland vs. Pennsylvania game, Breen Field

4 PM – Cherry Hill American (New Jersey) vs. winner of New York vs. East Hartford game, Edgewood Field #2
5 PM – Manchester South (New Hampshire) vs. winner of Vermont vs. Trumbull game, Breen Field

Thursday, August 17:
2 PM – Semi-final game
5 PM – Semi-final game

Friday, August 18: open for make-ups

Saturday, August 19:
5 PM – Championship game

CHAPTER FIVE

AN EASY OPENING WIN AGAINST VERMONT

Opening Day of the Eastern Regional, Tuesday, August 15, 1989 provided a breezy yet humid setting.
   If you're a real fan and not cheering for any one team, all you really want to see are well-played, close games. If your kids are playing, you're hoping they blow out the other team.
   At the end of the Opening Day of the 1989 Eastern Regional Little League Tournament at the Edgewood Little League Complex in Bristol, Connecticut, half of the crowd went home happy though many still bit their nails as they headed to their cars... while others trudged toward the parking lot in disappointment.
   This is a single-elimination tournament. If you lose, your season ends, right then and there. Your Little League career likely ends as well. You'll never play for the title in Williamsport.
   Oh well, move on. Did we have fun? Did we learn something important? Let's go swimming.
   The four first-round games took on a split personality befitting a character in a Stephen King horror story. The two games played at Breen Field ended up last-at-bat, 2-1 victories, while the two games played at Edgewood Field #2 finished as lopsided wins.
   As it happens, best-selling author King is in attendance, as one of the assistant coaches for the Bangor, Maine, Westside Little League, as that team lost a tough 2-1 decision to Westfield, Massachusetts. But King focused on one thing, he told Keith Freeman of *The Bristol Press,* "I'm just here for the baseball."
   Owen King, the author's son, put Bangor on the scoreboard in the first inning when he drew a bases-loaded walk. Westfield then tied the game in the second on Erik Leen's sacrifice RBI. Westfield won the contest in the bottom the sixth when winning pitcher Timothy Laurita came home on a

bases-loaded walk. Laurita, stellar, hurled a one-hitter complete game. The Westfield Little Leaguer fanned 14 and walked only four. Ryan Iarrobino garnered Bangor's lone hit. Matt Kinney, Bangor's tough-luck loser, tossed a three-hitter, striking out 10 and walking five. Anthony Melo notched two of Westfield's hits.

Massapequa, New York, edged local favorite East Hartford 2-1 in extra innings in an exciting finish to the first round of games that saw Massapequa's Anthony Skorupski hurl a no-hitter, striking out five and walking six. East Hartford grabbed a 1-0 lead in the second when pitcher Scott Soucy walked, moved to second on a groundout, took third on a wild pitch, and scored on the front end of a double steal. Massapequa's Michael Bekiers tied it up in the bottom of the second slapping a home run, one of only four hits allowed by Soucy, who struck out nine and walked six to earn the win. Massapequa won it in the bottom of the seventh when Chris Abbene scored on an error with the bases loaded.

Hitters dominated the other two games. Trumbull National drubbed Swanton, Vermont, 17-3 and Westminster, Maryland recorded a 14-4 win over Dubois, Pennsylvania, the only team in the Eastern Regional with a female player, Erin Henry, who not only pitched but played first base as well as shortstop.

Dubois recovered from an early 3-0 deficit against Westminster with four runs in the third inning on home runs by Thomas Thiebaud, Christopher Smiley, and the aforementioned Erin Henry to take a 4-3 lead. However, the Marylanders stormed back with two runs in the fourth, two more in the fifth, and seven runs in the sixth.

Lawrence Alvarez led Westminster with four hits and Jason Nusbaum followed with three more. Losing pitcher Erin Henry supported her performance on the mound for Dubois with three hits of her own. Westminster's William Staub struck out nine, allowing seven hits and walking but one to earn the win.

Carole Burns of the *Bridgeport Post-Telegram* summed up the atmosphere for Trumbull's opening game in Bristol: "At least 100 Trumbullites showed up for the first game Tuesday in Bristol to cheer on their homeboys. They brought with them horns, trumpets, applause, cheers and lots of sideline advice for Coach Tom Galla, provided only when he was out of hearing distance."

Tom Galla's string of lucky coin-tosses continued in Bristol, Connecticut, as Trumbull got the home team advantage in its Eastern Regional opener against Swanton, Vermont. Swanton's road to the Eastern Regional in Bristol included victories over LaMoille County, 7-2, Waterbury, 12-0, Bristol, 9-7, and Brattleboro, 14-7.

Today, a Trumbull Little League team took the field in a Regional game for the first time ever. You could almost feel the collective butterflies floating as Chris Drury stepped to the mound, ready to toss the first pitch of the game. Swanton's leadoff batter, Andrew Puttick, fouled off it off, but smashed the next pitch at Jason Hairston... who booted it. As Jesse LeClair squared for the sacrifice bunt, Drury threw it wide of the plate, out of Todd Halky's reach, allowing Puttick to advance to second. Drury's next pitch swooped low into the dirt, so Puttick took off for third, Todd Halky's throw got by Jason Hairston, and Puttick scored. Swanton took a quick 1-0 lead without a hit, providing a nervous start.

Next, LeClair attempted to bunt for a single, but Drury made a great play, flying off the mound and nipping him at first base for the first out of the game. This seemed to settle the boys down, and after the shaky start, Drury retired the side with no further damage.

Trumbull's offense got right to work in the bottom of the first. Drury led off with a sharp single up the middle. Halky sacrificed him to second, and Ken Martin's single to center moved Drury to third. After Andy Paul walked to load the bases, Danny Brown worked a walk to force in Drury for Trumbull's first run in the Eastern Regional. The Swanton pitcher then hit Dan McGrath in the leg, scoring Martin for a 2-1 Trumbull lead.

Though Vermont threatened in the second, Trumbull never looked back, as its offense took off in the home second when third baseman Jason Hairston, a small, fast kid whose gold-rimmed eye-glasses seemed to take up two-thirds of his face, smacked an 0-1 fastball over the center field fence for his first Little League home run, igniting a five-run second inning.

Jason Hairston remembers the moment well. "I remember exactly what happened. The umpire ticked me off, because he called a strike on a pitch that was high. I was upset that he had even called it, so I took the bat and hit it on the plate. When I saw the next pitch coming in high and because he called the last one, I thought I might as well swing. I put it over the center field fence." His Trumbull teammates mobbed him upon his crossing the plate.

Trumbull then loaded the bases on a walk, a single, and a hit batter before Danny Brown ripped a two-out, two-RBI double to right-center field. Dan McGrath continued the attack, slicing a single to left that brought in another run, and David Galla closed out the scoring with an infield hit. Trumbull expanded its lead to 7-1 after two innings.

The onslaught continued when Drury lined a single to center to open the bottom of the third and Matt Basztura doubled off the centerfield wall scoring Drury. Consecutive singles by Ken Martin, Andy Paul and Danny Brown brought in three more runs. Trumbull opened up an 11-1 lead after three innings.

Trumbull added three more runs in the fourth inning on three walks, two errors, and one hit, Chris Kelly's two-RBI single to left. The highlight of the inning: a David Galla blast down the right field line that put the crowd on its feet. Galla did his very best Carlton Fisk imitation, trying to will the ball fair, but alas, it curved just foul. The disappointment showed as Galla

30
Thor 9: Vensa

Contact Joeanne 203 483 9090

Allison Birch

1111

MIDDLETOWN
860 346 0306
03

Silver ST

Rushford — Allison
faxed 2x from Milford
once from us
3 confirmations

Cigna —
   Auth Team @
   1-800-244-6224
case manager
will get you to
   Rachid

he will personally
take care of getting
   authorization

Boyd Birch @ 30 WED
Allison
Birch @ 30 FRI
1:30 FRI

had barely missed his first Little League home run.

In the fifth, Trumbull put three more runs across with Danny Brown adding two more RBIs, bringing his total for the day to six.

Drury allowed just two hits over his five innings, while striking out four and walking four. Chris Kelly closed, tossing the sixth inning, allowing two unearned runs. Drury got a little rest so he could pitch again in two days...*should* Trumbull get that far. More importantly, he threw his normal 80 pitches, giving the coaches hope that he would indeed pitch again in two days...*if.*

The double-digit offense hadn't missed a beat, and neither had the pitching. Trumbull thumped the Vermonters, 17-3.

The starting nine led the 15-hit attack, each player collecting at least one hit on the day. Danny Brown (3-for-4, 1 run and 6 RBI), Ken Martin (2-for-3, 3 runs scored and 1 RBI), Chris Drury (2-for-4, 4 runs scored), and Dan McGrath (1-for-2, 2 RBI) paced the attack. Pinch-hitters Chris Kelly (2 RBI) and Harlen Marks also contributed hits. Jason Hairston's home run stands as a landmark for Trumbull National Little League, the first ever hit in Regional tournament play.

"The butterflies are gone," Galla told his team after the game. "Let's play ball now." In hindsight, what he might have told his team was "Let's pitch the ball, now."

When asked by Carole Burns of the *Bridgeport Post-Telegram* how he felt about the possibility of going to Williamsport and winning it all, Galla said he got "shivers" just considering the possibility. "It's all gravy from this point on," he said, "but we're not looking at it that way. We want to win it all. That may sound crazy, but if you don't think it's possible, then guess what? It's not going to happen."

Looking at how the players dealt with it all, Burns continued, "The players themselves however seem to take the noise and drama in stride. And at times, their mannerisms seemed to resemble those of professional ballplayers; they walked and talked like they were in the big leagues."

"Listen to Chris Kelly, who relieved Drury in the game against Vermont: 'I thought they were going to be tough but Chris really gave them good pitching,' Kelly said. 'We played a real good game.' Or Jason Hairston, talking about the first home run of his career: 'I was just trying for a single to start off the inning.'

"Are the boys mimicking the All-Stars they see on television or does this type of demeanor come naturally to athletes young and old? Of course, Jason Hairston also said the tournament was fun 'because you get to sleep in the same room with all your friends.'

"When you come out onto the field of the Eastern Regionals, a bigger stage, brighter lights, score as many runs as we did in against Vermont, and get a solid pitching performance, you feel good," Hairston affirmed. "You know you are playing a higher-caliber team [in Bristol], so

when you score a bunch of runs, show a significant amount of fire-power, and get a lot of clutch hits, you feel enthusiastic for your chances going forward. Every time we won a baseball game we were excited. There was no 'ho-hum, we won another game...' It was a big deal."
Thank goodness for boyish innocence.

John Heher, Little League District 2 commissioner and a coach in Trumbull National Little League for many years, was the first to jump on the Williamsport bandwagon, recalled Tom Galla. "He was the first to say this team was going to Williamsport, even before I thought we could. He really believed we would." After the win over Vermont, he said it again.

"After beating Swanton, Vermont, I was thinking, we're still hitting, still playing good defense, still pitching, so I was feeling good," Tom Galla told me. "John Heher comes over to me after the game, and I'm standing there with Bob [Zullo] and Ed [Wheeler]. Remember, Heher was the first one who said we were going to Williamsport before anybody else said that, and way before I said it, and he truly believed it. So John wants to chip in and suggests that we probably don't need to start [Andy Paul] against New Hampshire, because they can't be any better than Vermont, and we've got to win four games in five days. We took all this in, and Bob wouldn't let me look past anybody, so we didn't. We started Andy, and he pitches a one-hitter. So once again, we learned a lesson. I have tremendous respect for Bob; we couldn't have won it without him. We complemented each other."

After the big win, the fans in the grandstands shared the emotions on the field. Sandy Galla recalled: "We were joyous! It couldn't get any better than this! We were on top of the world!"

Later that evening at Trumbull's "home on the road" in nearby Southington, the Comfort Inn "...was *rocking*!" Sandy Galla remembered.

Also sharing the Comfort Inn were parents and fans from Massapequa and Brandywine. Sandy continued: "As we saw each other in the lobby and hallways, or at the pool, our smiles were warm, yet at arm's length. Each team was wishing that the other one would lose, but not out loud."

CHAPTER SIX

BITING NAILS AGAINST NEW HAMPSHIRE

The high heat and humidity continued on day two of the Eastern Regional, Wednesday, August 16th. Christopher Dalton provided that day's highlight, a no-hitter to lead Woonsocket, Rhode Island to an 8-0 win over Westminster, Maryland, the second no-hitter of the tournament. Rhode Island scored in every inning except the second to advance to the Regional semi-finals on Thursday. Dalton struck out eight and walked two in his win, and helped himself with two singles and two RBI. Second baseman Jeff Leduc backed him up with three singles. Dalton's single in the first inning put Woonsocket up 1-0, all the scoring he would need.

    Left fielder Evan Ciabattoni's game-winning single in the sixth led Brandywine, Delaware, to a 7-6 victory over Westfield, Massachusetts, and a place in the first of Thursday's semi-final games against Woonsocket, Rhode Island. Ryan Victor stroked three singles for Brandywine, while Greg Bevilacqua and Stuart Gornall homered for Westfield. Chad Bowers picked up the win while Joey Strebel took the loss.

    The third game of the day pitted the two pre-tournament favorites Cherry Hill, New Jersey, and Massapequa, New York against each other. Cherry Hill pounded the New Yorkers 11-3 as pitcher Chris Matarese allowed just two hits and struck out 12. At the plate, New Jersey shortstop Jason Flory and catcher Todd Groves paced the offense with a double and single apiece. Massapequa's Roland Clark and Anthony Skorupski homered in the loss. Cherry Hill would play in Thursday's second semi-final game, facing the winner of the Trumbull vs. New Hampshire matchup.

    In the consolation games played earlier in the day, East Hartford edged Bangor, 5-4, and Dubois, Pennsylvania blew out Swanton, Vermont, 13-1.

    Trumbull's second game in Bristol was a 4:00 PM encounter against Manchester, New Hampshire. Manchester caught a break, drawing a first-round bye, thus able to start the team's best pitcher against Trumbull. Trumbull countered with one of its two aces, Andy Paul. Trumbull has already chased away the nerves, but had New Hampshire? It was *their* first game in Bristol.

Trumbull ultimately squeaked by on a 1-0 pitching gem by Andy Paul to defeat Manchester, which appeared as if a misprint to readers after Trumbull's recent offensive onslaught.

Facing Manchester's ace, Romio Dagher, loomed a tall order for Trumbull and starting pitcher Andy Paul, but Paul stood his ground and pitched a masterful one-hitter, striking out nine batters and allowing only two runners to reach base.

"The New Hampshire game was a tough one." Jason Hairston recalled. "We didn't think they were going to be that tough. But it ended up being a pitcher's duel. That speaks a lot about our defense; we played a pretty solid defense that game against New Hampshire. We had been coached well, and we were able to execute. We knew what to do with the ball when it was hit to us, and what base to go to. We practiced this all the time."

Andy Paul's only rough spot came in the 4th inning when he gave up an infield single to Tom Masiero. Jason Hairston made a diving stop at the ball, deflecting it to Danny Brown, whose throw arrived late. Paul then walked the next batter, Matt Grenier, on five pitches. Manager Galla visited Andy on the mound and told the lanky right-hander with the intense "game face" to "...get mean." The message sank in. Andy Paul settled back in and struck out the next two batters to end the inning. It proved the only inning Manchester would put anyone on base.

Trumbull put the game's only run across in the bottom of the first inning when Chris Drury led off with a double down the left field line, and two wild pitches later, scored.

Another scoring opportunity arose later in the first inning when Matt Basztura walked and advanced to third on two more wild pitches. After Ken Martin struck out, Andy Paul walked, but Dagher got tough and fanned Danny Brown to end the first. It would not be the only time Dagher reared back and struck out a Trumbull batter in a crucial moment.

"After we scored the run in the first inning, I was thinking, that's just the beginning," Tom Galla remembered. "Then it became evident that the kid pitching against us was something special. I told Andy to just keep throwing bullets, because I'm not sure we're going to score any more runs against this kid. It was one of Andy's best pitching performances. But it wasn't as much a pressure situation as the California game. California always wins the US title, and New Hampshire isn't California, but they were tough."

In the third, David Galla walked and Ken Martin followed with a one-out single to center. Manchester's ace again bore down, putting away

Andy Paul on a called third strike and getting Danny Brown to pop up to second.

Though Trumbull's quiet bats seemed poised to mount a third rally in the fifth, when Ken Martin smacked a one-out double into the right-field corner, and Andy Paul followed with a walk, Dagher silenced Trumbull's bats again, striking out both Danny Brown and Dan McGrath.

On this day, Romio Dagher appeared nearly as good as Andy Paul, holding Trumbull's normally booming bats to just three hits and one run, while fanning eight. But "nearly as good" is not good enough on this summer day. It's tough to lose 1-0 in Little League. In the end, though, Dagher's lack of control proved his downfall, the six walks and five wild pitches his undoing.

Andy Paul totally shut down New Hampshire after the fourth inning, retiring the final six batters thanks to some excellent infield defense to preserve the 1-0 win and put Trumbull into the semi-finals against Cherry Hill, New Jersey. Andy so dominated Manchester that they never hit a ball out of the infield.

Franco Indomenico, writing for *The Hartford Courant*, said, "If you were there, you had to be impressed by each pitcher's big body, blazing fastball, and composure."

In the major leagues, they call it "composure." In Little League, they call it "downright awesome," the best way to describe what fans saw as Andy Paul out-dueled Manchester's Romio Dagher to advance Trumbull into the Eastern Regional semi-finals.

"It was a phenomenal pitching battle," said a relieved Tom Galla. "I was very nervous. But then I'm nervous even when we score a lot of runs."

"That was probably the best pitched game I've ever seen," recalls Todd Halky. "Andy pitched a total gem, as clutch as clutch could be."

After squeaking by New Hampshire, Dan McGrath "...felt bloody lucky mate, very lucky."

Again, David Galla: "We didn't have such a good game. When we start a game with Chris Drury in our lead-off spot, the expectation is he is going to get a hit. So when he got the hit and scored to put us up 1-0 right away, we were thinking, yeah, this is about right. Then both pitchers shut the rest of the day down; there was nothing after that. That was a tight defensive game; it was a game we needed, like Park City. We needed to experience the pressure of a close game. We had played a lot of blowouts, with lots of home runs, grand slams. The 1-0 win really woke us up and gave us the opportunity to think about going home. So that was a good experience."

David continued. "Andy's performance was dominant. He threw as hard as I'd ever seen him, really overpowering. He tossed a one-hitter, a shut-out. That is a well-pitched game. If it was a major league game, you'd pay good money to see that kind of game. We were very fortunate to come away with that win."

Sandy Galla called the win "...a real heart-stopper to say the least. We didn't like the way it was going, AT ALL! Our bats were quiet and we were not used to being held to so few hits. We couldn't pin down the problem, which bothered us. We always felt responsible for the way the game progressed and we were sure it was something we were doing wrong. Maybe we didn't pick up a coin for the day, who knows?"

After edging New Hampshire 1-0, the fans let out a collective sigh of relief, then adjourned for the evening to the Comfort Inn, where the partying was a bit subdued for the parents, but not so for the siblings. To them, a win is a win. Kids don't worry the way parents do. As the kids relaxed, the parents began focusing on tomorrow's opponent – Cherry Hill.

CHAPTER SEVEN

THE ELECTRIC COMPANY SHOWS UP AGAINST CHERRY HILL

Thursday, August 17th arrived, a hot, humid mid-summer afternoon, typical weather for Connecticut's dog days. By the end of the day, the teams who would fight it out for the Eastern Regional title on Saturday will know their fate: playing on Saturday for a berth in the Little League World Series in Williamsport.
In the first game, Brandywine knocked off Woonsocket 9-5 to take the first spot in Saturday's championship game. Chad Bowers, the only player back from last year's team that lost to Andover, Massachusetts 9-6 in the Eastern Regional finals, delivered the key blow, a three-run homer in the top of the fifth that broke a 3-3 tie.
"He gave me a fastball, chest-high and inside, which is just the way I like it," Bowers told Kevin Tresolani of Wilmington, Delaware's *The News Journal*. "I was just swinging to make contact. When I hit it, I knew it was gone." It stood as the only Delaware extra-base hit of the game.
After stroking the game-winning hit the day before against Westfield, Massachusetts, Evan Ciabattoni once again paced Brandywine's singles parade with three, followed by Joseph Mattair and Ryan Victor with two hits apiece.
The four-foot, eight-inch tall Victor also starred on the mound, tossing a six-hitter with 11 strikeouts to earn the victory.
"They were a fastball-hitting team so I started throwing curveballs," said Victor. The change of speed kept the Rhode Island hitters off balance all game. "My one curveball sinks, so I was setting them up with that," Victor noted.
Brandywine enhanced the reputation it earned in the district and state tournaments by coming back once again from an early 1-0 deficit

against Woonsocket. Thomas Tray's sacrifice fly in the second tied the game. Brandywine added two more runs in the third on singles by Ken Giles, Bowers, and Ciabattoni combined with a Woonsocket error.

Woonsocket tied it in the fourth, but Bowers' blast following Victor's single and Giles' walk put Delaware ahead for good, 6-3. While Woonsocket would close the gap to 6-5 in the fifth, Brandywine pulled away with three unearned runs in the top of the sixth to secure the 9-5 victory.

Brandywine's three runs scored on a controversial call by the first base umpire that few understood. As *The News Journal*'s Kevin Tresolani described it, "With two out and runners on second and third, Bowers was called out, then - two seconds later – safe at first on an infield grounder when the first baseman pulled his foot off the bag. Woonsocket, already heading off the field, then started throwing the ball around. Tray and Victor scored and Bowers circled the bases." Tresolani continued: "Woonsocket manager Marcel Godin said he couldn't understand how an umpire could make an out call, then a safe call, on a play of that nature. He wasn't the only one."

Though Trumbull expected to play Massapequa, New York, the pick to win the Eastern Regional, they caught a break when Cherry Hills pulled off an upset.

But is it really a break? After all, Cherry Hill easily handled Massapequa with an 11-3 victory in their second-round game, whereas Trumbull only squeaked by New Hampshire, 1-0.

After bumping into several of the Cherry Hill kids, even Tom Galla was impressed.

"The night before the game against Cherry Hill, Little League sent both teams to Lake Compounce, an amusement park in Bristol," Galla recalled. "Bob [Zullo] and I are walking around and we see these big kids, four of them over six feet tall. I said, 'Bob, who are these kids? They can't possibly be Little Leaguers.' When we walk onto the field the following afternoon, it turns out they are from Cherry Hill. I'm thinking, oh my god, they just beat up on Massapequa."

Not to worry, for the baseball gods would spare Galla's nerves this day.

Because Cherry Hill's No. 1 pitcher worked in the Massapequa game, Trumbull would "only" have to face Cherry Hill's No. 2, a slim lefty named Casey Fossum. Standing next to Cherry Hill's six-foot plus first baseman, Chris Matarese, Fossum appeared tiny since the top of his head barely reached his teammate's armpit.

Another break Trumbull caught? Back then, Little League had few minimum playing time or pitching limit rules. As Tom Galla explained it, "The only rule that Little League had [in 1989] about playing time or pitching limits was you could pitch every other game. That's it. In all honesty, that was too much, a lot too much. Early on in the Districts it wasn't bad with the games spread out, but in Bristol, we played four games in five days. Chris and Andy did all the pitching. That was too much, but we got away with it."

Tom continued, "And, there were no rules about having to play each kid [a minimum number of innings or at-bats]. So, since I wanted to win every game, even when we were winning big, I was reluctant to put everyone in, because we knew these were good teams that could come back at any time." He remembered one of the basic rules of Little League coaching: "*No* lead is safe."

Galla then related the third break Trumbull caught playing Cherry Hill.

"Chris [Drury] was going against [Cherry Hill]. As it turned out, Chris pitched the games against Cherry Hill and Taiwan that could have turned out so different if Andy had pitched, because Chris threw lots of junk and Andy threw the fastball. [Looking back], I'm afraid of what those kids might have done against Andy's fastball. I know against California Andy started with the fastball but switched over to the junk, and did fine. Overpowering pitchers don't always dominate in Little League; the better kids learn how to hit the number one early on. You need to have someone who throws the off-speed stuff to really succeed," he shared.

Was this another turn of the baseball gods in Trumbull's favor? It sure seemed like it. After all, Trumbull set its rotation in its first tournament game more than a month ago, when Galla started Andy Paul against Stratford American, and he never wavered from alternating his twin aces.

The size of the Cherry Hill kids didn't bother Dan McGrath.

"It didn't really matter," McGrath claimed. "Since I was little and extremely competitive, my father always reminded me that by being there, by being in that game or any game, that I had a right to win and size for me was never something I feared. I was an average kid in terms of height and not a bad ball player. I just remember being told by coaches too that we had earned the right to be there, that we were not lucky and that to take us lightly would be to their detriment...ha, how the game turned!"

Sitting in the bleachers before the game, Matt Sewell felt real concern. He witnessed the Cherry Hill vs. Massapequa game and "...was worried. Cherry Hill looked like the best team," Sewell volunteered.

Sandy Galla remembered the buzz going through the stands that afternoon before the game: "...we were shaking in our boots. [Cherry Hill] had squashed Massapequa...we were impressed. They were the roughest, toughest, meanest-looking group of 12-year-olds we'd ever seen. The entire team was *huge*! We thought the [Massapequa] team would be tough to beat and [Cherry Hill] had no trouble with them. *E-GADS*! Mothers chewed their finger nails and fathers paced uncontrollably. This would be the team that could beat us, if there was such a thing. We were scared, but we vowed that the kids wouldn't know it. We put on our *go-get-'em* faces."

"As a 12-year old, I was a little guy," recollected David Galla, "Four-foot-11 and one-half-inch, maybe weighed 86 pounds, soaking wet. So, we're playing a team and each one of their outfielders is six-feet tall. We had some big kids, Ken Martin and Andy Paul, but these other guys were huge and they had beaten up everyone before they played us. So, when I looked across the field at a 12-year-old who stands six-feet tall, it is intimidating. That changed very quickly though when we started hitting home runs left and right. But yeah, it was intimidating when I first saw them."

Trumbull played its third game in three days, with Chris Drury back on the mound against Cherry Hill, New Jersey on just two days' rest. Thankfully, it didn't really matter, as Trumbull's bats came alive, the runs plentiful, in an 18-6 rout of Cherry Hill. Trumbull's 15-hit attack included six home runs. While it looked easy and the *Bridgeport Post-Telegram* touted it as a "rout" in its headline the next morning, it wasn't.

As the crowd of 3,000 settled into their seats, Chris Drury stepped to the plate to lead off the game. Moments before, Tom Galla's 11-game winning streak of coin tosses to determine the home team…ended. Then, in a moment of terror for Coach Galla, Drury chased an eye-high fastball from Fossum for strike three. Not a good omen, when combined with the loss of the coin toss.

But Drury held an incredible performance record as Trumbull's leadoff batter. Fossum was just the second opponent to strike him out this post-season, the previous K occurring 16 days earlier against Park City American, a game Trumbull lost. Drury won't strike out again in the tournament. In the 16 games that Trumbull eventually played, Chris led off by getting on base 12 times, with 10 hits, including two home runs, a walk, and an error. For the entire tournament, Drury raked the ball at a .527 clip, with 29 hits, including six home runs, in 55 at-bats.

Talk about tough. Drury was as tough as they came; a gutsy, hard-nosed kid who led by doing what needed to be done. He didn't say much; he just got it done. Period.

"Even though Chris led off striking out, I wasn't worried," said Tom Galla. "Someone else would just have to pick him up, and they did."

Jason Hairston agreed. "We learned from the Park City game, when the coaches said just because Chris struck out to lead off doesn't mean we can't play with them; someone else just has to take the lead. I think this really helped us in the Cherry Hill game when he struck out again to lead off, especially because everyone had told us that we were going to get slaughtered. We came up big in that game; we learned that it's just not him."

The coach's words had sunk in – deep – with his young players.

Drury's misstep did not cause his teammates to fall apart. Following the Drury strike out, Todd Halky stepped to the plate and lashed a

UNLIKELY CHAMPIONS: A MIRACLE IN WILLIAMSPORT

shot that glanced off the third baseman's glove into left field. Matt Basztura then singled to right. A Fossum wild pitch moved both runners up a base before Ken Martin smacked a grounder that zipped under shortstop Jason Flory's glove, scoring pinch-runner Paul Coniglio. Fossum threw another pitch in the dirt that got by catcher Todd Groves, allowing Basztura to score, and then walked Andy Paul on four pitches. Danny Brown then delivered the key hit, a double down the left field line bringing home Martin and Paul, fronting Trumbull a quick 4-0 lead after one inning.

Cherry Hill countered in the bottom of the first when catcher Todd Groves smashed a two-out fastball from Drury over the fence in right-center for a three-run homer, cutting Trumbull's lead to 4-3 after one. The game took on the look of a potential slugfest.

Jason Hairston singled to center to start the Trumbull second, and Drury smacked Fossum's next pitch high and deep to right-center field. The crowd knew it was gone the moment it left the bat. Trumbull went up 6-3.

Cherry Hill's first two batters in the second reached on base hits, but Drury heard the crowd urging him to "get tough," and he did, retiring the next three batters to end the rally.

Both pitchers escaped bases-loaded jams in the third inning unscathed.

After the offensive "lumber slumber" of the previous day against New Hampshire, Trumbull's bats finally woke up with a home-run barrage in the fourth inning never before seen in the Eastern Regionals. Trumbull's number 3 through 6 batters – all four of them – "go yard."

Back-to-back-to-back-to-back.

Matt Basztura stepped to the plate – *Boom!* Fossum's first pitch flew deep into the center field seats. Ken Martin is next – *Boom!* Martin sent the 0-1 pitch over the center field scoreboard. Jason Kurtz relieved Fossum. Same result with Andy Paul – *Boom!* Kurtz's 1-and-2 pitch landed in the bushes in left field. Danny Brown swung at a 2-0 pitch – *Boom!* It's gone, deep to left field. As each batter crossed the plate, the celebration at home plate grew more joyous.

Unbelievable. Trumbull National has just blasted four consecutive home runs. No one can confirm the record, but apparently, no team ever accomplished such a feat previously in Little League Baseball tournament play. It's only been done seven times in Major League Baseball history.

The four titanic home runs on 10 pitches clearly rattled Cherry Hill, who had yet to record an out in the inning. Trumbull now led 10-3.

"Downtown" Danny Brown calls it "My one personal triumph. I wasn't known as a big hitter, the power dropped off when the line-up got to me, so it was a surprise to everyone, I think." Matt Sewell remembers sitting in the grandstand when the fireworks started. "When we came back with all those home runs, it was just fantastic!"

No one could know at that time that the Boston Red Sox would one day draft the then-11-year old Fossum with the 48th pick of the June 1999 draft. Fossum would make his Major League debut for the Sox in 2001. Wow, Trumbull is facing a future major leaguer on the mound. Can you really tell at that age he will make it to The Show? Is this really a break for Trumbull?

After the game, Galla thought Fossum "…was quite hittable" and he "…didn't think much of him. I guess that shows you how much I know." His assessment of Fossum wasn't that far off, though Galla didn't know that either. Fossum proved a very hittable pitcher during a nine-year Major League career.

Chris Kelly came to the plate, and the crowd almost groaned when the barrage ended, as he slapped a hard bouncer to shortstop Jason Flory, who promptly booted it. Harlen Marks followed with another bouncer to short, but this time Flory forced Kelly at second. Marks moved to second on Jason Hairston's walk. As Drury stepped to the plate, the crowd wanted more, and Drury did not disappoint, as his RBI double to right-center scored Marks.

Todd Halky popped up to third base for the second out.

Kurtz hit Matt Basztura with a pitch that glanced off his helmet, loading the bases for clean-up batter Ken Martin. As Martin stepped into the batter's box, the crowd loudly urged him to knock another one out, chanting "Let's go, Ken-ny! Let's go, Ken-ny!"

After Kurtz responded by nearly beaning him, Martin drove the 3-0 pitch high and deep to left field for his second home run of the inning, a grand slam. The crowd roared their approval. As Andy Paul stepped to the plate the crowd urged him to keep it going, but Kurtz finally fanned him to end the battering.

With nine runs, Trumbull put the game out of reach for Cherry Hill. Trumbull led 15-3 after four innings. The offense had not scored this many runs in an inning since their 13-run outburst nearly a month earlier against North End East Little League.

"The fourth inning was just unbelievable," Tom Galla smiled. "I was thinking, let's keep it going. Let's get another one and another one. I was worried that they would do the same thing to us. They were a powerful team."

"He was the right guy in that situation, just like he was against Taiwan. I know he was thinking, 'You might hit one off me but you're not going to hit four off me.' Chris was all over the place with his pitches. He threw a lot of balls out of the strike zone. He walked guys all the time but he kept the other team's best hitters off-balance with his junk. Chris was a great Little League pitcher, but he wasn't going to be a pitcher. I always thought he would be a catcher for the New York Yankees. He was good and he was smart."

"I was amazed when the guys hit all those home runs, especially because I wasn't a power hitter," said Todd Halky, who caught the game.

"I just laughed," recalled Dan McGrath. "How awesome a display was that? My favorite moment when watching the video is Matt Basztura's face...the guy had ice in his veins."

David Galla remembered that "When the guys went back-to-back-to-back-to-back, the excitement level in the dugout was off the chart. The guys were just going out of their minds. We knew we had an extremely talented lineup, especially the top of our lineup. And those guys really proved it that game. The pitchers we were facing were good. They threw the ball hard; they were throwing curveballs and throwing changeups. We were definitely facing a better caliber team and we were able to rise up to the challenge as we went along."

Drury kept Cherry Hill off the scoreboard in the home fourth, squelching any ideas they might have held about a comeback, although Cherry Hill added a run in the fifth on a hit and two walks, then scored two more in the sixth on a Chris Matarese monster shot into the trees in left.

Chris just looked at his coach in the dugout and mouthed, "Wow!"

It is too little, too late for Cherry Hill. Trumbull neutralized Cherry Hill's three runs with three runs of their own in the sixth inning. Singles by Halky, Martin, and pinch-hitter Dan McGrath loaded the bases. Halky scored on Danny Brown's grounder, misplayed by Flory, and Chris Kelly's single to right center drove home Martin and McGrath. Chris Fasano dropped a hit into left that reloaded the bases for pinch-hitter Cody Lee, but he struck out. Drury then popped out to center to end the inning.

Gloves flew high in the air as the team mobbed Drury on the mound after he struck out Jason Kurtz to end the game. The crowd roared in delight, "We ARE Trum-bull! We ARE Trum-bull!" Trumbull had knocked off the big boys from Cherry Hill, New Jersey, 18-6, to advance to the Eastern Regional championship game on Saturday against Brandywine, Delaware.

In pitching the complete game, Drury allowed eight hits and six walks while striking out seven. Before the game, Tom Galla worried about how Drury would handle the assignment on just one day's rest. After the game, Galla said, "Drury pitched five innings on Tuesday (two days earlier). I had no idea if he'd be sore, but we had to put him out there." Drury kept the fastball-hitting Cherry Hill batters off balance with his junk, including a change-up (the "dart pitch") that he learned from Assistant Coach Ed Wheeler. Afterward, one of the parents in the stands said, "Chris will sleep well tonight." Indeed, he would.

In a post-game interview, Assistant Coach Bob Zullo made it clear, "These boys came to play baseball." When asked to comment on the team's record-setting home run outburst in the fourth inning (five home runs including Ken Martin's grand slam), Zullo replied, "I haven't seen that many home runs in an inning either, but our boys just know how to swing the bat."

As Ken Martin stepped up to the microphone, someone asked how he felt about those home runs in the fourth inning. "I feel great!" he blurted. "After the first home run, they kept throwing me the curve and I finally hit it."

Chris Drury had pitched his second game in three days, so he is asked how he feels after pitching a complete game on such a humid day. "It got pretty hot out there, but it was alright," he said. A follow-up question: Did he panic after Cherry Hill scored three runs in the first inning? "Yeah, a little bit, but then I knew we could hit the ball." When asked if he was a strikeout pitcher, he said, "No, not really, I'm a groundball and pop-up pitcher."

Trumbull's sure-handed shortstop, Downtown Danny Brown, faced the microphone next, but he had lost his voice from all his screaming during the game, so Tom Galla stepped in and complimented Danny on his slick defense that day. "His great plays saved us lots of runs today," Tom declared.

"Because Trumbull had never made it out of the State tournament," said David Galla, "nobody knew who we were. There was no expectation of us being a strong team. So when you come in as the underdog, it's a lot easier to shatter expectations, which is what we did in the New Jersey game. You know, Cherry Hill, New Jersey, was supposed to beat us one hundred to nothing. They had big kids. They were considered to be the best team in the tournament, along with Massapequa, New York, who they crushed the day before they played us. Maybe we got lucky and only had to face their number two pitcher."

"How can you not smile when you've got a bunch of kids who can do what these kids have done?" a proud Tom Galla asked reporters after the game. "Yesterday, we get three hits, we steal a run, and we win 1-0 on a one-hitter. Today, we come back and we got a lot of hits and hit a lot of home runs. This team can do it all. They surprised the heck out of me. I never saw a team hit so many home runs. I just hope we saved a few for Saturday."

Galla continued. "That 1-0 victory yesterday frustrated our hitters. So this morning, we had a batting practice over at Forestville, who allows us to use their field. They are our biggest friends and biggest fans up here. And it was awesome, as awesome as what you saw out here today. After that, we were pretty confident that we would hit a lot better today."

Five players paced Trumbull's fired-up offense. Ken Martin gave a 3-for-5 performance, including two home runs, three runs scored, and six RBI; Chris Drury went 3-for-6, including one home run, two runs scored, and 3 RBI; Matt Basztura enjoyed a 2-for-3 day at the plate, with three runs scored and one RBI; Danny Brown hit 2-for-5 at the plate with a run scored and three RBI; and Chris Kelly delivered 2-for-4 on the day with two RBI.

UNLIKELY CHAMPIONS: A MIRACLE IN WILLIAMSPORT

The four consecutive home runs and five home runs in one inning stand as a Little League record, and earned the team a new moniker: "The Electric Company."

Andy Paul remembered talking with his dad about the Cherry Hill team years later. "My father stills says that Cherry Hill, New Jersey, was the most impressive-looking Little League team he has ever seen." Andy also recalls that game in his own way, "Cherry Hill was a cocky bunch and assumed they could beat us handily. Little did they know that we would proceed to play probably our best overall game of the entire summer. We were scorching hot that day in the field and at the plate. We rode this huge wave of momentum that game."

Bob Moseley, a sports writer with the *Bridgeport Post-Telegram*, likened Trumbull's offensive performance to "...a miniature version of the 1927 Yankees."

The Hartford Courant wrote, "Andy Warhol once said something to the effect that everyone will be famous for 15 minutes. The Trumbull Little League team is not exactly famous (yet), but it certainly was invincible during a 15-minute stretch of baseball in the Eastern Regional semi-finals at Breen Field."

Galla responded, "Just don't tell my kids they're awesome. They think they're ordinary. I tell them they're ordinary."

Many if not most considered Cherry Hill a talented team and clearly the tallest with their four "giant" six-footers. Trumbull would now play in the Eastern Regional championship game on Saturday against a scrappy Brandywine Little League (Wilmington, Delaware) team.

Years later, Tom Galla revealed that after this victory, he felt for the first time that his team really could go to Williamsport. "After the Cherry Hill, New Jersey, game, I thought we were going to Williamsport. I knew Brandywine was a good team, but they didn't seem to have the big, strong horses to get them there. So I thought we could beat them. Still, I was nervous, because I knew we could come out on the field and be flat, or they could come out on the field and just play out of their minds."

No one picked Trumbull to win the Eastern Regional, nor did anyone select Brandywine. Trumbull could now see the final obstacle on the road to Williamsport.

But Trumbull possessed a secret weapon.

According to Tom Galla's wife, Sandy, the preponderance of home runs against Cherry Hill loomed an intimidating statistic to their next opponent. She gleaned this from a conversation with her counterpart, the Brandywine, Delaware coach's wife the night before the teams met in the Eastern Regional championship game.

Sandy Galla's conversation with the Brandywine coach's wife took place in a meeting room in the Comfort Inn, where both teams in the finals lodged. It "...kind of announced our intention to win the whole pot," Sandy recalled. "She actually brought up the point that we had hit so many [home runs] and I simply agreed that it was an extraordinary number," Sandy said. Sandy then added insult to injury by commenting that six home runs "were, more or less, routine."

Both women had it right – this team could really light it up.

"Though I'm not sure if the Brandywine kids saw our game against Cherry Hill," Tom Galla mentioned later, "I'm sure the buzz was going around about what we had done. So, they may have been intimidated."

Even though Trumbull found its offense again against Cherry Hill, analysts speculated they remained overmatched against Brandywine. No one expected them to win, no surprise there …no one outside of Trumbull had given them much of a chance.

That evening, a local Trumbull musician, Bill Leete, went back to his hotel room and wrote an impromptu song about what he had witnessed that day against Cherry Hill. He called it *"Trumbull National Little League – the Electric Company."* Andy Paul called it "A hilarious song which kind of made that game into an instant cult classic with its own theme song. I remember hearing the taped play-by-play call on the radio afterwards and the announcers were going nuts."

Later that evening, both teams met with Kyle Herrington, a representative from Little League Baseball in Williamsport, and were told to arrange for rooms near Williamsport. The winner of the next day's game would use them. What might have been unthinkable a few weeks ago approached reality…and reality was approaching *crazy*. To think that Trumbull remained one of eight teams in the US from the thousands who had started…*incredible*.

CHAPTER EIGHT

A DAY OF DESTINY WITH BRANDYWINE

The day of destiny for Trumbull: Saturday, August 19th, when they faced their final hurdle on the road to Williamsport, once again presented a typical, hot and humid mid-summer New England evening. The forecast threatened thunderstorms, which could appear at any time. An overflowing crowd of more than 5,000 fans packed Breen Field for the 5:00 PM game. Fans sat and stood everywhere.

Trumbull's ambition? Become the first team from Connecticut to advance to the Little League World Series since Stamford in 1981.

It proved a significant and historic day for ESPN as well, the emerging network headquartered in Bristol, Connecticut, since its 1979 inception. This is the first live event ESPN would broadcast from the center of its universe – Bristol, Connecticut.

Today these 28 youngsters, aged 11 and 12 years, would play to a national television audience for their very first time.

Playing a game on television?

"A huge deal back in the day," recalled Andy Paul. "Pitching on TV was a little nerve racking at first but I remember settling in and doing what I had done all the games prior, which was just to do my best and listen to the coaches and Chris behind the plate."

"I was worried that the kids were going to be nervous," said Tom Galla, "but they certainly didn't appear to be nervous."

His son David remembered it a bit differently. "That was the first time we played on television, so the TV cameras were intimidating."

Ed Wheeler wasn't worried about the kids being nervous because the game would appear on TV.

"They were a confident bunch of kids, really loose before that game, ready to play, ready to make the trip to Williamsport. It was hard not to be [confident] after how we played against Cherry Hill. I was very confident that day, more confident than any other game we had played. That's when I told them they could shave my head bald if they won. I had quite a head of hair back then, still do. The kids were getting 'zips' and asked me why I didn't get a 'zip.' So I told them if you win, I'll get my head shaved."

ESPN's Tim Brando opened the broadcast of the Eastern Regional Little League Championship, welcoming the audience. "For years, Bristol had been the home of amateur baseball in the northeast." Brando offered. "Today Bristol welcomes some of the top Little Leaguers in America. This afternoon it could be a field of dreams; a berth in the Little League World Series waits."

ESPN's Tim Brando had it pretty much nailed, right at the start, "Delaware can pick at you, manufacturing runs, while Trumbull does rely on heavy-duty power."

He also made it clear that starting pitcher Andy Paul "…can be overpowering with that great size (5-foot-6, 131 pounds) and has excellent control. He throws a fastball and what he calls a dart ball, like a change-up."

Delaware's Chad Bowers would oppose Andy Paul on the mound. Brando's color analyst in the ESPN booth, Rick Wolff, called Bowers "Mr. Perfect" because he had thrown a perfect game earlier in the season. Well golly gee, Mr. Wolff, doesn't that make Andy Paul "Mr. Perfect" as well? Paul pitched a perfecto in the tournament opener in July.

Bowers, no slouch at the plate either, led Delaware into the Eastern Regional tournament with a home run in the state championship game, and powered Brandywine to a 9-5 victory over Woonsocket, Rhode Island on Thursday with a single, a three-run homer, and five RBI to earn its berth in the Eastern Regional finals.

If anyone experienced any pre-game jitters, no one let them show.

Dan McGrath said, "No, I was a typical kid, was probably daydreaming half the time I wasn't in the field." Jason Hairston doesn't remember noticing the television cameras. "It was just another game. Maybe other people noticed, but there was a pretty large crowd, more than we usually saw."

David Galla remembers the Brandywine game. "We knew the game was going to be televised, one, because we were told it was going to be on television, and, two, ESPN had an 18-wheeler with a satellite dish parked behind the third base dugout. They also had 100-foot booms set up down each base line and there was a cage in centerfield with a camera in it. Early in the game, I think we got wrapped up in the fact we were playing on TV. So, you're looking around to see if you're on TV, and then you get comfortable that you're on TV and realize the pitcher is still trying to get you out."

Delaware wasted no time, picking away at Andy Paul in the top of first. Chad Bowers started a two-out rally with a sharp grounder to third.

UNLIKELY CHAMPIONS: A MIRACLE IN WILLIAMSPORT

Jason Hairston back-handed it neatly, but on what should prove the inning-ending play, his throw to Trumbull's 5-foot-10-inch first baseman, Ken Martin, sailed high, and Bowers took second base.

Cleanup hitter Joseph Mattair walked, followed by an Evan Ciabattoni liner to left. McGrath made a nice play to hold Bowers at third, loading the bases for catcher Darren Dombrowski, who promptly blooped a single just beyond the reach of a diving David Galla, racing out from second base into short right field. Bowers crossed the plate easily but Chris Kelly's throw home nearly nipped the second runner when catcher Chris Drury grabbed the throw and nearly tagged out Mattair.

Brandywine had scratched and clawed a quick 2-0 lead. The inning ended without further damage as Andy Paul got Andrew Resini on a called third strike. Brando called it "A real pitcher's pitch, on the black."

Though Andy looked hittable, he didn't worry. "I knew our team was capable of putting up a lot of runs, plus their pitcher wasn't intimidating. That team wasn't nearly as good as Cherry Hill and we knew it."

If Brandywine felt comfortable getting to Paul, it quickly morphed into discomfort, as they witnessed Trumbull's power at the plate. The Connecticut team registered a nine-hit, 10-run first inning, sparked by Matt Basztura's two-run homer and a three-run double slapped by Jason Hairston. Trumbull recorded their biggest opening inning of the post-season.

As Chris Drury stepped into the batter's box, the camera focused on Trumbull National's Tom Galla. "Boy, he's got a lot of intensity," Tim Brando observed. "He played ball at the Division 3 level at Marietta College in Ohio, where he caught major leaguer Kent Tekulve."

Delaware quickly learned why Trumbull considered Drury, 6-for-13 with one home run and seven runs scored in the Eastern Regional, more than just a table setter. The entire Trumbull team looked up to Drury as their leader, the one to get them started, to set the right tone, as he usually did every game.

Drury continued in that role, providing the leadership, showing the way. He set the tone for the game and got Trumbull rolling by lacing a 1-1 pitch from Bowers down the left-field line, hustling into second, sliding in just ahead of Ciabattoni's throw.

Brando complimented Drury: "Boy, he's got a nice, pure swing, a classic stroke."

"Tom Galla told us the impact his team may have offensively in a game could rest on the first at bat of Drury," Tim Brando added.

Rick Wolff continued. "He [Galla] said he had to talk to the team and say, 'Hey, look, if this guy gets a home run it could be a fluke, or if he strikes out, not to worry, just go with the flow, there's a whole game to play.'"

After Dan McGrath struck out, Matt Basztura lined Bowers' 0-and-

2 curveball just under the glove of a diving Kevin Fitzpatrick at third, scoring Drury for Trumbull's first run. It provided some satisfaction to Basztura after swinging and missing Bowers' first two offerings, both curve balls, the pitch Basztura has struggled with all season.

Ken Martin then lined a double to left that moved Basztura to third. Andy Paul follows with a hard shot off Bowers' leg that scored Basztura. It has started...

"They sure have some productivity out of that lineup at three, four and five. Kind of like the Little League version of Mays, McCovey, and Jim Ray Hart," Wolff reported. "They have really been nailing the ball. This looks to be an offensive game."

Following Paul's shot off Bowers' leg, the Delaware pitcher appeared injured. He walked around, trying to shake it off, so his coach Tony Deldeo paid a visit to the mound. The umpire allowed Bowers to throw a few pitches to "test it." He stayed in.

Bowers got Brown to hit a slow bouncer to shortstop Brendan Kennealley that forced Andy Paul at second, but Martin scored the go ahead run. Chris Kelly walked, and David Galla singled under second baseman Andy Resini's glove to load the bases.

Number nine hitter Jason Hairston broke it open with a bases-clearing double into the gap in left center, scoring Brown, Kelly, and Galla, the latter just sliding under the tag of Brandywine catcher Darren Dombrowski.

Drury whacked a double to right center to score Hairston, and McGrath doubled off the left-field fence to bring Drury home. Brandywine's early 2-0 advantage evaporated into an 8-2 Trumbull lead.

"The Trumbull crowd is pumped up," said Brando, and, in the background, the trumpet of Paul Coniglio's dad John led the charge.

"This is some barrage of fireworks. Bowers is throwing a pretty good game but these guys are swinging the sticks like there's no tomorrow," Rick Wolff added.

Delaware's Tony Deldeo mercifully replaced the limping Bowers with his second baseman, 4-foot-9-inch, 85-pound Andrew Resini. "He didn't seem right after that," Wolff said, referring to the shot to the leg that Bowers took off the bat of Andy Paul.

As Matt Basztura stepped to the plate to face Resini, rain began to fall. Basztura took an "excuse-me" check-swing on Resini's first pitch, a fastball. The ball easily cleared the wall in left, bouncing off a car parked beyond it; but it's foul. He wouldn't hit the next one foul. Matt can hit the fastball, but lately he's seen more than his share of curveballs. Is he thinking curveball? Another fastball arrived, this one eye high, and Basztura hammered it to deep left center, nearly reaching the trees beyond the bleachers. The two-run homer put Trumbull up 10-2.

Though it's been drizzling since the first pitch of the game, it started to rain a little harder as Ken Martin entered the batter's box. Tom Galla knew if they do not finish the first inning, they will have to start the game over and lose the ten runs they have scored. He also knew that he had no pitcher if they have to play tomorrow. Andy Paul's start would go to waste, and Galla can't start Drury.

The injury to third pitcher Matt Sewell once again loomed large. Knowing that they need to end the inning before the game is called, Tom Galla gives Martin the strikeout sign. Martin looks puzzled as he stares at his coach, but he takes two ugly swings and looks at the third strike to end the inning, almost walking toward the dugout before the third pitch crossed the plate. Tom Galla sighed in relief. His son David called it "an intentional strike out," and it's another big break for the kids from Trumbull.

"Did he just take those pitches on purpose to get the inning over?" asked Tim Brando. Brando then explained to the audience that in Little League, a game is official after 3½ innings, but if they do not finish the first inning, then the two teams must start all over again.

"Every pitcher's dream is to have a huge cushion in a big game so you can just go out there and get outs," Andy Paul shared. His dream had come true. Now all he had to do was focus on finishing the game.

The Trumbull crowd now chanted, "Will-yams-port! Will-yams-port!"

In the field, the Trumbull boys felt good after their 10-run outburst. As Dan McGrath put it, "It was sweet…you listen to the chatter prior to the game with the experts and they get caught up in how big players are, etc. It's the same chatter we have in our local games with kids and they look at size first and forget that smaller player have the same abilities."

"What can I tell you," Tom Galla began, "the kids were *great*! We had some nerves early on, but we figured they did too. That's a scrappy team over there. We didn't want to let up on them. We ran the bases aggressively. If they were nervous, we wanted to take advantage of it. We didn't want to stand around and wait for something to happen."

Brandywine's Kevin Fitzpatrick immediately got things started in the top of the second with a double down the left field line, but Paul bore down and easily retired the next three batters.

Trumbull produced nothing in its half of the second; Delaware followed suit in their third.

Drury opened the Trumbull third with a liner over the shortstop's head. "He bats like he's on fire, a sweet swing. He's a player," exclaimed Tim Brando.

Dan McGrath, whose family will soon move back to Australia, followed with a double into the left field corner, pushing Drury to third. "Tom Galla will have to convince his [McGrath's] family to stay awhile longer if they get to Williamsport," says Wolff.

Resini finally got Basztura out on a slow curve. Then Martin, a tall, handsome kid with a deep tan and thick dark eyebrows smashed Resini's second pitch into the trees over the left center field bleachers.

"The yard won't hold that one," Rick Wolff declared. "That one's out of the complex." It's Martin's third dinger in two games, and his tenth of the post-season. "He's hit a bunch of homers for us," said Galla. "He's been great. He came in hitting .641 for the tournament." Trumbull now enjoyed an eleven-run lead, 13-2.

Brandywine scored three quick runs in the top of the fourth on four hits and a walk, but Paul again never let it get too far out of control, finally ending Delaware's last gasp.

The final two runs came in the home fourth on a pair of two-out RBI singles by Danny McGrath and Matt Basztura. Galla led off with a blooper to right, his third hit of the game, moved to second on Jason Hairston's sacrifice bunt, and scored on McGrath's single. McGrath advanced to second when Delaware's right fielder let the ball get past him and then made it home on Basztura's soft liner into right field, extending the Trumbull lead to 15-5.

Andy Paul opened the sixth by easily retiring Bowers and Mattair. Pinch-hitter Josh Jacobs held the tough task of keeping Brandywine's flickering hopes alive. As Andy prepared to throw his two-strike pitch to Jacobs, the Trumbull crowd rose to its feet as they sensed their children are about to realize their dream. Andy's game face turns into a smile. His teammates stood behind him, focused, ready, waiting for that last pitch, and their faces clearly told the tale. They knew what they were about to do, where they would go next.

The coaches sensed it as well. "Feel it, feel it Andy!" Bob Zullo shouted to his pitcher, The television camera zoomed in on a smiling Tom Galla, the tension and intensity in his face gone, replaced by a glowing smile. "That's a happy coach there," Tim Brando observed. Andy blew a fastball by Jacobs. *Game over! Trumbull wins!*

"They're on their way to the Big Show," Rick Wolff pointed out, with Tim Brando adding "The Trumbull coaches are jubilant, but why not?"

"As Andy was getting ready to make the last pitch," Tom Galla said, "you're feeling pretty good about what's happening, maybe getting a little ahead of yourself thinking 'we've won this thing and we're going to Williamsport.' That was pretty exciting. Who would have ever thought that that was going to happen, even as hard as you've tried to make it happen, and how difficult it could be? Now it was there." Williamsport, here we come!

As Delaware Manager Tony Deldeo, a salesman for Clairol, crossed the field to congratulate the winning coach, you could read Tom Galla's lips as he replied, "Thank you, I appreciate it." Deldeo had wished him well.

Tim Brando related how he had spoken to Tom Galla before the game, and that Galla had explained that he and his coaches had "...mapped out a plan to make it to the Little League World Series. And now they're there." As the TV camera again focused on Galla and Zullo embracing in the dugout, Tim Brando continued, "Galla has waited a long time, from Division 3 as a player to a winning coach."

While pitching remains important, so is offense, and the "truly remarkable offensive output" by Trumbull in the last two games of the Eastern Regional was, as Tim Brando pointed out, "The difference between a short bus ride home to Trumbull and a trip to Williamsport." And the awesome offensive output did not belong to just a few players.

It wouldn't rate as Andy Paul's best outing, as he only fanned three. But he started the most important game of the tournament so far, and although Brandywine had tagged him for an uncharacteristic five runs on 10 hits and three walks, the Trumbull offense bailed Andy out. Bothered by a stomach bug, Andy Paul needed every ounce of that Trumbull offense that day.

"Andy gutted it out," Galla remarked about his pitcher who worked on just two days' rest. "He didn't feel well, but we scored a bunch of runs for him early and that helped."

After the last pitch, Paul, who stood much taller than Drury, grabbed his shorter, stocky battery-mate and whirled him around in celebration. Then, while his teammates ran around the field waving the championship banner, Andy Paul sat in the Trumbull dugout, a wet towel wrapped around his neck, sick to his stomach. Paul, bothered by a virus for a couple of days, fought off the gremlins and pitched a complete game, while also helping himself with three hits and a RBI.

Andy Paul, who punched Trumbull's ticket to Williamsport, recalled the moment. "It was a huge relief and the sudden shock of what we had accomplished hit me. I remember coming off the mound and feeling really sick, almost like a panic attack but also feeling dazed and exhausted. I didn't take the victory lap around the field that day with my teammates with the Eastern Regional Champs banner because of it. There were a few people attending to me in the dugout. I was fine. I think the whole experience just leveled me at one time and I had to take some deep breaths."

Jason Hairston does remember the coaches saying "…hitting can be contagious. I think the Cherry Hill game really got our bats going again for the championship game [against Brandywine.] It carried over for sure."

"Unless something catastrophic happened," David Galla said, "I felt pretty comfortable we were going to win that game [with a 15-3 lead]. The whole last inning, we were all counting outs. That's pretty typical in sports. Two more to go, one out to go, gloves in the air, let's go party. Then, you run for the pitcher's mound to celebrate with your team. The pile gets knocked over and unfortunately in Little League you're not smart enough to know that it's going to hurt if you're at the bottom. To have that feeling that you were going to continue to play. We knew the next step, we were going to Williamsport."

"Then, we remembered that we were going to be able to shave [Assistant Coach] Ed Wheeler's head." David continued. "That was the most exciting thing we had done in a long time. We were really excited to do that. We all just thought that was the coolest thing going. It cost him nothing and was a fun incentive to keep us focused on the fun side of the game. So, the game is over, out comes the chair right there at home plate, here come the clippers. So at that point my father says, if we win the World Series, you can shave my head, not really expecting that we were going to win the World Series."

Trumbull's number one through five batters hit a collective 14-for-20 with 11 RBI in the game.

Basztura went 3-for-4 with four RBI, including a two-run homer, while Martin went 2-for-4 with three RBI including a three-run smash, and McGrath was 3-for-4 with two RBI. "This is just a dream come true," said Martin.

Drury, behind the plate in this game, went 3-for-4 on the day, with three runs scored and a RBI. David Galla had also contributed with a 3-for-4 game and two runs scored.

But the day's true hero, the player who broke it open for the Trumbull kids in that crucial first inning after they had fallen behind early, proved their diminutive third baseman, Jason Hairston, whose bases-clearing double sent the message to Delaware that every one of these Trumbull kids could hit, including the number nine batter. Asked about his fine day at the plate, Jason could only remember that "...we got to shave coach's head."

Afterwards, Rick Wolff spoke with "winning coach" Tom Galla and his assistant Bob Zullo. "What a tremendous, tremendous win," Wolff began, to which Galla replied, "These guys have been terrific throughout the whole tournament. We're just going to try to keep it going."

Rick Wolff: "You guys really hit the ball today."

Bob Zullo: "These guys know how to play both ends of the game. They know how to hit. They know how to field. They know how to do everything. They're really a great bunch of kids."

Rick Wolff: "You have a tremendously balanced attack...you just hammered the ball, a real Murderers' Row."

Tom Galla: "I'd just like to say that Bob (Zullo) has been the batting instructor since July 1st. And all of our successes are the result of his work, his patience, his constant reminding. That's where it's coming from."

Rick Wolff: "And of course, Andy Paul had a real solid performance today on the mound."

Bob Zullo: "A nice job, yes, especially to go out on national TV and pitch the way he pitched. He did a real nice job. It's unbelievable!"

Rick Wolff: "As it has started to rain here in Bristol, your fans from Trumbull must be thrilled as well."

UNLIKELY CHAMPIONS: A MIRACLE IN WILLIAMSPORT

Bob Zullo: "Yes..." as the fans cheered, drowning him out.

Once the post-game interviews ended, the team surrounded Assistant Coach Ed Wheeler to collect on his promise to have his head shaved if they won a berth in Williamsport. As they stood at home plate, electric clippers, courtesy of Dan McGrath's father, got hooked up to an extension cord and the hair-clipping party began, each kid taking "shear" delight at clipping off a clump of Wheeler's hair. If they return from Williamsport as champions, Tom Galla loses *his* hair next.

"When this team first got together," Galla said, "I asked them *why* we were together. They looked at me like I was crazy. I told them the idea is to go to Williamsport. I reminded them of it a couple of times." Wonder how Coach Wheeler looks now?

Tony Deldeo's wife's worst nightmare had come true; Trumbull pounded out 18 hits to roll over Brandywine 15-5.

"Trumbull National was now crowned the 1989 Eastern Regional Champions..." Galla would say later. Trumbull National did something no team from Trumbull has ever done. First, they won the State tournament and now they were bound for Williamsport – completely new territory for a Trumbull Little League team.

Tom Galla told *Bridgeport Post-Telegram* sports writer Chris Elsberry that his stomach "...was doing flip-flops all the way" as his team "...ran roughshod through the Eastern Regional field." Now they would make the trip to Williamsport. Would his stomach continue its gyrations? They would now sail unchartered waters.

The next day, those waters grew deeper. Trumbull rode a wave to a berth in the Little League World Series. "This is tough," said Galla. "Now I know what it is like to be in the minor leagues, going from town to town, staying in motels. But I think we can stick it out."

As relaxed as the boys looked, their parents watching from the stands appeared anything but. As the team won game after game, their anxiety grew, as did their superstitious rituals. Such is the life of a Little League parent.

Once the on-field celebration ended, new anxieties arose. "We didn't know there was more to come," Sandy Galla remembered thinking. "How much can one person take?"

The joy of winning one tournament created new challenges for the parents. Taking care of things back home might go on hold...again. There were bigger worries. So many things to do...in so little time!

Such as...

What colors would the team be wearing – do we need to coordinate T-shirt colors? Who's ordering the T-shirts? How many does Blanchette's have? Take them all. Get as many as you can. They need to be ready for the Davenport, Iowa game on Tuesday. Who will pick up the T-shirts? Who was going straight to Williamsport? Do we have enough rooms for everybody? Where is Danville, anyway?

That night, an exhausted Tom Galla joined the parents and fans for a celebration and a replay of the game on TV. Finally, the rigors and exhilaration of the past few days caught up with Tom as he crashed for the night on a "real bed." He fell asleep thinking he would deal with Williamsport in the morning.

How have Eastern Regional champions done in Williamsport? From 1957, when Little League established the regional tournaments, through 2000, when the Eastern Regional was reorganized into the New England Region and Mid-Atlantic Region, Connecticut teams have had some success:

State	Eastern Regional Champions	Record in Little League World Series	Winning PCT	Little League Champions
Connecticut	10	15–14	51.7%	2
New Jersey	9	21–9	70.0%	3
New York	8	13–11	54.2%	1
Pennsylvania	6	10–8	55.6%	1
Maryland	3	2–7	22.2%	0
New Hampshire	3	2–7	22.2%	0
Massachusetts	2	2–4	33.3%	0
Rhode Island	2	3–5	37.5%	0
Maine	1	1–2	33.3%	0
Total	44	69–67	50.7%	7

CHAPTER NINE

GOING WHERE NO TEAM FROM TRUMBULL HAS GONE BEFORE

After their East Region championship win over Brandywine, Donald Trump offered to fly the Trumbull team to Williamsport, but Little League officials got wind of it and nixed the deal. Instead, early the next morning, Sunday, August 20th, the team boarded a bus for the six-hour ride to Williamsport.

Later that morning, the parents returned to Trumbull to do laundry, repack for what they hoped would be a week away from home, and get ready for the ride to Williamsport. A few gathered at their home field, Unity Park in Trumbull, to carpool or pick up laundry for the kids whose parents couldn't make it to Williamsport until later in the week, with everyone anxious to see what awaited them.

After the mayhem earlier in the week, with kids from 12 teams overwhelming the facilities, the last night in Bristol turned quiet. As teams suffered elimination, they left, so, after beating Brandywine, only the Trumbull boys and their coaches remained on Saturday evening.

Tom Galla appreciated the serenity of the moment when he said, "The next morning after breakfast, they loaded us on a bus for the ride to Williamsport. It was a quiet ride, a good time to catch up on some sleep. On the bus, we had a chance to speak with a Little League official, Andy Konyar, a good guy, about what we could expect. It was nice to get a little head start on what we were driving into. It was a nice, relaxing ride. Matt Sewell was with us, although we paid for that later. Little League officials didn't like that we had done that. He was no longer considered to be part of the team."

"I put Matt [Sewell] on the bus that took the team to Williamsport," said Ed Wheeler, "even though I couldn't go on the bus. They made a bit of a stink when I put Matt on the bus. He was pretty upset. Tom backed me up on that and Matt got back on the bus."

The road from Trumbull – no, make that *Bristol* – to Williamsport runs a bit more than 250 miles. Riding along Interstate 84 through Connecticut into New York, across the Hudson River at Peekskill, and ultimately Pennsylvania, the view transforms from suburban Connecticut into thickly covered forests of Pennsylvania's Delaware Water Gap National Recreation Area. As you turn south towards Interstate 80, there are brief glimpses of urban Scranton, then rolling farmland and bucolic hillsides as you head west toward your target – Williamsport.

After leaving Interstate 80, the last 15 miles north into South Williamsport, where the Little League complex actually resides, present a fairly nondescript scene, lots of farmhouses and open farmland, but also run-down commercial strip malls with numerous signs pointing the way to *Clyde Peeling's Reptiland*. This area has seen its better days. Oh, and get your camera ready, because you also pass by the Federal Correction Institute at Allenwood, Pennsylvania.

None of the Trumbull kids has ever been here.

The view changes dramatically once the Little League complex comes into view. The tree-lined hillside that overlooks Howard J. Lamade stadium, the practice facilities and dormitories forms a natural amphitheater for the tens of thousands who will witness the championship game later in the week.

As the bus pulled into the complex set across the Susquehanna River on about 66 acres just a couple of miles south of downtown Williamsport, the kids got their first look at Little League's home as they stepped down off the bus after the six-hour ride. Seeing Lamade Stadium for the first time sends chills down your spine...

...and that view *still* sends chills down Todd Halky's spine, every time he visits. "Seeing the field for the first time was cool, pretty cool, still is today. Back then, it looked like a campground more than it does now, with bunk beds, ping pong tables... Since we weren't allowed to go swimming, even though all the other teams would go swimming, we just played lots of ping pong. I guess the coaches didn't want anyone to get hurt or sick. We practiced, ate, played ping pong. For most of us, being away from home for the first time, it felt like a summer camp. We all got along pretty well, busted each other's chops, like kids do."

To Jason Hairston, the "...view from the top of that hill was amazing. That's what I remember as we pulled up and looked down at the field. And I think that is when it really hit me. We had two things on our mind, one, wow we're going to play on that field, that's an awesome field. The other was, look at that hill, we can roll down this hill. I don't think we even had cardboard boxes; we just lay down and rolled." Danny Brown joined Jason in wanting to also roll down the hill. What 12-year-old *wouldn't* want to do that? Kids know how to have fun.

UNLIKELY CHAMPIONS: A MIRACLE IN WILLIAMSPORT

The first time he viewed Lamade Stadium, Brown said, "It was cool. But, I thought it was a bit unusual that the field didn't have chalk lines [to mark the foul lines]. There was a white tape that was nailed into the ground, which I thought was strange. I guess they didn't have to re-do the lines after every game; they were permanent."

"The experience of seeing Lamade Stadium for the first time was great," David Galla recalled. "We were shot when we got to Williamsport. We had been on the bus for six hours or so. It was a wave of emotions. You want to get started. You're excited to be there. You're drained from what had happened previously. Then you look out over the field and seeing that hill, it seemed to go on forever. The field was way down at the bottom of that hill. We had never played on anything like that. We knew we were looking at a place where a lot of people are going to be there in a week to watch the championship, whether you are or not."

Danny McGrath had never seen anything quite like it. "It was much cooler than what I had seen on TV, a stadium built for kids. The centerfield 'wall' of grass was daunting to look at knowing it could be filled with people!"

"Honestly, awestruck seeing it, especially from the top of the hill," Andy Paul said. "It really looked like a mini-Major League stadium and was so different from Unity Park and the other ballparks we played in. It is a beautiful complex."

Can joy be any purer than when a 12-year-old experiences it?

It held the same effect for Tom Galla. "Seeing the field was awesome. I'm sure as a visitor it's very impressive, but as a participant it was magnificent. When you look at it, it's just incredible. Then when we walked down the steps to the field [for the Taiwan game] and heard the crowd chant, 'U-S-A! U-S-A!' ...it was very emotional."

Once Trumbull arrived in Williamsport, the team had little time to think about what was happening; it proved a bit of a blur. Lots of administrative tasks presented themselves, such as getting their housing assignments...scheduling practices...completing medical exams. With just 48 hours to the opener on Tuesday afternoon, they had little time to soak it all in...not a lot of time to absorb the setting...not even a lot of time to focus on the task ahead. But they had plenty of time to see the kids from Taiwan, the favorites, the titans they know they have to beat to bring home the trophy.

At 3:00 PM, the Trumbull team stepped off the bus into the Little League compound, excited to arrive until...they see the kids from Taiwan, who appeared "...very polished and dressed in similar warm-up suits," recalled Tom Galla.

He remembered their first day in Williamsport...

"There were things that had to be done that first day. They gave us windbreaker jackets when we first arrived, then later they gave us uniforms.

We also had to go to the infirmary to meet with a doctor who examined each of the kids. That's when we first met the kids from Taiwan, because they were in line waiting for their physicals. It looked like they had been there for a while and were dressed in their practice uniforms. They looked very professional; everything was perfect. Our kids looked like normal kids, dressed in different shorts, tee shirts, and sneakers."

"I thought we fell out of the bus like Keystone Cops compared to the regimented Taiwan team," quipped Ken Martin.

"Our kids' eyes got wide open," Galla said. "That's all we've heard about for about 10 years is 'Taiwan this, Taiwan that.' We don't have to worry about Taiwan until about three games from now and that's the last thing I want them thinking about. So we took the kids right out and drilled them harder than we have all season. That brought them back to earth. I told them I'm being this way for a very good reason. We've got to make sure that we understand what we're here for. We have to understand that we have to bring it up a notch now, maybe two or three notches from the regionals."

"Afterward, I told them that I didn't want them thinking about those guys [Taiwan], but wanted them to focus on Davenport, Iowa, who we would be playing in two days. They seemed to focus, and didn't seem to be in awe of anything that was going on. It's the only time we were intimidated in our stay at Williamsport," Tom Galla continued.

If every Little Leaguer aspires to play in the Little League World Series, then surely every Major League baseball player dreams of someday earning a place in the Baseball Hall of Fame in Cooperstown, which sits on the shores of Lake Otsego, the source of the Susquehanna River, a mere 206 miles north of Williamsport.

Each year during the Little League World Series, South Williamsport becomes the home to hundreds of 12-year-olds, their families, their fans, and most of all, baseball. Is there any sport more pure than Little League baseball?

The influx of baseball fans overwhelms this small Pennsylvania town and its surrounding communities. Hotel rooms are scarce, restaurants packed. Traffic jams every main thoroughfare. Entrepreneurial neighbors' yards meet the demand for additional parking spaces for the large crowds attending every game.

The fans come for many reasons: some to watch their kids or grandkids, nieces or nephews, or friends play; or to support their home town team; others make the trip just to be there because they are baseball fans. Still others attend because "…if you build it they will come." They just love watching baseball.

After the long drive from Trumbull, the parents finally arrived at the Days Inn in nearby Danville, Pennsylvania. They wasted little time, checking in, unloading their vehicles, and "immediately got back in our cars to drive to Williamsport," Sandy Galla recalled. "We couldn't wait one more minute. Our hearts were pounding and blood was rushing to our heads. The first view over the hill was *magnificent*! We had *arrived*!"

Coach Tom Galla described the Trumbull team's collective frame of mind as they came through the Eastern Regional on their way to Williamsport: "Fired up, intense every single time they hit the field. Perfect attitude, no cockiness, just downright aggressive." When they arrived in Williamsport, Galla wanted to take the pressure off the kids. "The kids are great. It's the coaches who are scared to death," he said.

"There's so much talk at the regionals, 'oh it's such an honor to be here, win or lose.' It's true, but it's not why you're here. You're here to win and we're going to try to win…We're the underdog. I love it. That's where I want to be," Galla added

It's also the right way to go into a series where if you have just one bad game you find yourself watching the championship game from the stands or on TV at home, and not from the dugout. Underdog status can actually often relax a team, making it easier to deal with the expectations foisted upon the favorite.

While Galla's attitude might seem pretty intense for Little League, when you get to Williamsport, no coach wants the kids to go home lamenting the fact that they blew their chance.

"Pretty intense" is how Jim Carpenter, a sports writer for the *Williamsport Sun-Gazette* in 1989, remembered Coach Galla. "From the get-go once he arrived in South Williamsport, Trumbull manager Tom Galla exuded confidence in his team. He said more than once that his squad relished its underdog role and in games leading up to the championship it was evident why – the Trumbull National Little Leaguers were fundamentally sound, played great defense and showed more mental toughness than many youth teams exhibit. The latter was a tribute to Galla and his coaches."

When asked about Taiwan, Galla said, "I get the feeling that they're almost military. We're not military, but we're competitive, real competitive. I don't think you can compare an American team to them. It doesn't mean they're going to beat the American team. If we keep playing the way we played in the regionals, just hitting the ball. We've got good pitching and excellent defense. We're solid all across the line and if it continues, we're going to be tough." He continued, "Now I think it's a mental thing and that's *my* job, so I'm going to do my best."

David Galla recalled that "…though we had been on TV, we knew there was going to be media everywhere. My dad and our coaches, Bob Zullo and Ed Wheeler, did a great job of shielding us from the media pressure as much as they could. They told us to just answer their question, keep it short, don't go on too long. Be truthful in whatever you say to them. It is a good lesson that I still carry with me today. All of us have been doing interviews since we were 12 years old. So at this point in our lives we are more comfortable answering questions without going too far. It's served a lot of us well throughout our lives. Certainly, it was a different level of scrutiny when we got to Williamsport. I think we handled it pretty well...

"Some of the guys wanted to talk and some didn't," the younger Galla continued, "so, those who wanted to talk did, and those who didn't, didn't. Because we were so young, my dad did most of the talking with the press to protect the kids. But, we really didn't know what hit us until [we won the title]. Being a 12-year-old kid with a microphone in your face is a pretty cool thing. I think we handled it well. It was also different back then. At that time, [the Little League World Series] just hadn't gained the huge international following that it [has] today."

"I don't think we were [ready for the media attention when we got there]," Jason Hairston recollected. "We were just one team out of many. All the teams had stories just like us. I didn't think we were anything special. It was fun. I still remember when we were filling out our profiles, they put us in this one room, we were told, just fill out who your favorite team is and who your favorite player is. Well, Cody was hysterical that day. He started filling out his profile out loud, making jokes about the answers. And then we all started laughing about the questions and would answer our own profiles with [silly responses]. No one really told us what these were for. We were asked to fill them out so we did. Anyway, five days later, you're on ABC-TV, 'What's your favorite thing about the USA?' My answer was, 'girls.' So, everything from that profile went on TV."

Dan Brown doesn't "...remember talking to too many people. We were somewhat sequestered so the media never bothered us too much. I probably would have shied away from them if I saw them coming. I don't think I wanted any part of that. I wasn't comfortable talking to the press, if ever. I really stayed away and hung out in the ping pong area more than anything else. I'm not sure that I was dodging the press, but I also don't think I was the focus of their attention very much. The press was probably more focused on the pitchers and the guys who hit all the home runs and maybe Dave [Galla] because he was the coach's son."

"When we get to Williamsport, the other teams were coming in," David Galla remembered. "Everybody is sizing each other up, doing things that 12-year-olds normally do. We saw the ping pong table, so we wanted to play ping pong. The food there wasn't that good, so we were starving all the time because we were drained from playing so much baseball. We all kept looking at the pool, but we were not allowed to go in it. I said to myself, one day I'm going to go back and swim in that pool."

"As 12-year-olds, they wouldn't talk to the media," Tom Galla recalled. "If they did talk, it was usually a one- or two-syllable answer. I'm not sure why, whether it was because they were shy, or because of their age.

UNLIKELY CHAMPIONS: A MIRACLE IN WILLIAMSPORT

I think at that age maybe they weren't equipped to give great answers. So, I got a lot of attention, and I enjoyed it."

"The media kind of haunt you," said Ed Wheeler. "As a matter of fact, Chris Drury had a lot of trouble with them. They would turn what he said around. The media wasn't fun for me. I avoided them as much as I could. Tom handled all that, he was good at talking to them without sticking his foot in his mouth."

A little bit about the players...

Just before the team's arrival in Williamsport, Galla named Drury and Martin the team's co-captains. "They deserve it and it was necessary," Galla said, "because Chris and Ken are like adults on the playing field."

At 5-feet, 1½ inches, 126 pounds, Chris Drury bats leadoff as the best pure hitter on the team. He's also a crafty pitcher who throws lots of junk – a curve, a changeup and a knuckleball. If you stand in the batter's box beware, because Chris will come at you with different speeds and every imaginable arm angle. Deception is his game, his off-speed stuff a perfect counterpart to Andy Paul's fastball. However, his control rates nowhere as good as Andy's.

"He throws lots of balls," recalled Tom Galla. But, Drury proves a tough and determined kid whose Pee Wee hockey team won the U.S. Amateur American Hockey Championship in April. The kid with what one reporter described as "a cherubic face" would develop into one of the country's premier collegiate and professional hockey players.

As Tom Galla says, "He'll bend a little, but he's never broken." "This kid's got the biggest heart you'll ever see in baseball," Ed Wheeler added. "There's no player at 12-years-old who can give you what he gives you."

Drury played catcher when he didn't pitch, thus his involvement in calling every pitch of every game. The coaches trusted him and rarely interfered with his pitch-calling. His teammates respected him, and looked up to him as the face of the team and its leader.

Tom Galla described Drury this way: "Chris was a great Little League pitcher, but he was never going to be a pitcher. He was good, he was smart, and he was a great hitter."

Andy Paul, at 5-foot-6-inches, 131 pounds, filled the role of the team's "other" starting pitcher, and the hardest thrower. His fastballs often reached 70 miles per hour, equivalent to more than 90 mph from a Major League hurler. He learned how to change speeds with the "dart pitch" that Ed Wheeler taught him. He used it on occasion to keep batters off balance. But his heat burned so hot he didn't need to resort to the "dart" often. When not pitching, Andy played the outfield and hit in the middle of the batting order as a key member of the team's "Murderers' Row."

The 5-foot-10-inch, 140-pound, power-hitting Ken Martin played first base. Kenny can blast a ball out of the park with the best hitters anywhere, it's called "whack-power," and being so tall, he provided a great target for throws across the infield as the team's first baseman. Not surprisingly, Martin could also play basketball better than any of his Trumbull teammates.

Dan McGrath stood 5-foot-2-inches, weighed 104 pounds, and played the outfield, but could also pitch. As a native of Melbourne, Australia, his presence on the roster gave the team an international dimension. The blond-haired, freckled-faced left-hander had lived in Connecticut for four years while his dad, who worked for the Australian government, fulfilled an assignment with Sikorsky Aircraft, the helicopter manufacturer. The family had planned to return to Australia earlier in the summer, but stayed a little longer so Dan could play on the All-Star team.

Centerfielder Matt Basztura, at 5-foot-4-inches and 125 pounds, could run faster than any other kid on the team. His powerful bat earned him the nickname "Matt the Bat."

Danny Brown, a solid defender at shortstop, made all the plays look routine. Standing 5-foot-4-inches and weighing 112 pounds, he rated the most athletic kid on the roster. Along with Jason Hairston at third base, they formed a strong left side of the infield for Trumbull. His teammates called him "Downtown (Danny Brown)."

Jason Hairston, one of the "little guys" on the team at 4-foot-7½ inches, and but 75 pounds, got the label "Little Big Man" as the team's sparkplug. He played third base, and while he didn't make every play, he often made the spectacular play. Tom Galla described him as "a real competitor."

Todd Halky, a 4-foot-11½-inches, 99-pound catcher, another member of the pint-sized catalysts on the team, described himself as "…a scrappy player, always able to make contact with the ball, [and] get on base."

Tom Galla's son, David, at 4-foot-11½-inches and 86 pounds, another of the team's smaller players, played second base. "I was a defensive specialist," said David when told that he did not commit an error during the entire tournament. "I was not a big hitter, usually batted eighth or ninth every game. I knew how to play my role; a left-handed hitter who slaps it around a little, a line drive guy. That's why I was so excited when I almost hit a home run that one game. I might have hit a couple of doubles but that was it; I mostly got singles."

Cody "Gomer" Lee stood 5-foot, ½-inch tall, 105 pounds. "Gomer" kept the mood light as the clubhouse comedian and practical joker. He earned the nickname "Gomer" for his "Gomer Pyle" routines. "He keeps the team going," Ed Wheeler commented. "He's always got a funny crack to make, and always has a smile."

Harlen Marks, at 5-foot-½-inch, 95 pounds, could hit the fastball better than any of his teammates and proved a pinch-hitting specialist, while

5-foot-1-inch, 103-pound defensive ace Chris Kelly could fill any of the outfield positions as well as pitch an inning or two in a pinch.

Coach Galla used four-foot-10½-inches, 90-pound Paul Coniglio as a talented and speedy pinch-runner with solid defensive skills in the outfield, and added 5-foot-1-inch, 93-pound Chris Fasano to the roster after Matt Sewell's injury.

Prior to falling off his bike and breaking his arm delivering newspapers in early August, Matt Sewell had started every game in right field. His ability to get on base was top-notch, and he could always be counted on to deliver in a pinch as the team's third pitcher.

Once Trumbull began play in Williamsport, per Little League rules, they could only have two adult coaches in the dugout. As a result, Ed Wheeler was the third man out. As the third base coach, Wheeler filled a key role on the coaching staff. As Tom Galla put it, "He would sit with the kids in the back of the bus and be into their heads and be their friend and the whole bit. I think between him being their friend and me being the bad guy, because I was always the tough guy most of the time, and Bob Zullo being both ways, I think the kids realized we were all in it together."

"This is a three-year dream," said Ed Wheeler. "Three years ago we said this team could go to Williamsport. And then when it finally happened, we didn't believe it." Asked when he began to believe the team could make it to Williamsport, "Though I wasn't overconfident, I knew we had a shot. We went through the Districts pretty easy. In the States we were doing well too. I knew if they kept playing up to their potential, we could go all the way. When we got to Bristol, we saw some good teams, and knew we would have to get lucky, which we did. We got a good draw. We didn't get Cherry Hills' number one pitcher, who was unbelievable. We played a good game against them, and all of a sudden started whacking home runs. If we had had an off game, they could have killed us. All the way, I thought we could do it, but I knew we had to be lucky. I know baseball too well."

CHAPTER TEN

"HELLO MR. GALLA. YOUR ASSIGNMENT, SHOULD YOU CHOOSE TO ACCEPT IT, IS...TO WIN"

Little League marked a special year in 1989 as it celebrated its 50th anniversary, with special events and commemorations held every day of the tournament to recognize what had transpired since Carl Stotz's idea became reality in 1939.

You'll find Little League's headquarters on U.S. Highway 15 in South Williamsport, a mile or so south of downtown Williamsport. To the left of the Headquarters building stands the Little League Baseball Museum. The players live in a complex of dormitories behind and below the Museum during the week-long tournament.

You get to Lamade Stadium by walking around the left side of the Headquarters building and descending a hill, a steep hill. I found my first view of the stadium almost overwhelming. The covered grandstand of Lamade Stadium, built in 1959, goes from the left-field foul-pole, curves behind home plate, and finishes its swing at the right-field foul-pole. It can seat nearly 10,000 in its grandstand, and another 30,000 or more on the grassy berm that surrounds the outfield.

Behind and below this gorgeous stadium you'll find Lamade Stadium's near-twin ballpark, Volunteer Stadium, built in 2001 with a seating capacity of approximately 5,000. Beyond that, several more ball fields exist to accommodate team practices.

There were two tournament brackets for the 1989 World Series: one bracket included the US teams from the four geographical regions of the country – East, Midwest, South, and West; the other bracket held the four international teams from around the world – Europe/Middle East/ Africa, Far East, South America/Caribbean, and Canada.

UNLIKELY CHAMPIONS: A MIRACLE IN WILLIAMSPORT

The schedule of tournament games for the week ran as follows:
Championship Bracket:
Tuesday, August 22:
  Game 1 – Taiwan (Far East) vs. Saudi Arabia (Europe), 2 PM
  Game 2 – Trumbull (US East) vs. Davenport, Iowa (US
    Central), 5 PM
Wednesday, August 23:
  Game 3 – San Pedro, California (US West) vs. Tampa, Florida
    (US South), 2 PM
  Game 4 – Toronto, Ontario (Canada) vs. Maracaibo, Venezuela
    (Latin America), 5 PM
Thursday, August 24:
  Game 5 – US Championship, 2 PM
  Game 6 – International Championship, 5 PM
Saturday, August 26:
  Game 8 – Championship Game, 4 PM
Consolation Bracket:
Wednesday, August 23:
  Game A – Game 1 loser vs. Game 2 loser, 10 AM
Thursday, August 24
  Game B – Game 3 loser vs. Game 4 loser, 10 AM
Friday, August 25:
  Game C – Game A loser vs. Game B loser, 10 AM
  Game D – Game A winner vs. Game B winner, 1 PM
  Third Place Game – Game C winner vs. Game D winner, 4 PM

    Once Trumbull National arrived in Williamsport, the team became the focus of the national media, just as the other teams there that week. Just eight teams remained, each vying for the Little League crown out of the thousands that had set out two months earlier in hopes of reaching the Little League World Series.
    Though eight teams played for the Little League title, the favorites emerged even before the teams arrived in Williamsport, before the first pitch was thrown. As *Williamsport Sun-Gazette* reporter Jim Carpenter remembered, "Historically, teams from the Far East, Latin America and either the US West or US South, were tabbed prohibitive favorites due mainly to their being able to play baseball year 'round. In fact, going into the 1989 Little League World Series, teams from the Far East had won 18 of the previous 22 titles, including 13 by teams from Taiwan – among them, the last three in a row."
    The record bore this out, with one exception. Since International competition commenced in 1957, the Far East champions had clearly dominated (18 champions and one runner-up). The other 14 titles belong to Latin America (two wins plus three second-place finishes), while the US South and West had brought home six title between them (plus 19 second-

place finishes). As expected, the US Central had just one championship (1959) and five runners-up, while no teams from Europe or Canada have won the title, though Canada played in the 1965 championship game, losing to Windsor Locks, Connecticut. The surprise is that the US East has won five titles since 1957, the last being in 1975, and finished runner-up three times.

Carpenter continued: "Other than records, we didn't know much about the teams before they arrived in Williamsport. There was no regional television coverage in those days and we (the press) relied on reports supplied through Little League International headquarters, in South Williamsport."

While the coaches had to deal with the media as they advanced from the Districts to winning the Regional, they have never seen anything such as what they now faced. Who could they talk to? No one from Trumbull had ever experienced this kind of media coverage because before this, no one from Trumbull has made it to Williamsport.

Galla and his staff also worried that the attention from television stations and newspapers could puff up the egos of the players, who might start "believing their own press." Galla knew that this kind of attention could cause the kids to lose focus on the games, or get discouraged if the press labeled them the weak team from the East. To guard against this, the coaches prohibited the boys from watching television and reading the sports pages.

Another big decision the coaches made: "No Swimming." They wouldn't let the boys go to the swimming pool in the housing complex Little League has for all the players, known as The International Grove. The coaches knew one thing for sure, 12-year-olds love to "roughhouse," and pools provide the perfect place to get hurt having that kind of fun. The team already lost Matt Sewell to an injury and could not afford another.

As in Bristol, the Little League World Series in 1989 is single elimination. If a team loses, it drops into the consolation round, eliminating it from competing for the championship. To advance to the final round, a team must win all three of its games over a five-day period.

No room for error.
No recovering from a bad day.
Do or die, or, maybe, do or go home.

Speaking with the media after their practice on Sunday afternoon, Trumbull National's Galla understood quickly the Trumbull status of underdog, and just as quickly, he relished that role. But that did not mean he wanted his kids to consider themselves underdogs or the "weak team" from the East. Let the other teams think what they will about the East team. *This* team can play baseball.

Trumbull hit the ball well nearly every tournament game, averaging more than 11 runs per game, despite a shutout in their only loss and only scoring one run against New Hampshire. More importantly, the pitching staff, led by dual aces Chris Drury and Andy Paul, proved themselves tough to score on, allowing just 2.5 runs per game while maintaining excellent control with just 31 batters walked in 13 games.

Trumbull's "Electric Company" arrived in Williamsport having compiled some astounding batting stats - the team had hit a cool .440 (159 hits to their opponents' 68), outscoring the other teams 155 to 32 while launching 31 home runs.

Ken Martin led the way, slugging 10 home runs with 32 RBI while hitting .600. Andy Paul followed with eight home runs and 22 RBI while hitting a lofty .559. Leadoff hitter Chris Drury raked the ball at a .532 clip, including six home runs and 17 RBI. Adding sparks to the Electric Company's output: Matt Basztura (.475, 4 HR, 15 RBI), Dan Brown (.286/2/16 RBI), Dan McGrath (.467/0/6), Cody Lee (.375/0/3), Todd Halky (.435/0/6), David Galla (.292/0/3), Jason Hairston (.333/1/8), and Chris Kelly (.400/0/5).

Little League named the housing complex in Williamsport "The International Grove," a name that did little to describe its real character in 1989; it looked more like a military barracks, with its eight bunk beds for the kids and two more beds on the other side of a divider for the coaches. Within this fenced-in complex you'd find the second building, known as "The Pavilion," where the kids had their meals each day, sitting at one table as a team, and hanging out between practices and games.

"The food wasn't good, cafeteria food, kind of like what you get in college. But we were kids," Todd Halky remembered.

After just spending a week living with all the kids in an elementary school room in Bristol, Tom Galla and Bob Zullo faced another week living with the boys in "The Grove" in Williamsport. "At The International Grove, I felt a bit trapped having to spend 24 hours a day with 14 kids, but they did lots of things for the kids, like parties, movies and lots of ice cream. But we were somewhat sequestered, with restrictions regarding the times when the parents could visit with their kids. There was a fence surrounding The Grove from the outside world, which is where the kids would usually meet their parents."

Most of the time, the kids did a pretty good job of amusing themselves with the activities usually expected from any group of 12-year-old boys. The scenario also provided the opportunity to mingle with the kids from the other teams.

"There was lots of stuff to do there," Jason Hairston remembered, "play ping pong, there were pool tables, and we played whiffle ball with the Taiwan team. There was swimming, but we were the only team that didn't do that." There were also televisions, though the coaches tried to keep them from watching too much about what was happening in the tournament.

Dan Brown recalled "…getting big into the trading pin thing. Still have them. I traded the Trumbull pins I had for pins from other teams."

"This was an exciting part of the whole experience," thought Dan McGrath. "I had a chance to play table tennis against Chris Sabo, who played with the Cincinnati Reds at the time. A couple other pros came by the camp area. Just to hang out and talk with them was pretty cool."

Dan Brown also played ping pong with Chris Sabo, but remembers being "…disappointed that he wasn't wearing the goggles he wore when he played. Not sure who won. We played a lot of ping pong. I also remember hanging out with the security people and asking them to give us rides in their golf carts."

"Johnny Bench was there…" the morning of the California game, David Galla added. "I think it was a Bubblicious [bubble gum] deal. Chris [Drury] pitched to Johnny Bench, and I think he struck him out. All the teams were there for that…" and Tom Galla added, "Johnny Bench was there talking about hitting and asked Chris Drury to go to the mound to throw him some pitches, and I'm not sure what was going on, but Johnny couldn't hit any of Chris's pitches."

"We had a little bit of a run in with the first baseman from Taiwan [the 5-foot-8-inch, 175-pound, Ming-Lan Hsu] while playing table tennis. Go figure, there was a little controversy with him and Chris in the final game," Dan McGrath recalled. "Years later I would face him and the pitcher, Chien-Chih Lee, when representing Australia in a game versus Taiwan. A mate of mine had Lee stay with him while they were here in Melbourne…back in '92."

During one of the team's practices, Dan Brown remembered seeing the Taiwan kids show up for practice on one of the side fields. "The Taiwan team arrives for practice suited up in uniforms, white shirts and white pants, an orange or red hat, and each of them had the same bat bag and same shoes on. We were all in "jams" and had different stuff on, like we were playing on a sandlot."

After the team practiced Monday afternoon on the Lamade Stadium field, Tom Galla joked with *Bridgeport Post-Telegram's* Chris Elsberry when asked if he was nervous. "The kids are great. It's the coaches who are scared to death. They told us not to worry, that there would *only* be about 12,000 to 15,000 people in the stands" to watch the opening game against Davenport, Iowa.

Galla continued: "Our kids don't seem fazed. I guess the regional game helped." The Eastern Regional championship game two days earlier before a national television audience on ESPN and more than 5,000 Little League fans squeezed into Breen Field in Bristol, Connecticut, had apparently taken a bit of the edge off for the kids.

Though Tom still likes to give credit to his wife Sandy for the idea of using signs during the games to tell the kids where to throw the ball, she insists it was John Coniglio's idea. She just made the signs using file folders and black markers purchased at a local office supply store.

"It was getting very crowded on the hill, so noisy with the large crowds, that the kids couldn't hear what the coaches were telling them to do," Sandy explained. "Then they tried hand signals but those didn't work, so we did the signs. They were a lot easier to see. They really worked well."

The kids may have seemed calm because Tom Galla had instilled them with a high level of confidence, a particular ability of his. He was good at that. Of course, it also helped that they were peaking at the right time, with the pitching strong and the bats alive. It's nice to peak when you need to…as it certainly beats the alternative.

Continuing his interview with Elsberry, Galla said, "All the kids are peaking right now. Paul, Basztura, Martin, Drury…they're all hitting the heck out of the ball. And the little guys are coming through, too." Galla credited Assistant Coach Bob Zullo. "Everybody's driving the ball and Bob should get all the credit in the world. The kids are laying off the high stuff and are really a lot more determined at the plate."

"One of my best memories in Williamsport," recalled Todd Halky, "was when they got all the pitchers and catchers from all eight teams together under the third base bleachers [before the first game], so they could watch everybody's motion, to make sure they were legal, [that they] weren't balking. Then the Taiwan guys got up to throw, and it was like, whoa, their pitches were really popping. We were told not to say anything to the rest of the guys."

"I don't really think we were worried or anxious about being there, or nervous about losing," Todd Halky maintained. "I don't think we ever went into a game thinking we were going to lose. If we were playing a game we just felt we could win it."

Ed Wheeler remembered telling the kids that "the other teams got here the same way we got here, so you aren't going to see any softies." He was not trying to scare them but rather trying to keep them focused, level-headed.

"Before the Davenport game, we had only practiced once on the stadium field," remembered David Galla, "so I was a bit worried that the hops weren't going to be true or something because I didn't really know the field. In the end there was no need to worry because the field was well manicured. But all we really wanted was to start the game. We had practiced enough, we were ready to play. We were just happy to get on the field, see our first pitch, swing the bats, and be in a live game situation."

As he sat in the stands on Monday afternoon watching Davenport practice, Tom Galla wasn't sure what to expect from Davenport, and didn't seem to know much about them. "Heck," he said, "they could beat us 20-0."

CHAPTER ELEVEN

GOLDEN GLOVES QUIET THE DAVENPORT BATS

Tuesday, August 22nd arrived with a warm and muggy dawn and the possibility of thunderstorms; temperatures would reach the high 80's, same as yesterday, with more of the same forecast for tomorrow.

The 43rd Little League World Series opened this afternoon, with the first game pitting Aramco Little League from Dharhan, Saudi Arabia (representing Europe) against one of the favorites, Kang-Tu Little League from Kaohsiung, Taiwan (representing the Far East). First pitch scheduled for 2 PM.

Dhahran, located in central Saudi Arabia, came to Williamsport with an 8-0 post-season record. This marked their fifth appearance in Williamsport. Manager Mark Tucker hoped his third trip there in as many years would prove the charm…

Statistically, Dhahran's numbers looked as good as Taiwan's. They had scored 112 runs while allowing only two, 14 runs per game en route to the Europe Regional championship played at Ramstein Air Force Base in West Germany. However, two games skewed those number a bit: a 50-0 win over an Israeli team playing Little League for the first time, and a 22-0 pasting of Norway. Still, their pitchers had done well, tossing six shutouts in eight games, allowing only a single run in each of their other two games.

Manager Mark Tucker, a land surveyor from Grand Rapids, Michigan, who worked with Arabian American Oil Company, knew it would be tough, despite what the numbers said.

If you want to win the Little League World Series, you need to play solid baseball. You also need a few lucky breaks along the the way. Dhahran drew the short straw, learning their opening game opponent would be pre-tournament favorite and three-time defending Little League World Series champion, Taiwan. Their task was neither easy nor one that the other International teams envied. No one wanted to play Taiwan, certainly not in your first game.

Taiwan is always tough, and Tucker knew his kids would have to play outstanding baseball to upset Taiwan. Oh, by the way, not only was Taiwan the three-time defending Little League champion, but their record over the previous 20 years in the championship game stood a glittering 13-1; their lone loss a 6-0 shutout by Kirkland, Washington in 1982.

The good news? Tucker and his assistant, Cornell Seymour, from Brunswick, Georgia, who also worked for Arabian American Oil Company, had three kids returning from last year's team that played in Williamsport. Even in Little League, experience rules, especially *Williamsport* experience. They also had a truly international team, with kids born in cities across the US as well as others from Iran, Italy, Indonesia, England, and Saudi Arabia.

Tucker knew what his kids had to do. "Our pitchers are going to have to do real well and we're going to have to make some plays in the field because they're {Taiwan} going to hit the ball. They're good hitters and they're not going to strike out. And we're going to have to get some hits. That's probably the key, hitting for us. There's not much you can concoct in the way of strategy for Taiwan. We're just going to have to go out and play our game."

Kaohsiung's (Taiwan) Manager Wu Chin-Ming spoke through an interpreter before the contest, saying, "We have good pitching. We have good hitting. Everything is just fine. We have confidence." An 11-0 record entering Williamsport should give you *plenty* of confidence. [Author's note: Officials of the Taiwan team did not provide the team's exact record, but indicated they had played many games while losing none. They could only provide information regarding five of their games prior to the Regional event.] Taiwan also has some "nice size," as teams from Taiwan seem to exhibit every year.

It came as no surprise that they had outscored their opponents 88 to 7, allowing less than one run per game while pitching seven shutouts in those 11 games. Taiwan performed even better in the six-game Far East Regional event played in Seoul, Korea, scoring 52 runs while allowing none in the six games. Their only close games came as 3-0 and 1-0 wins against Japan and Korea, respectively. The basic winning formula in baseball at any level is to score more runs than your opponent. Taiwan did it better than that - they usually scored early and often and almost never let the other team score, the best of both worlds in baseball: dominating offense and smothering pitching and defense. They breezed through games.

Manager Wu continued, "Our boys work very hard and we play solid, sound baseball. It is an honor for us to represent the Far East Region and to defend the World Series championship."

Dhahran gave Taiwan some pause for worry, taking an early 3-0 lead in the World Series opener. However, Taiwan rallied from this early deficit to score eight runs in the second inning and eventually defeat

Dhahran, Saudi Arabia, 9-4.

Taiwan loaded the bases off Dhahran starter Chet Frank, but could not push across any runs in the first inning. So, when the European champions score three runs in the top half of the second, the crowd reeled in shock. Doug Huisman led off with a double to left and Brian Kruse followed with a single to right field to get Dhahran started. One out later, after a delayed double-steal moved both runners up a base, and Jason Spice poked the first home run of the Series, just clearing the 204-foot, right-center field fence giving Dhahran its short-lived 3-0 lead.

Any dreams that Dhahran could spring the big upset quickly dissipated in Taiwan's half of the second. Taiwan's bottom three hitters got the offense rolling. Ming-Chieh Hsu got hit by a pitch, Kuan-Lung Chen singled to left, and Chin-Chih Huang reached first on an error by Dhahran shortstop Khalio Abdelrasoul to load the bases.

At 5-feet, 8-inches, 175 pounds, Taiwan's first baseman, Ming-Lan Hsu, didn't look like a twelve-year-old. He didn't play like one either. He stepped to the plate and crushed Chet Plank's next pitch high and deep to right-center field. It easily flew over the fence for a grand slam. Dhahran's lead had quickly disappeared with no outs. Taiwan's starting pitcher, Hsin-Lung Tseng, stepped into the batter's box and smacked one to right field, but Jason Spice misplayed it into a two-base error. A passed ball got Tseng to third, and he scored on a fielder's choice by Chien-Chih Lee.

Mark Tucker visited the mound, pulled Plank, and brought in second baseman Doug Huisman to pitch. At this point, he just hoped to stem the bleeding, but clean-up hitter Chen-Lung Yeh welcomed Huisman with another long shot to right-center field. It, too, cleared the fences, increasing the Taiwan lead to 7-3. They reloaded the bases, scoring another run on a RBI single by centerfielder Kuan-Lun Chen. Dhahran struggled to finally get the last two outs. It would be a struggle to come back from an 8-3 deficit against Taiwan, and Dhahran didn't.

Each team scores a run in the fifth inning, providing Taiwan's final 9-4 margin

Dhahran's pitchers struck out five and only allowed six hits, but their seven walks and their three errors stung. Taiwan's winning pitcher Hsin-Lung Tseng threw a great game, allowing just four hits and walking none while striking out six. Their defense showed some holes as they committed two errors, unusual for Taiwan.

After the game, Dhahran's Manager Mark Tucker said, "One thing about Taiwan, they always come ready to play baseball. They put the bat on the ball and you've got to play defense and you've got to pitch good also. I'm proud of my team. They played real well apart from that [second] inning. That was the difference."

Tucker continued, "I'll predict this much – no one will come that close to beating them. That means they'll win the World Championship."

UNLIKELY CHAMPIONS: A MIRACLE IN WILLIAMSPORT

What do land surveyors know about the future anyway? Probably as much as an accountant… [Author's note: I'm a CPA.]

Tom Galla and his coaches watched the game and recognized the strength of Taiwan's first four hitters. They had front-loaded their batting order with their very best hitters.

"That prompted Bob and I to talk about what we would do if we got into that type of situation, what we would do to somehow get through it, by doing something a little unorthodox, which is what we ended up doing," Galla shared.

In the second match-up of the day, Trumbull National faced Central Regional Champion Davenport East Little League from Davenport, Iowa, located on the eastern border of Iowa about 70 miles south of Dubuque. First pitch would leave the mound at 5 PM.

Davenport posted an 18-2 record through the Regionals, but Manager Hank Hemmen, an accountant by day and a Little League volunteer for 18 years, didn't seem very confident when asked about his team's chances.

"It's really difficult to project where we're going to be," Hemmen commented. "We're sure to play three games and we're going to play three games in our style." All teams play three games with the first-round losers dropping into the losers' bracket. "This team is a group of hardworking, good boys, who make fun out of all they do," he added. "We have excellent team spirit and good defense. Our strength is playing basic fundamental baseball and the ability of our first eight batters to hit a home run."

"The key is going to be our pitching," Hemmen continued. "The hitters always scare you as you move to different levels. We have good pitchers, but I really don't know how good the hitters are going to be." Davenport's top pitchers included right-handers Adam Shockey, Matt Jacobs, and Antwan Hanes. Hemmen finished by saying that there was no more pressure playing in Williamsport.

The real question remained how far Hemmen and his assistant Rick Rizzo, a construction superintendent, could lead their squad. In their 20 tournament games, Davenport outscored opponents 140 to 67, putting up double digit run totals in six games, and pitching three shutouts.

Davenport had edged Jeffersonville, Indiana, 1-0 to win the Central Regional tournament, coming back after losing to Jeffersonville 6-3 earlier that day. This was Davenport's second trip to Williamsport, the first coming in 1975 when Southeast Little League represented the Central US.

Before their Series opener against Davenport, Iowa, Trumbull Manager Tom Galla said, "We just have to keep playing the way we played in the regionals, just hitting the ball. This is a fantastic group of kids who have come a long way. We are thrilled to be one of the eight teams in the Little League World Series. Our bats have been hot and cold but there has always been someone to pick us up and get the job done."

Drury got the nod for the start (it was his turn in the rotation) and he would, as usual, bat leadoff. "Drury is an intimidating presence as a lead-off batter," says Galla. "He's already hit three lead-off homers and four or five doubles off the fence in that spot, while McGrath is an excellent line drive hitter with a great eye at the plate. Basztura's real aggressive and can hit with power. Martin, he's hitting something like .700 and has ten homers. He's just awesome. Paul's a free swinger who's hit seven or eight homers. Brown has also come on lately, hitting a lot of line drives, while Halky is a real good contact hitter who'll rarely strike out," Galla added.

The eight and nine hitters are his son David, who went 3-for-4 against Brandywine, Delaware, in the Eastern Regional championship, and Jason Hairston, the team's defensive specialist at third base. "That's why he's there," said Galla. "He makes the tough plays look easy. And he goes to his left so well that we can cheat Brown over more toward second base and that makes him a better shortstop."

The Trumbull nine played nearly airtight defense, committing just 10 errors in their first 13 games. If you expect to win in Little League, you *must* play solid defense. It is vital.

Just before the game started, Tom Galla lost the coin toss to determine the home team. Similar to the Cherry Hill game, losing the coin toss means Trumbull would bat first; only the second time Trumbull has not held the home advantage. This would prove a game in which they really would relish having "last ups."

Jason Hairston didn't remember being anxious before the first game in Williamsport. "We were naïve kids back then, just trying to get ready to play the game. We knew it was going to be a tough game. But we weren't worried." After all, it was just another game. Sort of…

But, from the first pitch, there came a sense that this game might be different. Trumbull's offense had scored early and often throughout the tournament, failing to score in the first inning just three times this summer. Chris Drury continued his incredible hitting with another leadoff hit, this one to center. Todd Halky sacrificed Drury to second, but Davenport starter Matt Jacobs retired Basztura and got Martin to pop out, stranding Drury. This will definitely be a different game; a *tight* game. Every play will count; with every run hard earned.

As Trumbull took the field in the bottom of the first, catcher Todd Halky remembered "…standing there, looking at my family in the stands, and seeing the large crowd watching us. It was pretty cool. As the game started, I was nervous. When the second batter popped one up behind home plate, I was nervous that I might miss it. But I caught it. I relaxed pretty well after I caught it. The crowd noise never really bothered me; I didn't pay much attention to it."

Trumbull broke the ice in the top of the second, taking advantage of Davenport starter Matt Jacobs' wildness, five walks and five wild pitches.

Dan Brown walked and moved to third on two wild pitches. After Dan McGrath popped out to short for the second out of the inning, David Galla and Jason Hairston each work walks in between three more Jacobs wild pitches, one of which allowed Brown to score the game's first run. It is Trumbull's first run in Williamsport, *ever*. Drury walked to load the bases, then Todd Halky walked to bring home Galla. Matt Basztura struck out to end the inning. Trumbull grabbed an early 2-0 lead without getting any hits.

In the bottom of the second, Matt Basztura made a spectacular, home-run-saving catch of Adam Shockey's drive deep to center field that appeared headed over the fence. Stretching as much as he could, Basztura reached high over the fence to glove it, preserving Trumbull's 2-0 lead.

"He's our best outfielder, obviously, and showed us why," observed Tom Galla to the *Williamsport Sun-Gazette*. Matt's teammate in left, Dan McGrath, called it the key play of the game: "Basztura's catch in center field was simply perfect!"

Ed Wheeler considered it the big play of the tournament. "When Matt Basztura reached over the fence and took back that home run against Iowa, he probably saved that game for us. It was a close game."

In the third inning, Trumbull loaded the bases again when an errant pitch hit Andy Paul, and Dan Brown and Dan McGrath drew walks. But the threat ended when pinch hitter Harlen Marks looped a soft liner to shortstop Dan O'Brien, who doubled up Andy Paul at third base.

Drury looked strong in the early going, giving up just one hit and striking out four through three innings, but Davenport tied it up in the fourth. Drury walked Tate Featherstone to open the inning, then one out and two Drury wild pitches later, William Plambeck's single knocked in Featherstone for Davenport's first run.

Antwan Hanes followed with a double, pushing Plambeck to third. A third wild pitch by Drury allowed Jeff Megraw, pinch running for Plambeck, to score the tying run, and the score stood 2-2 after four.

As if he wasn't already nervous going into this game, Tom Galla's stomach now began performing loop-de-loops.

On the mound, Drury showed some wildness, and, when at the plate, Davenport seemed to pitch around him. After his single to lead off the game, Davenport walked Drury three times; perhaps intentionally?

Davenport held the heart of the batting order hitless, and had just rallied to tie the game. Trumbull hasn't been tied or behind this late in a game since their loss to Park City American nearly three weeks earlier in the District 2 tournament, thus justifying Tom Galla's gastronomical instability.

At this point, anything could've happened, and usually did, when 12-year-olds play baseball. Andy Paul, beaned by a pitch in the third inning, crashed his ninth home run leading off the fifth, a deep drive over the right-center field fence off Antwan Hanes, who relieved Jacobs in the third, giving Trumbull the lead once again.

The fifth inning continued with David Galla ripping a two-out single to right-center field and advancing to third on Jason Hairston's single. Drury's third straight walk filled the bases. If Davenport tried to work around Drury, their strategy failed this time when Cody Lee's bases-loaded walk scored Galla. Drury got an insurance run and Trumbull carried a 4-2 lead into the bottom of the fifth.

Davenport responded by putting the pressure back on Trumbull and Drury in the home fifth, putting two runners on with two outs. Matt Jacobs lashed a single over third base that scored Tate Featherstone to bring Davenport within one. That insurance run looked pretty good right about then, and looked even better when Drury finished the inning. After intentionally walking clean-up hitter Plambeck, Drury got tough with Antwan Hanes, retiring him on a comebacker that Drury fielded cleanly. Unlike Davenport's apparent "walk Drury" strategy in the top of the fifth, Trumbull's plan to walk Davenport's dangerous clean-up hitter worked. Trumbull headed into the sixth and final frame nursing a very slim 4-3 lead.

Hanes walked Martin to open the sixth. Andy Paul followed, driving Hanes' first pitch to deep center, but it settled into Shockey's glove for the first out. Hanes settled down and retired the next two Trumbull batters easily.

Drury returned the favor in the bottom of the sixth, putting Davenport's first two batters away quickly on pop-ups, then he closed out Davenport when number eight batter, Matt Loper, slapped a grounder to shortstop Dan Brown, who threw to Martin at first for the final out. Trumbull had won their first game in Williamsport, 4-3.

Tom Galla would later say, "It was an ugly game. Nothing real good was happening. It was one of those games you win and say, 'Oh boy, I hope we play better the next time.'"

"It was a tight game," Todd Halky remembered. "We played good defense, but didn't hit the ball particularly well; we played small ball that day." Dan McGrath called the game "...bloody exciting; it was surreal."

"The first game wasn't a big deal," Dan Brown commented, "it was just another game against another baseball team, as Coach Galla had prepared us. I remember being real nervous just before infield practice, but once they hit me a couple of balls, I was ok. You have to just focus in and play baseball. It's the only way to survive, otherwise you'd just freak out."

After the offensive output during the Eastern Regional, David Galla said, "Yeah, this was another close one. We had won a lot of games big, hit a lot of home runs, but when we were in tight games, we got the hits that we needed to squeak it out. Andy's home run [leading off the fifth] was certainly another. We also got some real good pitching from Chris. After the game, the coaches talked to us. I think they were a little worried because we didn't hit the ball well against Iowa, even though we had won. I think it was Bob Zullo who said to us that 'this field is the same size field we've been playing on all summer. You're gonna hit. We just have to go out and play baseball.'"

Drury, who improved his pitching record to a sparkling 7-0, gave up just four hits, while striking out six and walking three. Davenport's pitchers matched Drury in allowing just four hits, but their 12 walks and seven wild pitches opened the door wide enough for Trumbull to walk through and take the game.

After the game, Galla commented, "I couldn't be happier. I'm thrilled. Nothing could be better. We're back on TV." ESPN would broadcast the US Championship game on Thursday on a tape-delayed basis.

When asked why the middle of the batting order had struggled, Galla replied, "The same thing happened against [New Hampshire] the week before in the Eastern Regional. We had a lot of opportunities, but couldn't generate anything when we needed to. We should've hit the ball a lot better than we did. Davenport was tougher than they looked in the dugout."

When asked what happened to Drury in the fourth inning, Coach Galla answered, "He always throws a lot of pitches. He always has a wild inning where he'll walk the wrong kid. He probably was tiring. The kid is just a gamer. It's hard to pull him out of the game."

A light rain fell as the game ended; the heavier rain didn't hit until after the game, but the 150 Trumbull parents and friends in the crowd of 10,000 at Lamade Stadium didn't seem to mind the moisture. Alice Marks, mother of Harlen Marks, expressed how all the Trumbull parents and fans felt, saying "It's incredible. I can't believe it, that a town like Trumbull could have such good talent."

The dedication of everyone who followed and supported the team was "unequalled" according to Sandy Galla. Imagine, as Sandy Galla did, what they had to put up with. "Who else would sit through hard seats, hot days, soggy hot dogs and warm soda?"

You could pick out the Trumbull parents and friends in the crowd; they stood out in their yellow- with-green-lettering T-shirts that read "Trumbull National" on the front and "Eastern Regional Champions, 1989" on the back.

"We sold 150 in less than a day. We could have sold 300 shirts," reported Dick Mulrooney, who had the shirts made up at Blanchette's in Shelton. So, after the first batch sold out, the call went back to Blanchette's for another 150 T-shirts.

"People from Trumbull are so geared up, so wound up for this whole thing. We're hoping we're going to give them something to really be happy about," Galla told reporters after the game. "This win was big in itself. You came here thinking you want to win your first game ... and now you've got to start thinking about winning your second game," he continued.

Indeed, the Trumbull contingent stood at the ready, armed with air-horns, pom-poms, signs and, of course, the trumpet of John Coniglio, who got the Trumbull crowd started with blasts of "Charge" on his trumpet. Maureen Maher, a neighbor of one of the players, "...just got caught up in this a couple of weeks ago. We had to come." She brought homemade pom-poms with her, and her two daughters. [Author's note: In 2001, Maureen's daughter, Traci, married David Galla. "It was great to see her there. We'd been friends for a long time," David recalled. "I guess it worked out." I agree!]

So many came, they took a block of 50 rooms at the Days Inn, some 30 miles south on Interstate 80 in Danville.. Almost everyone expected to stay for the week. Winning pitcher Chris Drury's mom, Marcia, said, "I've got to go [home] after the game, but we'll be back later in the week. I never thought they'd get this far. It's so exciting just to be here...the kids have done so much." It seemed like all the parents had to change work schedules or vacation plans – didn't anyone expect Trumbull to play in Williamsport in late August?

Ken Martin's family cut their annual vacation in Martha's Vineyard short a week so he could get back in time for all-star practice, while Harlen Marks missed out on a trip to Disney World. Don't you go to Disney World *after* you win the title, not before? Oh, sorry, that's in the big leagues...

Chris Kelly's mom Kathy said, "We usually go to Rhode Island but gave it all up to be here. It's a wonderful experience, a dream come true." Mariann Fasano, mother of Chris Fasano, added, "It's fantastic, it's a dream come true. I'm here with my five kids. It's just great."

Jason Hairston's dad George joked, "I suggested to all the parents that they quit their jobs. No, really, this is so important. It's a once in a lifetime experience with your child and it's great to be able to enjoy it."

Even though Matt Sewell couldn't play, he traveled to Williamsport to cheer on his teammates.

When the parents finally got back to their rooms in Danville, they were sedate compared to previous evenings, and worried. The Davenport game proved difficult. Everyone knew the competition would only get tougher. Then they realized that the Tampa, Florida parents, who also lodged in Danville, had yellow T-shirts as well. "*Yellow! Oh, no!*"

Years later, Tom Galla seemed a bit baffled as to why the Trumbull bats fell so quiet against Davenport. "I didn't think we faced any exceptional pitchers in Williamsport, yet the hitting cooled off. Maybe it was nerves, though I didn't see nerves. Even trying a little too hard can throw you off in baseball. You've got to be loose."

Finally, the boys returned to their "luxurious" accommodations at The International Grove. David Galla remembered being "...excited to have won, but it was a close one. Everybody was anxious. We had all been together for about two and a half weeks, and needed to let off a little steam, so we had a little fun that night in the barracks, you know, just some kid's stuff."

The media blitz, which started after the Iowa game, would get more intense as Trumbull continued to win, and it wouldn't stop for a *long time*.

Tom Galla: "The Iowa game had not been on television, but the next game against California would be. [Television announcer] Al Trautwig wanted to talk with me and each of the kids. He asked them questions, which they would use during the game."

CHAPTER TWELVE

TWO FAVORITES FACE OFF

Wednesday, August 23rd arrived, yet another sunny and hot start to a playoff day, with thunderstorms forecast for the afternoon. In a 2 PM game, the two US favorites would face off, with the winner moving on to the US Championship game the following afternoon. Will it be Western Regional Champion, San Pedro, California's Eastview Little League or Southern Regional Champion, Tampa, Florida's Northside Little League? Regardless, one will emerge as Trumbull's next target.

On a day free of competition, Trumbull practiced. The extra fields available in Williamsport made practices much easier to arrange than in Bristol. The coaches took time out to carefully observe San Pedro and Tampa play. It's abundantly clear that both teams have game. The respective strength of their pitching, hitting, and defense will determine the winner, as will their ability to maintain composure under the pressure of playing in the Little League World Series. Wednesday, August 23 held much at stake.

The experts, whoever *they* were, had anointed one of these two teams as the team who will play in Saturday's title game.

San Pedro, located about 30 miles south of Los Angeles, would make its first appearance in the Little League World Series. The team compiled a sparkling 16-1 record with its team of 12-year-olds. As with most teams who make it to Williamsport, San Pedro proved an offensive juggernaut, having outscored their opponents 195 runs (11.5 per game) to 75 (4.4 per game). Their road to Williamsport wound through the Western Regional tournament held in San Bernardino, California, and included wins over Sitka, Alaska (18-3), Portland, Oregon (1-0), Missoula, Montana (14-5), and Pearl City, Hawaii (3-2) – a 10-0 loser to Taiwan in the 1988 Little League Championship game.

San Pedro Manager Joe Dileva, an insurance agent with eight years of Little League volunteer experience, described their scenario. "We have had an outstanding effort and we are just happy to be here. These kids are on Cloud Nine. We're just going to be playing one game at a time and just have fun and play baseball."

Given that experts often favor the West teams to win, Dileva made it clear that this "history of the West" did not impress him, that it provided no edge to his team whatsoever.

"I don't think we have an advantage against anybody," Dileva insisted. "All of the teams are pretty good. They wouldn't have made it here if they weren't," he told reporters. The keys to his team's successful journey to Williamsport have been "...defense, hitting and pitching."

"Hitting has really brought us along. We've been down in a lot of games and come back in the last inning," Dileva continued. San Pedro's entire roster boasted a wealth of good hitters, he pointed out, but the real punch has come from Victoria Brucker, Gary Sloan, Tim Harper, and Mike Lennox.

The media immediately focused on 12-year-old Victoria Brucker, only the second girl to play in the Little League World Series. The first, Victoria Roche, played a limited role with Brussels, Belgium in 1984, serving mostly as a pinch runner. Victoria Brucker, however, did it all for the Californians, batting clean-up, playing first base, and pitching. In All-Star play she held a 4-0 pitching record and led San Pedro with nine home runs.

San Pedro Assistant Coach Nick Lusic, who coached Brucker during the regular season, said, "She's one of our power hitters. She's been playing major league Little League for two years." Clearly star material, Brucker emerged as the winning pitcher in the Western Regional finals against Pearl City, Hawaii.

Imagine the media attention and resulting pressure this amazing young lady faced as a 12-year- old female playing a key role for her team in the Little League World Series. Her coaches said she handled the extra attention well, labeling her "very level-headed." Dileva seemed pleased with how Brucker handled the attention... and herself.

When asked if the atmosphere in Williamsport put her in awe, Brucker replied, "No, not that there's anything different except that there's teams from other countries." If anything, she seemed a tad sheepish. "She gets kind of embarrassed when everybody's putting all the attention on her. She doesn't feel that she's the star of the team. She just wants to be one of the players," Lusic explained.

Because she could not stay with the rest of the (male) players housed at The International Grove, Little League made special arrangements for her to stay with a local resident, Kim Massetti. Brucker's hostess saw the impact of the media pressure on the young player, saying, "She is in a tough role here. She's getting so much [attention from the] media. She hasn't been able to walk two feet without somebody snapping a picture of her." In the end, Brucker made it clear that she just wanted "to play baseball" like all the other players.

Tampa's offense, while not quite as overwhelming as San Pedro's, had scored 120 runs (8.6 per game), but they recorded an even stingier record than San Pedro on defense, allowing only 37 runs (a mere 2.6 per game).

Tampa returned a team to the Little League World Series for the seventh time, and placed second in 1975, 1980, and 1981. Their road to Williamsport traveled through the Southern Regional tournament played in St. Petersburg, Florida, and included wins over Biloxi, Mississippi (7-0), Bellvue, Tennessee (11-6), Lake Charles, Louisiana (3-0), and Taylors, South Carolina (8-4).

When asked what he expected in Williamsport, Tampa Manager Tony DeFrancisco answered directly: "To win it."

And why not – would you expect any other response? After all, Tampa arrived in Williamsport with a perfect 14-0 record, the only United States team undefeated in tournament play in 1989. [Author's note: In case you were wondering, three of the four International teams carried perfect records into Williamsport.]

DeFrancisco explained his well-founded confidence. "We've got just the team to do it. We've just got to have a good game, that's all. We've got to get everything working together, the hitting, the fielding and the pitching," he affirmed. According to DeFrancisco, "We have a good attitude, good pitching, good defense, good hitting, and never give up. These kids play as a team, show good sportsmanship and are extremely dedicated."

When asked for his formula to get the kids ready to play, he answered, "...just let the boys have fun and play baseball." He might have suggested this strategy to the Little League Board of Directors, for it remains a founding and sacred tenet of Little League Baseball.

DeFrancisco continued, "They're psyched. They're ready to go. Let them play baseball. They know what they're here for and they have the spirit for it."

As Tampa's Kenny Nightlinger walked to the mound to throw the first pitch on the second day of competition, 10,000 fans jammed into the grandstand or sat on the hillside, ready to take in what everyone considered a preview of Saturday's title game. The fans would enjoy an exciting and history-making day, as Victoria Brucker slapped the first-ever hit by a girl in a Little League World Series.

Angel Quintero opened the game with a lead-off single and moved to third on pitcher Tim Harper's double. Quintero scored the first run of the game on Gary Sloan's groundout. One out later, Steve Williams clubbed a towering home run to make it 3-0.

UNLIKELY CHAMPIONS: A MIRACLE IN WILLIAMSPORT

Two runs are usually not much in Little League, but when they come at the wrong time, well…they can loom huge. So, after the game, losing Manager Tony DeFrancisco made it clear that Williams' home run did a lot of damage to his team's psyche. When Tampa got the second out, DeFrancisco felt his team would exit the first inning in good shape if they took their ups down by only one run. Instead, they trailed by three.

"I think if we got out of the first inning it would have been a different ballgame. That one that the kid hit over was a big blow. That was the game right there," DeFrancisco later realized.

In the bottom of the first, San Pedro's Tim Harper retired Tampa one-two-three, crushing any Tampa hope of rallying back quickly. Nightlinger handled San Pedro in the top of the second without any further damage.

Tampa broke the ice in the home second when Harper loaded the bases on three straight one-out walks. A wild pitch that catcher Ryan Albano could not block allowed Mario Torres to cross the plate with Tampa's first run. A ground out brought in Jon Eisner, and Tampa trailed by only one run, 3-2. But that proved as close as it would get.

After the game, DeFrancisco further lamented, "When we got to within 3-2, I thought we might be able to come back on them. But we didn't get the hits we needed, when we needed them."

Another history-making moment transpired in the third inning when Victoria Brucker walked following Gary Sloan's lead-off homer, moved to second on a single by Steve Williams, and scored the first run ever by a girl in a Little League World Series when Joe Sulentor doubled.

After Williams scored on a wild pitch, Sulentor crossed the plate on a double-play. Chris Hevener's pinch-hit solo homer knocked Nightlinger out of the game, but it is too late. San Pedro's five runs broke the game open, and they led, 8-2.

Tampa fought back with two runs in their half of the third on a two-run double by future Major Leaguer Kevin Cash that scored Mike LaBarbara and Nightlinger.

San Pedro added to their lead with three unearned runs in the fourth to then lead 11-4. In the bottom of the fourth, Tampa loaded the bases, but only scored one run, on a wild pitch by Harper.

Victoria Brucker scored her third run of the game in the sixth inning after leading off with her historic single to left field. She moved to third on a Mike Lennox single, and Ryan Albano's two-out single brought her home.

Harper shut down Tampa in the sixth when shortstop Williams grabbed a grounder and whipped it to first basemen Brucker, who made the force and then fired the ball back across the diamond, nailing William Kickham at third for the game-ending double-play and a 12-5 victory for San Pedro.

San Pedro's starter, Tim Harper, experienced some control issues, giving up five walks and throwing two wild pitches, but with a 14-hit, three-homer attack, you usually win.

After the game, San Pedro Manager Joe Dileva summed it up: "We came out and hit the ball hard. We got a little sloppy and couldn't find the strike zone for a while, walked a few guys, but other than that our team played really good. We've been fortunate hitting the ball. We do play the long ball once in a while, but we don't live by it."

Tampa's DeFrancisco provided his perspective on the same six innings: "I knew California could hit. I don't think they have the pitching to make it all the way."

Defensively, his team committed just one error and turned two double-plays, with Brucker, who played flawless defense with 10 putouts and two assists, in the middle of both. Trumbull's Tom Galla, who saw the game, said, "She's a player. She's legit."

Asked about how Brucker fared now that the media attention had swelled after her performance against Tampa, San Pedro coach Nick Lusic said, "She's had a lot of pressure on her. She was trying to hit the long ball. She's been hounded for three days now. We're talking CBS, ABC from New York, and The Regis Philbin Show wants her. Every half hour we get messages. It's kind of an honor. She's handling it pretty well, but doesn't want to be the focus."

It didn't take Trumbull Manager Tom Galla long to see what his troops faced. He had seen enough. "They've [San Pedro] got a real good hitting team," he said. "The key is going to be to try and put pressure on them." How do you put pressure on a team that just blasted a pretty good team 12-5? "We'll have to come out strong and try to score early," Galla noted.

What did Galla know that no one else knew? Yesterday, Trumbull National, a team that had scored a ton of runs in the Eastern Regional, throttled back a bit, struggling to edge Davenport 4-3. Was it a case of first-game jitters? After all, how often do 12-year-olds play a game in front of 10,000 people?

"I hope we got our butterflies out of the way in that first game," said Galla. "We had so many walks (12) and wild pitches (7) handed to us, and we just couldn't get any runs."

When you really look at San Pedro's pitching stats, you realize the pitching can't be too bad. Rule Number One - All the teams from the West can hit. Rule Number 2 - No team gets to Williamsport unless they have some pitching.

Down deep, Galla worried. He knew California could hit and that another four-hit attack by his boys won't get it done unless…the bats wake up or Trumbull pitching shuts down a pretty good offense. He hoped for the kind of day they enjoyed against Cherry Hill. He wanted to command the dugout Saturday, directing his team, not sitting in the stands watching San

UNLIKELY CHAMPIONS: A MIRACLE IN WILLIAMSPORT

Pedro.

"I wasn't confident that we could beat California after I saw them play Tampa," Ed Wheeler remembered. "That team hit fastballs like nobody's business. When we got to Williamsport, we weren't supposed to win at all. We weren't supposed to beat Iowa. All the teams were good teams. I knew we had to be lucky and good to win."

The pressure weighed squarely on Galla and his staff, not the kids. They had tried to keep the daily routine unchanged each day with a batting practice in the morning, then giving the kids the rest of the day off. "We don't want to break up the normal routine," Galla said. "We just need to hit the ball. No major corrections."

Why did all the pressure land on Galla and his staff but not the kids? After watching San Pedro rough up Tampa, why wouldn't the kids feel intimidated?

Because none of the kids saw the game – the Trumbull coaches had not allowed their squad to watch the game until the very end, when the outcome held no doubt.

"Our coaches didn't want us to watch in the stands because they didn't want us to be intimidated," said Trumbull's Cody Lee, as he and his teammates hung out in the housing complex lounge during the San Pedro-Tampa game.

"Once we knew we were playing California," said catcher Todd Halky, "we knew they were going to be tough just because they were from California...and they were pretty big. We also knew it was a big game because the winner would be playing for the championship."

"We knew we had Andy pitching [against California]," David Galla remembered. "We knew he was going to come out and throw a good game. Still, we were feeling more pressure, because it was a bigger stage and the games were getting tighter, and we weren't hitting home runs like we had been. We knew we all had to step up. It wasn't a big deal that California was heavily favored; every team we played was heavily favored. So we had nothing to lose."

Whenever they went over to Lamade Stadium, the Trumbull kids found themselves the center of attention. Todd Halky said, "We were standing outside the fence and all of a sudden all these people came up and started asking us for our autographs. I guess we're the hometown team here in Williamsport. We must have signed 20 baseballs. It was fun."

"The stadium is real exciting with all the people, and the press and everything. It's really fun," Andy Paul added.

The Trumbull coaching staff firmly held to "The Swimming Pool Rule," having decreed upon arrival that the swimming pool, usually the most popular area of the complex, remained off-limits to Trumbull. Cody Lee said, "We don't get to use it [the pool] because our coaches are worried about us." But he quickly added, "The ping pong is awesome." Todd Halky joined in, "Yeah, we love the ping pong."

Andy Paul, who would pitch on Thursday against San Pedro, described the excitement in his hometown upon their favorite sons rising to the challenge in Williamsport. "Trumbull has never even won a state competition game let alone a regional, so this is real exciting for the town and for us," he beamed.

Paul and his teammate Ken Martin thought they had a good chance to defeat San Pedro. "I think we need to have our pitching as usual and we need to hit a lot better than last game," said Martin. Paul chimed in, saying that he would "...try not to give the San Pedro batters any good pitches to hit by keeping the ball down and away, trying to get them to hit ground balls."

When asked how he would pitch to San Pedro's Victoria Brucker, who has hit a team-leading nine home runs coming into the series, Andy Paul said, "I'll probably pitch to her the same as anybody else, go right after her and try to strike her out."

"Everybody said the East and Central teams are the weakest. We'll see about that," Tom Galla said, once again nervously relishing his team's role as the underdog. But he knew his ace Andy Paul could get it done.

"We'll have our work cut out for us," he conceded. Trumbull may be the underdog, but Galla liked his chances. All they need is one more win. If they succeed, they will play on Saturday…for the title.

Wednesday's second game, a 5 PM start, matched another tournament favorite, Maracaibo, Venezuela's Coquivoca Little League (representing Latin America) against Toronto, Canada's High Park Little League.

There's a good reason why Maracaibo, making its sixth appearance in Williamsport, held respect as one of the pre-tournament favorites: undefeated post-season play (16-0), scoring more than eight runs per game and tossing nine shutouts. Though no team from Venezuela had ever won the Little League championship, Maracaibo's Manager Sabas Alvarado, speaking through an interpreter, made it clear what he thought about his team's chances, exclaiming, "I want to win it all. I want to play three games and win, win, win."

Maracaibo dominated the Latin America Regional tournament, defeating Panama (13-0), Ecuador (13-6), Curacao (6-0), Guatemala (18-7) and Mexico (7-0), with three of the five wins shut-outs, two of them no-hitters by Johnny Gonzalez.

They exuded tremendous competitive spirit, so little wonder that Alvarado feels so optimistic. "It is a thrill of a lifetime to participate in the Little League World Series. I want to represent the Latin America region with spirited play and sportsmanship," he continued,

Richard Perry, manager of the High Park Little League team, described his team as "Solid. We're not going to overpower anyone with our bats. Our pitching is solid, but not incredible. Defense, we have made some mental mistakes in the past. Hopefully they're past us and we can come down here and play defense and not beat ourselves. I feel we have a good chance to get by Latin America if we don't beat ourselves. It is our privilege to represent Canada." He summed it all up: "We will play hard and enjoy this great experience."

The High Park Little League is but the second team from Toronto to make it to Williamsport. Their 15-2 record in the Canada Regional tournament held in Edmonton, Alberta, included wins over Moose Jaw, Saskatchewan (7-1), Gordon Head, British Columbia (5-0), and Glace Bay, Nova Scotia (5-4). After losing to Confederation Park, Edmonton, Alberta (7-4) in their first meeting, Toronto came back to knock off the favored Edmonton squad (10-2) for an unexpected championship.

The best way to describe this game is "wild," as Maracaibo came back from a 6-2 deficit to advance to the International championship on Thursday against Taiwan.

Toronto loaded the bases with one out in the first inning off Maracaibo starter Jose Melendez on two walks and a single by Miguel Manriquez, but Melendez fanned the next two batters to escape the jam unharmed.

In the bottom of the first, Maracaibo started quickly when shortstop Alejandro Marquez worked a walk, scrambled to second on a wild pitch, and took third on Fernando Nava's sacrifice. After Johnny Gonzalez's sac fly put Marquez across for the first Maracaibo run, Ismel Zabala followed with a single. Toronto third baseman Miguel Manriquez's error allowed Freddy Ferrer to reach first and Zabala to reach second. Toronto starter Kevin Kim's second wild pitch advanced both runners, and a passed ball charged to Toronto catcher Bill Epner saw Zabala score Maracaibo's second run.

Then a six-run outburst in the second inning gave Toronto a 6-2 lead. Melendez hit Bill Epner to open the inning, struck out the next batter, and walked Dylan DeGiota before Mark DaSilva, the smallest player on any roster, singled to load the bases. Kristin Chraba singled home the first Toronto run. Another single, this one by Kevin Kim, scored DeGiota for the second Canadian run. Miguel Manriquez then clobbered the ball over the 204-foot centerfield fence for a grand slam. At that point, Maracaibo Manager Alvarado pulled Melendez for Erlin Stela, who retired the next two batters to end the inning.

In the bottom of the second, Maracaibo sought to cut the Toronto lead and put two runners on with two outs, but the rally ended when Johnny Gonzalez's shot to the warning track in center died in the webbing of Mark DaSilva's glove.

After keeping Toronto off the board in the top of the third, Maracaibo grabbed one run back in the home third on a one-out round-tripper to center by Freddy Ferrer. Toronto grabbed that run back in similar fashion in the top of the fourth on Kevin Kim's blast over the right-field fence.

No problem and no pressure. Trailing 7-3 and with time running out, Guillermo Rincon and Alejandro Marquez singled to open the fourth and chase Toronto starter Kim, who had now thrown more than 70 pitches.

"We had hoped to make the change before the wheels fell off," Toronto Manager Richard Perry said. "Kevin had thrown a lot of pitches. We knew he didn't have much more gas."

Reliever Dylan DeGiota loaded the bases when he hit the first batter he faced, Fernando Nava. A wild pitch followed, which brought Rincon home. Gonzalez singled to reload the bases and Ismel Zabala's single scored the second Maracaibo run of the inning. Gonzalez scored another run when left fielder Andrei Shklar misplayed the ball, cutting Toronto's lead to 7-6. Freddy Ferrer followed with another hit that scored Zabala to tie the game. DeGiota got Jose Melendez to hit into a double-play, but Ferrer came home and Maracaibo grabbed an 8-7 lead. Rafael Torres capped the inning with a solo home run, putting Maracaibo on top, 9-7.

Maracaibo made it 10-7 in the fifth as Guillermo Rincon reached first on an error and ultimately scored on Fernando Nava's sacrifice bunt.

Reliever Erlin Stela kept the lid on Toronto in the fifth and sixth to earn the victory. His four- and-two-thirds-innings effort reigned supreme, allowing just one run on two hits while striking out four and walking no one. Everyone in Maracaibo's line-up contributed to their offense output; while Toronto's top four batters accumulated their seven hits and seven RBI.

Miguel Manriquez found his zone at the plate for Toronto, going 3-3 for the day, including a grand slam.

"They're a fine ball club, but I don't think we played our game today," Toronto's disappointed manager Richard Perry reflected after the game. "I look at the scoreboard and see four errors under our column and I think that played a big part in it, too."

After his team had scrambled back from a four-run deficit, Maracaibo Manager Sabas Alvarado seemed very relaxed. "I was never worried," he told reporters.

CHAPTER THIRTEEN

THE "DART PITCH" SILENCES SAN PEDRO'S BATS

Thursday, August 24th delivered a beautiful "Let's play two!" day for a game, partly sunny and very comfortable. Trumbull's Tom Galla woke up knowing his boys faced their day of reckoning.

The US championship game, the first game of the day, matched West champion San Pedro against the underdog East champion, Trumbull National. ESPN would televise the 2 PM game with Al Trautwig handling the play-by-play, joined by Jim Palmer, providing color commentary, and Mike Adamle, reporting on the field.

The winner would advance to the Little League title game on Saturday, televised nationally by ABC on *Wide World of Sports*.

Knowing there was so much on the line, the anxiety in the stands moved up a few more notches as the first pitch neared. Then, ESPN told the parents they had to sit in the same order as their children were batting. The anxiety grew almost too much to bear. Sandy Galla called it "unnerving." What about the parents' superstitions? How would this change in seating arrangement forced upon them affect the kids and the game? Oh my...what else?

As David Galla put it, "As I know from my experience coaching my kids, the parental anxiety is always higher than that of the player, and they have their superstitions same as the players do. They sat in the same order during the Districts for every game. The one game that we lost, someone in that group, I think it was my mom, brought a video camera. They were never allowed to videotape again, as if that is why we lost the game. Then, when we got to Williamsport and the games were on live TV, the network people broke them up and made them sit in the same order as our batting order so that as their kids came up the cameras could find the parents easily.

That was a big deal because they had all sat in a specific order for [the previous] 14 games and now they were broken up."
The umpires for the US championship game comprised:
Home plate – Benito VanDerBiezen (Aruba)
First base – Denny Burkett (Shelby, Ohio)
Second base – Dwayne Tuggle (Amherst, Virginia)
Third base – Jerry Francour (South Milwaukee, Wisconsin)
Left field – Rich Cobble (Swampscott, Massachusetts)
Right field – Duncan MacDougall (Edmonton, Alberta)
Nerves jittered before the game. Dan Brown said, "You just freak out until you get on the field. Seeing the sea of yellow shirts and our fans going berserk each game really helped. I think we had the dominant fan presence there at each game. Looking into the stands and seeing so many people you know from town, like some girls from my middle school, was great. A large portion of the town came [to watch us], and not just family members. Paul Coniglio's dad had a trumpet. It was cool. All that [support] definitely helps."

David Galla didn't remember feeling "...intimidated by the television cameras that we knew would be there when we got to Williamsport because we had already played on television at the Eastern Regional finals" in Bristol the previous week. "We got that out of the way so that when we got to Williamsport, it wasn't a big deal. But some of the other teams may not have been on television so it was probably intimidating. The pressure of being in a single elimination tournament, in front of a huge crowd and having TV cameras everywhere was probably tougher on the other teams."

But David did remember, "We were certainly feeling more anxiety because we knew we were playing for the US championship. We knew that if we just played the game we knew we could, we would have a pretty good shot [at winning]."

"As we took the field for the California game," Tom Galla said, "the crowd was a lot bigger, the television cameras were all there, and I'm looking around, thinking, oh my god, this is starting to...[get intense]. I know I would have been very nervous if I had to go out there to play. The kids went out there and played fine, played great..."

As usual, Galla felt nervous about what he saw as a strong California batting order. "California was a lot like Taiwan. They had three or four strong, strong hitters, and then a bunch of normal kids, kind of like us."

If you arrived late for the game you missed a few critical moments early on in the proceedings. The nearly 20,000 people had barely taken their seats when Trumbull ace Andy Paul served up home runs to three of the first six batters he faced to start the game. San Pedro knew how to hit the long ball. In post-season play, 11 different members of the team had each hit at least one home run. They could go yard.

Andy Paul remembered California as "...an intimidating team because they had a few very big, developed players that looked beyond puberty and about 16 years old, and one who had a five o'clock shadow."

"We knew the West Coast teams seemed to win more than any of the other teams," agreed Dan Brown. "We looked at [California] as a bit of a novelty because they had a girl on the team. We thought that was funny. It wasn't mean but we were amused [as 12-year-old boys] they had a girl who was their clean-up hitter. She was pretty good."

After getting San Pedro's leadoff batter Angel Quintero to ground out to shortstop Dan Brown, Andy Paul, who would share a birthday the next day with Coach Tom Galla, then tried to sneak a fastball by shortstop Tim Harper (5-feet, 6½-inches, 124 lbs.). Big mistake No. 1. He then tried to sneak another fastball by centerfielder Gary Sloan (5-feet, 7-inches, 149 lbs.). Big mistake No. 2. Harper, nicknamed "Pit Bull," and Sloan can hit the fastball, and they hit two of Paul's pretty far. Harper smashed Paul's first pitch to right-center while Sloan took Paul even deeper to center on a 0-2 count. It's Sloan's 10th home run of the postseason, and San Pedro quickly jumped to a 2-0 lead.

"The power of San Pedro is on display in the first," Al Trautwig announced. Tom Galla wasted no time going to the mound to talk to his pitcher, and his catcher, Chris Drury.

"The ball is up. You have to keep it down. You can't give it to them at the waist or above," Galla told his battery. "Now look, that's only two runs. That's no big deal. Let's come right back at them now. Let's get the ball down. Let's work them with the off-speed, ok? Come on, go get 'em."

Standing in left field, Dan McGrath remembered thinking, "S**t! (Or whatever you think when you are 12 years old... and worried.) It was deflating, but I knew it was early."

David Galla recalled his thoughts when San Pedro hit those two home runs. "We're playing California, who is heavily favored, and they're pumping them over the fence. That was concerning," he said. "After getting hit around a little, Andy did a real good job coming back to take control of the game. That's not easy to do when you're 12 years old; it's not easy to do when you're 30."

Andy Paul followed his coach's advice, keeping his fastball down and mixing in a good curve against cleanup hitter Victoria Brucker (5-3½, 137 lbs.). She took a called third strike on an inside curve ball.

Andy Paul worried when facing Brucker for the first time that he might hit her. "I remember just not wanting to hit her, honestly. I know that is a funny thing to think about on such a big stage. After we won the title and got back home, I had to answer a lot of questions about playing against Victoria; she was a great story that everybody latched onto during that tournament."

Number five hitter Steve Williams (5-feet, 3-inches, 128 lbs.) went down swinging on three curve balls for the third out of the first inning. Trumbull trailed 2-0, early.

San Pedro's starting pitcher, Steve Williams, came in undefeated in post-season play, and as Al Trautwig pointed out, "He's exhibited good control." His repertoire comprised a good fastball and a good curve.

"When we got out of the inning and came to bat in the bottom of the first, we were a bit shell-shocked," David Galla recollected. The Trumbull crowd sat there a bit shell-shocked as well, and stirred nervously.

In Trumbull's half of the first inning, Chris Drury, leading off as always, smashed a 2-2 curve right at shortstop Tim Harper, who couldn't handle it. Jason Hairston, who had moved up to the second slot in the batting order, got hit by an errant Williams pitch. Matt Basztura followed, working his way on base with a walk to load 'em up for slugger Ken Martin.

This provided the perfect setup for Trumbull slugger Martin, who led the team with an on-base average exceeding .600 and 10 home runs. Trumbull could really use a shot in the arm... or, better yet, a shot over the fence, anything to wake up the bats. Martin's good eye earned him a walk, pushing Drury across with Trumbull's first run.

San Pedro Manager Joe Dileva hustled out to the mound to speak with Williams, who seemed bothered. "Don't worry about it," Dileva counseled him. But Williams' emotions have already taken control. His manager encouraged Williams to "...relax, and do your job. Let the defense help you get out of it."

The bases remained loaded for Andy Paul, who has hit eight homers, as he stepped into the batter's box, and the crowd cheered their encouragement Paul smashed a hard grounder to San Pedro's second baseman Iggie Galaz, who gloved it but, instead of going for the easy double play, threw to catcher Ryan Albano, who caught it a moment before Hairston could score.

Trumbull's crowd groaned in disappointment seeing the tying run cut off. The score remained 2-1, but by passing up the almost assured double play, the Californians may have left the door open just a crack for the kids from Connecticut.

Dan Brown followed by smashing a line drive at pitcher Steve Williams. Williams snagged it and pivoted to throw the ball to Mike Lennox in an attempt to double up Basztura at third to end the inning, but in rushing his throw, he twisted his right knee. His throw landed in the dirt and got by Lennox. As the ball rolled down the left-field line, Basztura scored the tying run.

With Williams grimacing in pain on the mound, San Pedro Manager Dileva paid him a visit; then decided to leave him in the game. Williams' next three pitches to Danny McGrath traveled way outside.

UNLIKELY CHAMPIONS: A MIRACLE IN WILLIAMSPORT

That's it, Dileva had seen enough. He replaced Williams with centerfielder Gary Sloan, moving Williams to third and Lennox to center. Sloan's first pitch couldn't find the strike zone and McGrath walked, reloading the bases. As McGrath trotted to first, he thought that San Pedro's pitcher felt the pressure. "He fell apart and we felt we had them there and then. He was not used to the pressure and we capitalized."

Cody Lee stepped to the plate and hit a comebacker to Sloan, who couldn't handle it and, instead of getting the sure out at first, threw home. Andy Paul hustled to score ahead of the throw, giving Trumbull the lead, 3-2, all without the benefit of a base hit.

Dave Galla got Trumbull's first and only hit of the inning, sending Sloan's 0-2 pitch just beyond the reach of shortstop Tim Harper into left field, scoring Martin. Trumbull now led 4-2. Al Trautwig pointed out "…there are smiles around and cheers from the stands for the team from Trumbull, Connecticut…" as the television camera panned the crowd.

Trumbull had batted around and the bases were still loaded as Drury came to bat for the second time in the inning. Sloan nearly beaned Drury before walking him, bringing home Dan McGrath for Trumbull's fifth run of the inning. Hairston's sharp one-hopper to Harper forced Drury at second, and San Pedro finally got out of the disastrous first inning, now trailing 5-2.

After the scare in the top of the first, Trumbull had capitalized on some sloppy play by San Pedro. Four walks, a hit batter, two errors, and some bad decisions allowed Trumbull to quickly get back in the game. With a three-run lead, "…things get a bit easier," David Galla smiled. "Suddenly, the strike zone seems a lot bigger for the pitcher. It seems a lot easier to make the plays."

"So, when Andy gets out of the first inning, and we came to bat in the bottom of the first," recalled Tom Galla, "well, their pitcher just fell apart. He didn't want to be there from the beginning, I guess. And it got progressively worse, real fast. His uniform was too tight; he kept looking at his dugout. It was sad to watch. The game was over in that first inning, as far as I was concerned. Looking back at it, they had nerves, we didn't. Andy settled down, and they came in with somebody better but he wasn't great. They gave us the game."

Andy Paul opened the second inning with another letter-high fastball, which Joe Sulentor promptly smashed over the right center field wall, and San Pedro crept to within two, 5-3.

San Pedro's early power outburst clearly worried the Trumbull fans. The only good thing about the San Pedro slugfest is that each home run came with the bases empty.

Tom Galla worried as well. He quickly stepped out of the dugout, calling Drury over for a quick meeting with Andy Paul, telling Andy and Chris, "Andy, you've got to keep that ball *down*. Let's go, relax, and shake it off." Galla suggested that Paul try Coach Wheeler's dart pitch.

It's really the first time he will use the dart pitch as his number one toss. Everyone in the San Pedro line up could hit the fastball, so Galla figured the dart pitch would keep them off-balance. Andy could use the fastball as his off-speed pitch today, as long as he kept it out of the strike zone.

"It worked and I got my confidence back," Andy recalled. "Coach Galla told me to keep the ball low and Chris called a great game [behind the plate]," Paul said. "Chris was super. I was used to blowing people away with my fastball and they didn't even flinch at my velocity and just stroked them out of the ballpark with ease. That was a huge blow to my ego. I remember feeling embarrassed personally and worried about us being blown out, all because of my performance. I was terrified of letting my team down."

"We wanted to see how Andy's speed was and we challenged them," said Drury after the game.

"Andy had thrown his fastball by everyone until he got here," said Tom Galla. But his fastball wasn't getting by anyone today.

Galla timed it perfectly. Call it good timing, luck or whatever you want to. Trumbull's ace was getting hit hard and their bats had been dormant since arriving in Williamsport. Trumbull needed something to happen, and quickly, or everyone would watch the championship game on Saturday from the stands. And no one wanted that.

Whatever Galla said worked, as Paul settled down and easily retired the next three batters, the bottom of San Pedro's order, to escape the inning. From that point, Paul returned to form. He held the slugging Californians to just one hit the rest of the way, a one-out single in the sixth inning, and Trumbull's defense played to near perfection, committing just one error.

"Once Andy settled down, I felt pretty good about our chances," said David Galla. What a great birthday present for Andy Paul and Tom Galla.

"Now I'm feeling better," said Tom, "a bit more relaxed than I had been in the first inning, until the first kid up in the second inning hits one out and I had to go see Andy again, and tell him to just throw the dart pitch. No more fastballs. When I came back to the dugout, I said, I hope he can throw the dart pitch. He had not thrown it that many times; didn't need to. He might throw it once in a while, but now it was going to become his number one pitch. He threw and did just beautifully with it. They couldn't hit the dart pitch."

Once Andy got out of the second inning, Tom turned to Bob Zullo and asked, "How many runs are we going to have to score today to beat this team, because of the way they were hitting home runs? Who knows how many they would have hit if Andy wasn't able to adjust."

"I knew they had good power, especially the girl," said Paul. "They were swinging when the ball came out of my hand, so I went with the off-speed curveball, the dart pitch."

Twenty-five years later, Tom Galla remembered how Andy turned it around in the San Pedro game.

"Andy was a power pitcher," Galla said. "If he'd have kept throwing fast balls they would have scored 20 runs that day. Andy could have folded after those three home runs, but he didn't. He sucked it up and got through the game, somehow, leaving all he had on the field that day. He had nothing left when it was over. Andy should have come home as big a hero as Chris [Drury] because of what he accomplished against California.

"Unfortunately that's not the way it works. The guy who wins that final game is the big hero but, if it hadn't been for him there wouldn't have been that last game. So I always say it's a situation that could have caused someone to crack but he didn't. He was 12 years old."

Looking back at what Andy Paul did that day on the mound, on that stage, Dan Brown called the San Pedro game "…probably Andy's finest pitching performance because of all the adjustments he had to make. He threw some fastballs early that got turned around pretty good, and he essentially learned how to throw an off-speed pitch during the game. It was really an amazing feat. He became a finesse pitcher right there in the middle of the game. You see lots of Little League pitchers implode when they're used to blowing the ball by everybody then have a few fastballs that get turned around on them. He did not cave in at all. [Andy's reaction and adjustment] was really quite a mature performance for someone that age."

Dan continued, "In the same game, you could see the opposing pitcher [who struggled] crumble right there on the mound, somewhat embarrassingly. His coach, who [had a microphone on for television], shamed the kid for crying on the mound. It was difficult to watch later."

After the game, Tom Galla said, "Andy…had never pitched that way before, but he shifted gears right there in front of 20,000 people, and turned the whole game around."

Years later, Chris Drury described to Jeff Brantley of *ESPN Magazine* how to throw the dart pitch. "I could throw a hundred of them without putting any strain on my arm. You just kind of hold the ball without touching any of the seams, and then you short-arm it, like a dart. You don't twist your wrist or anything, but the ball drops like a curveball. From 60 feet, six inches, it probably wouldn't work. But it was the perfect pitch from 45 feet."

The only other moment when San Pedro looked like it might mount a rally occurred when Andy Paul walked number two hitter Tim Harper with one out in the third and then promptly balked him over to second. This presented Tom Galla with the chance to use a strategy that Jim Palmer and Al Trautwig would call into question in the championship game. Trumbull intentionally walked San Pedro slugger Gary Sloan, who hit a home run in the first inning. It put the tying run on first with the clean-up hitter coming to the plate.

As Victoria Brucker, whose game-winning home run in the Western Regional had brought San Pedro to Williamsport, stepped into the batter's box, the question became what should Andy Paul throw her? He struck her out in the first on a fast ball, but the dart has kept the California kids off stride since then. After the game, Drury said, "We'd throw two or three in a row and they never seemed to know what was coming..."

It's a fastball. Brucker drives it high and deep to center. Harper surprised nearly everyone and tagged up at second as Matt Basztura settled under it, gloved it, and made a perfect throw to Jason Hairston, doubling up Harper to end San Pedro's rally. Inning over!

As Jason Hairston celebrated, Jim Palmer called it: "A perfect play by Trumbull!" Trumbull's rooters join in the moment, chanting, "We ARE Trum-bull! We ARE Trum-bull!"

Trumbull scored its final run in the home third without a hit to bring the score to its final tally of 6-3. Cody Lee walked with one out to get things started, and David Galla reached when San Pedro misplayed his sacrifice bunt attempt. Drury followed with a grounder to short, but Williams' error allowed Lee to score Trumbull's final run. Al Trautwig pointed out how San Pedro's "weak fundamentals have really hurt them today."

Trumbull finally recorded its second and third hits of the game in the fourth, on a single by Martin and a double off the left field wall by Dan Brown. However, the rally faltered when Dan McGrath bounced one to third baseman Anthony Pesusich, who nabbed Martin at the plate on a nice play by catcher Angel Quintero. Quintero followed with another terrific play to end the inning when he threw out Brown trying to advance to third on a passed ball.

When Andy Paul struck out Joe Sulentor for the second out in top of the sixth, you could hear someone in the dugout chanting, "One more out! One more out! One more out!" Three pitches later, Trumbull erupted in joy when Andy Paul struck out Mike Lennox for the game's final out. "They are the best Little League team in America," Al Trautwig pronounced.

With the final out, a flood of emotions surged from the boys, ranging from joy, relief, and excitement for having won, to fear, uncertainty, and anxiety regarding their next step, the next game, and their next opponent. But at that moment in time, it was all good.

Tom Galla made it pretty clear how he and all the Trumbull fans felt when he said, "A lot of people told me we were supposed to be the weakest team here. Well, I'm happy being the underdog. Everyone was asking me who is Trumbull, Connecticut? Well, they know now."

Bridgeport Post-Telegram writer Chris Elsberry tagged Galla's words well: "They do indeed. They're the United States champions. They're the underdogs no longer. In fact, they're one game away from being the top dog."

UNLIKELY CHAMPIONS: A MIRACLE IN WILLIAMSPORT

"You start with such high hopes," Tom Galla said, "but you know you're crazy if you think you can actually get there. I had those hopes again, and this year we showed that hopes and dreams can come true."
As the wave of emotions subsided, a wave of media attention hit them like nothing they had ever experienced.
It began immediately after the game when a camera crew from ABC-TV got in the faces of the celebrating kids, asking the group to exclaim in unison, "We just won the US championship. Good Morning, America!" It aired the next morning, and ABC introduced the "Good Morning America" audience to the boys from Trumbull. Their star is born!
Tom Galla remembered how the media quickly swooped in on him… "I was not prepared at all for the media onslaught after we beat California, although I should have been, because we had already been talking with the media. But once you beat California, it is really big news because you're going to the final game, and Taiwan doesn't speak English, and the kids won't talk, so they want to talk to me. So I talk to everybody. And when I talk to them, I get 10 times more excited than [normal] because I am living the dream. It was special."
While it may not have looked very pretty, Trumbull had actually taken advantage of everything that San Pedro gave them. Trumbull produced six runs on just four hits and four walks, with San Pedro's four errors greasing the skids. Andy Paul pitched very effectively. Though the numbers didn't beam as brightly as some of his previous outings, they still glowed. He had allowed just four hits, although yes, three of them were home runs in San Pedro's early display of power, and walked three while striking out six. Andy Paul had faced the challenge of the slugging Californians… and he won.
After the win, Andy Paul emerged emotionally drained from his effort in this, their toughest game against their toughest opponent to date. He also felt quite satisfied with Trumbull's newfound status as the US champions, "…glorious in its own right," he said.
"I was very proud of myself and our team that day," Paul related. "I was mobbed by my family after the game and I think it was the happiest I ever saw them in my life. That feeling of being congratulated by all your family and friends from your hometown as you exited the playing field was one of the most emotionally gratifying moments of my life."
Years later, Todd Halky remembered "We had another tough game hitting against California, another one of those tight games. But we got lots of help because they didn't play that well in the field, and we did play good fundamental ball that day. After we won the game, I remember running around the field with the rest of the guys carrying the US championship banner, thinking this is just crazy, we're the best team in the country."
"Looking back, the kids from California were talked up," Dan McGrath said, "that the game with us would be a cake walk and perhaps

they would be a better match with Taiwan who blasted their semi-final game opponent. Again, I was not nervous; [I was] quite relaxed. Our coaches were the ones who did the stressing for us."

"Winning that game was awesome," declared David Galla. "People were cheering for us and the crowd started chanting, 'U-S-A!.U-S-A!'"

Playing against the girl "...didn't fuss me," McGrath continued. "She was good enough to make the team and play; she should be respected the same way we respect the boys. She could flat out hit too, a threat we wanted to make sure wouldn't hurt us." David Galla agreed, "She was good, a good player, a good hitter."

"Starting out, I didn't have any special strategies for the California game," Tom Galla admitted. "We were trying to get Andy to keep the ball down in the strike zone because they had hit those three balls out on high fastballs. So when I went to the mound to talk to him, and Andy said he was trying and then he said something about the mound. I looked at the mound and it was flat. This was not what we were accustomed to. All the other fields we had played on had a small mound, a hump, a Little League mound, but there was no hill on the main field in Williamsport. Andy struggled and could not adjust; he had difficulty keeping the ball down against California…

"Chris didn't have the same issue because he was not a power pitcher; his junk was all over the place," Galla continued. "Andy had really good control, very few walks, and lots of strikeouts. Chris walked people, would go to 3-2 counts all the time, would get guys to strike out on pitches [gesturing] up here. It was a different approach. Chris always made the games more exciting. We always knew he was such a competitor that he was going to get through it, even if he went 3-0 on somebody, we'd sit there and say, no worries, he'll get this kid out. And more often than not he did. Chris will bend but he won't break."

Thursday's second game saw the two international pre-tournament favorites square off, with first pitch at 5 PM. Tom Galla took a seat and watched the game.

Tom had spied the Taiwan coach watching Trumbull play California. "Taiwan watched our game [against California], and probably watched our Iowa game, too. They couldn't have been too impressed with what they saw. So, naturally they start their number one pitcher against Venezuela, which I don't think was unusual. Typically, the South American team was the second strongest team in Williamsport, back then. They would naturally throw their best pitcher against them. And it seemed as though they had six pitchers, Taiwan, but the guy that we saw, though he was unorthodox with the submarine pitch, he wasn't overpowering."

Maracaibo's Sabas Alvarado saved his ace, Johnny Gonzalez, to face Taiwan for the International championship and a slot in the World Series championship game on Saturday. At 5-feet, 2-inches, 112-pounds, the 12-year-old, undefeated in the post-season, has tossed two no-hitters and a one-hit shutout, and struck out 42 batters in just 17 innings.

Similarly, Kaohsiung Manager Chin-Ming Wu went with his ace, Ming-Lan Hsu, against Maracaibo. At 5-feet, 8-inches, 175-pounds, Hsu carried more heft than former major league star Pedro Martinez did when he signed with the Dodgers in 1988; at that time, Pedro stood 5-feet, 10-inches, but weighed just 135 pounds.

Betty Speziale, the first female umpire in Little League World Series history, stood behind the plate calling balls and strikes that day. With 12,000 fans packing Lamade in anticipation of a tight contest between these two powerhouses, Speziale officially signaled the start of the game with a hearty "Play Ball!"

Kaohsiung took a quick 2-0 lead in the top of the first on Maracaibo mistakes. Taiwan's best hitter, Hsin-Lung Tseng, singled, and after moving to third when Chien-Chih Lee's sacrifice bunt was misplayed by first baseman Ismel Zabala, crossed the plate on Freddy Ferrer's passed ball. Lee moved to third on that passed ball and scored on shortstop Alejandro Marquez's error. Maracaibo escaped further damage when they caught Chen-Hao Yeh, who had walked, and Chih-Hao Hsu, who reached on the Marquez error, attempting to steal.

In the top of the second, Taiwan batted around, scoring five times with two out, led by Chien-Chih Lee's three-run homer. A one-out single to center by Ming-Chieh Hsu got the inning started. Kuan-Lung Chen sacrificed him to second, and Chin-Chih Huang walked to put runners at second and third. Ferrer's second passed ball of the game allowed the runners each to move up a base.

The next batter, lead-off hitter Ming-Lan Hsu, stepped in the box. While not Taiwan's best hitter, at 5-feet, 8-inches, he is physically intimidating, and thus a scary batter to face, especially when followed by three hitters that Tom Galla labeled "tough." Hsu drew a walk to load the bases. Marquez's second error of the game allowed both Ming-Chieh Hsu and Huang to score, and Taiwan led, 4-0. Lee followed with a blast over the wall to make it 7-0. The going got tougher when the next two batters also reached base, one on a hit and the other on a walk.

Manager Alvarado didn't want the game to get any more out of control than perhaps it already had, so he removed his ace Johnny Gonzalez for left fielder Darwin Borges. You pull your ace in the second inning when you're served a large piece of reality pie. Three errors and a 7-0 deficit in the two innings provided that pie. Borges reached down deep and retired Chi-Yi Chang to finally end the inning. At that point, although only the end of the second inning, the Fat Lady probably got the nod to get her music ready…

In the end, the drama proved minimal, as Taiwan's Ming-Lan Hsu appeared as advertised, a hard-throwing ace, really bringing the heat. Some said he could throw it over 70 MPH. He shut down Maracaibo on just three hits, while striking out seven and walking no one. In fact, he was perfect into the fourth inning until shortstop Chien-Chih Lee misplayed a grounder, allowing Fernando Nava to reach base. Lee atoned for his miscue with a spectacular diving catch of a smash off the bat of Freddy Ferrer to end the inning. Losing pitcher Johnny Gonzalez's one-out single to left in the fifth broke up Hsu's no-hitter, but Gonzalez went nowhere, as the next batter hit into an inning-ending double play.

Maracaibo held Taiwan scoreless in the third and fourth innings, but Taiwan increased their lead in the fifth to 9-0 when pitcher Ming-Lan Hsu doubled, advanced to third on a wild pitch, and came home on a Ferrer error. Chen-Lung Yeh's homer to right made it 9-0.

Kaohsiung closed out the scoring with four runs in the top of the sixth, the big blow a three-run line drive launched over the center field fence by left fielder Hsin-Lung Tseng. Crossing the plate ahead of Tseng were Ming-Chieh Hsu and Kuan-Lun Chen, who both reached on Maracaibo errors.

Venezuela tried to spark a late rally in the bottom of the sixth when its first two batters, Darwin Borges and Guillermo Rincon, both reached on singles, but the threat ended just as quickly as it started when Marquez flied out and Fernando Nava hit into a game-ending double play.

Taiwan's 2-3-4 hitters accounted for all seven RBI, with each hitting a home run for the Far East champions. The other six runs scored on Maracaibo miscues – six errors, two passed balls and four wild pitches. In fact, only two of Taiwan's 13 runs were earned.

That evening, the Trumbull kids headed back to the barracks, ate dinner, and hung out for a while with their parents. After the parents left for their hotel in Danville, the boys got to be kids again for a little while. "We got to be goofy again," said David Galla. "Later, the coaches said, look, we have another game to go, so we have to keep our heads on."

David continued... "In those two days between the US championship and the World championship game, we talked to more reporters than we knew what to do with. There was a lot of pressure building up to that game. The coaches did the best they could but you walk into practice and there would be a microphone shoved in your face. The reporters would hang out by the fence of the compound, ready to talk to you. There were always certain people they wanted to talk to more than others. They wanted to talk to Chris, they wanted to talk to Ken, and they wanted to talk to Andy. We were a team of all-stars who had some superstars. Those guys learned very early how to deal with immense media pressure. I was fortunate that I wasn't one of those guys."

The next day [Friday], they held a light practice, just to keep everybody loose. David remembered his dad telling them that "...the other team was heavily favored, but let's just go out there and show them what we can do. We knew they [Taiwan] were heavily-favored; [but] we knew that we had one more baseball game to play; and we knew that we wanted to win that baseball game."

Life in The Grove had settled down. As teams lost, they went home, and with fewer and fewer kids around...well, it grew quiet.

CHAPTER FOURTEEN

THE US CHAMPIONS PREPARE TO FACE A DYNASTY

It's Friday, August 25th, the day before the Championship Game, a day "...as stunningly beautiful as it gets any summer, anywhere," according to Owen Canfield of *The Hartford Courant*. With no game today, Tom Galla had the kids on one of the auxiliary fields: time for some practice.

And there's plenty of help available. Ed Wheeler tossed batting practice, as usual, while Bob Zullo hung out near the batting cage, giving the kids some final batting tips. Andy Paul's dad, Ken, squatted behind home plate, catching batting practice.

During practice, Tom Galla got word that the media had asked for a meeting with Chris Drury. "They wanted Chris and the starting pitcher from Taiwan for a photo-op," Galla commented. "The other kid showed up with two of his friends, and Chris is by himself. Well, they were kind of looking at him, snickering. Who knew what they were talking about, and who knows what they were thinking. Maybe they were so convinced nobody could beat them, this was just a formality. All I know is back in those days, I believe Taiwan showed up with teams that probably weren't quite as legitimate as our teams."

Those kinds of concerns had made the rumor rounds for many years, but what do you do about it? You play the game, that's what you do. At the same time, you can understand what Galla said and how he felt. Remember his first encounter with Taiwan when they first arrived in Williamsport and he saw their players; they looked so regimented, so military-like.

Sure, Little League had rules about residency and population size for each league, wherever anyone played the game, but those who want to can always find some way to work around the rules. Unlike US kids, who

UNLIKELY CHAMPIONS: A MIRACLE IN WILLIAMSPORT

went to different schools, the Taiwanese kids had all attended the same school, and followed a daily routine that specified practice in the morning before classes, then school, and then more practice after classes. They did this all year long; all legitimate and all within Little League rules.

Taiwan Manager Chin-Ming Wu said the Taiwanese had dominated the Little League World Series in recent years because they practiced seriously and played baseball 12 months a year, while American kids usually only play in the summer save for warmer climes.

Manager Wu created a bit of confusion when he announced Ming-Chieh Hsu as his starting pitcher after his team's win over Maracaibo on Thursday, but sent Chien-Chih Lee, who usually played shortstop, for a publicity photo shoot with Trumbull starter Chris Drury on Friday morning.

The confusion may have arisen because Chin-Ming Wu had dug himself a bit of a hole by using his two best pitchers in Taiwan's first two games. Speaking through an interpreter, Wu said that he had gone with his best pitcher in Thursday's game against Maracaibo because "...they were the second best team in the tournament," but quickly added that, "the East team [is] very good too. We must be very careful against certain batters in their lineup."

Andy Paul remembered feeling intimidated by the Taiwan kids, not because of their size, but because they looked so militaristic. "They all had matching equipment and practice uniforms, haircuts, etc. It was like a military style baseball team. The whole week they just kept to themselves, mostly because that was their style but they also had a different language and culture as well."

Later that morning, in a conversation, Tom remembered how soundly Taiwan beat the US teams the last three years. So soundly, in fact, that ABC had ended the broadcasts and switched to other programming. "Finally I said to myself, boy, it would be awful to end this whole wonderful experience by getting murdered by these guys in the final game," Galla admitted.

That's when Tom called Don Schaly, his coach at Marietta College, for advice. Schaly told Galla he was kind of surprised to hear from him, but that he had followed the games on TV.

"I've been thinking about you...I need your help. These guys aren't hitting the ball," Galla remembered telling Schaly. "I told him how they'd been killing the ball all the way here. That I didn't really think the pitching was that much tougher here. Their bats were silent. How can I get these kids to start hitting?"

Surely, a man in the College Baseball Hall of Fame must have some way to awaken Trumbull's slumbering bats. Schaly provided sage advice, brilliantly simple and direct. "You've done everything you can do. All you can do is try to relax them. Tell them you love them. Tell them to go out and play. Have some fun." Clearly the pressure of playing at such a high-level, with so much at stake had finally registered with the boys.

Galla continued, "So we did. We met with them. We sat them down in right field. I talked real soft, real slow, and told them how proud I was of them, how I loved them. That's when I told them, you make one good play in the field, one routine play. Great! You did your job for the day. If you get one hit, you did your job for the day. If you make a spectacular play but later commit an error, just don't worry about it. Go on from there. Have fun. I was just trying to maybe take some pressure off. Again, you never know what works or what doesn't work."

Parents populated the area around the batting cage, watching, chatting, and anticipating what tomorrow would bring to their children… and to Trumbull. A legion of sportswriters from newspapers across the state and television crews from Connecticut's local television stations, Channels 3, 8 and 30, circulated among the adults, each reporter looking for a new story to tell the folks back home for the evening newscast or the morning edition of the paper. "The kibitzers joked and kidded on the sidelines," observed *The Hartford Courant*'s Owen Canfield.

Paul Coniglio's dad, "Bugle Boy" John, known as much for his trumpet as for serving as Tom Galla's de facto press secretary, held court, telling stories amidst plenty of nervous laughter.

On another field nearby, the kids from Taiwan mirrored the Trumbull kids: practicing…just another bunch of kids hitting, throwing, and catching.

After their tough one-and-a-half-hour workout on Friday afternoon, a reporter asked Tom Galla, "Does Trumbull really have a chance to win this game?" "Heck yes…definitely," Galla shot back quickly.

"[Taiwan] is a great team," Galla continued. "They've got all the history behind them and everybody knows that they're the frontrunner and we're the underdog. But that's okay because we've been the underdog many, many times already. And guess what, we're the team that they have to beat to be the world champions. And we're going to go after them, because we want to be world champions real bad."

"What about the Trumbull kids?" another reporter asked Galla. "What do they think about their offensive malaise since arriving in Williamsport?"

"They're just off a bit, but they feel confident; so I hope it comes together Saturday. That's what we need," Galla responded. "They've been giant-killers in the past," he added, referring to the New Jersey team that made these kids from Taiwan look small. While his public persona appeared confident, inside, as always, Tom Galla worried.

Taiwan Manager Chin-Ming Wu and his assistant Chi-Hui Tung put their kids through the same routine as Tom Galla, but before a smaller audience than Trumbull. Except for the coaches, no one else watched the Taiwan kids, save for the team's translator, Chien-Chung Yang, a candidate in a master's program in construction management at George Washington University.

Through Yang, Taiwan's Wu said he and his players do not want to disappoint their fans back home, so everyone will try his best. Wu's employer, the electric power company in Taiwan, supported Little League in Taiwan in a major way, allowing Wu to spend half his day working and the other half coaching.

Andy Paul recalled not being able to sleep well that Friday evening. "I remember very vividly having a conversation with my father the day before the championship game about how tired I looked. I think it just all caught up with me after I pitched the US Championship game. I remember not being able to sleep that well in the cabin; it was basically one big room with all of us in bunk beds. It wasn't the most ideal place for getting good quality rest before the biggest game of our lives."

Ten years later, Ken Martin related a story to *ESPN Magazine*'s Jeff Bradley (*"The Kid's Alright"*) about the night before the title game, when Chris Drury went outside after dark, alone, just before "lights out." Martin followed his friend outside...

> "What's up?" asked Ken.
> "Get lost," Chris replied.
> "What?" Martin countered.
> "I said get lost," Drury repeated.

Ken's best friend "wanted to be alone," Martin recalled, "but I didn't want to be alone. I was nervous."

Standing on the hill above Howard J. Lamade Stadium, Drury said he was going to walk down to the field and sit in the stands for a while. Martin told him he couldn't do that because the field was locked up at that hour. Drury scoffed and began to walk to the field. That's when Martin alerted a security guard, who told Drury to go back to the bunks.

But before Drury called it a night, he had some business to attend to. "He looked at me," said Martin, "and said – 'I'm going to kick your butt right now.'" And right there, the two teammates dropped the gloves and started throwing haymakers. "We fought and rolled around until we were both worn out."

Then, "...we just walked to the bunks and went to bed. The next morning, we just went back to being best friends," Martin finished.

Well past midnight, Galla and Zullo still strategized, discussing how they will pitch to each kid in the Taiwan lineup the next afternoon. They knew the first four batters could hit the ball, and make up the heart of the Taiwan line-up. In their two games in Williamsport, Taiwan's fearsome foursome went 8-for-22 with five home runs, 14 RBI and 14 runs scored. They would prove difficult to retire.

The two men discussed the possibility of intentionally walking a batter to keep the scoring under control. If they could limit the damage from the top of the Taiwan batting order to one or two runs in the early innings, Drury could handle the rest of their line-up, they figure. Then all the coaches need to do is bring their own bats back to life. Finally, sometime after 1:00 AM, Galla and Zullo called it a night.

"Tomorrow…tomorrow…it's only a day away," or, in this case, even closer. Sleep fast, Tom. Good night, Bob!

Jim Carpenter of the *Williamsport Sun-Gazette* recalled talking about the upcoming championship game with one of his newsroom colleagues. "The night before the championship one of my reporters and I had become aware that Trumbull was given little chance of winning, yet we thought that, based on what we had seen of the [Trumbull] National Little Leaguers thus far, winning wasn't out of reach. What transpired the next day proved us to be correct."

Because of the "national expectations" for Taiwan, they probably faced more pressure to win than Trumbull did to even keep it close.

CHAPTER FIFTEEN

CHAMPIONSHIP SATURDAY

Saturday, August 26th ...Championship Saturday: another Chamber of Commerce morning in Williamsport...

Owen Canfield, sports columnist for *The Hartford Courant*, described the atmosphere in Williamsport on Championship Saturday:

> [It is] baseball with the velvety trimmings of kids and country in Pennsylvania sunshine; corny, red-white-and-blue stuff; family stuff. There is much about the Little League with its official logos, trademarks, acronyms and corporate sponsorships that is too stiff and legal and promotional. But this would be difficult to ruin – 75-cent hot dogs, with or without sauerkraut, and comparable prices for the other items on the menu.
>
> And the fall-fair atmosphere; there were almost as many fans basking on blankets on the high bank behind the outfield fences as there were in the stands. Babies jumped and bounced in playpens. Umbrellas were opened against the sun. Kids walked among the people selling ice cream sandwiches, soda pop and newspapers. Everyone – not just the sportswriters – got in for nothing. The hat was passed; several hats. That's the Little League system.
>
> It was a splendid day. South Williamsport became a village Saturday, a village of some 40,000 packed around a little fenced-in green place and kind of looking at and looking after some kids and celebrating real baseball. Real baseball.

Bridgeport Post-Telegram sports writer Chris Elsberry put the challenge the Trumbull Little Leaguers faced into perfect perspective with a whimsical opening to his story on the morning of the championship game entitled *"Trumbull squad facing 'Mission Impossible.'"*

The setting is right out of Mission Impossible:

Good morning, Mr. Galla…You are looking at a team from Taiwan, perennial champions in the Little League World Series and solid favorites to win again this year. Your mission is to defeat the team from Taiwan and bring the World Championship back to the United States for the first time since 1983. Good luck, Tom…

It really *did* seem impossible in so many ways. Trumbull, a small New England town of 35,000 people, faced the most feared and most dominant team in Little League history, Taiwan. They would play Kang-Tu Little League from the southern port city of Kaohsiung, a metropolis of nearly three million residents. Teams from Kaohsiung won their two previous appearances in Williamsport [1974 and 1977].

Manager Chin-Ming Wu spoke through an interpreter, saying, "We haven't won the championship for a long time. If we win, there will be a tremendous welcome party."

Taiwan's official name is the "Republic of China" but it is now called "Chinese Taipei" due to diplomatic pressure exerted from the People's Republic of China. It exists as an island nation in East Asia, located about 110 miles off the southeastern coast of the People's Republic of China. At 14,000 square miles, Taiwan occupies a space about two-and-one-half times larger than Connecticut, but its population of 23 million dwarfs that of Connecticut [about 3.6 million as of 2014].

Taiwan's incredible record all-time in the Little League World Series stands an imposing 17 title wins [and three runner-up finishes] in 28 appearances through 2013, and they have won 80 of the 98 games they have played in Williamsport, or an incredible 81.6 percent. Through 1989, Taiwan's record looms even more imposing, as they had won 43 of the 45 games they played, winning 13 titles in their 15 appearances between 1969 and 1988.

While we may consider baseball America's pastime, those in Taiwan have elevated it to an even higher level. To understand, consider these words on a banner that hangs in a ballpark in Taiwan: "Baseball is the kind of sport that can exercise your body, your character, and your wisdom. It can stabilize your life, and the achievement in baseball is not inferior to economic achievement." [Author's note: Epilogue 2 provides a more in-depth perspective on the importance of baseball in Taiwan.]

UNLIKELY CHAMPIONS: A MIRACLE IN WILLIAMSPORT

Trumbull's bats maintained "radio silence" since arriving in Williamsport; the "Electric Company" suffering a blackout. The offense simply sputtered. Trumbull managed just eight hits in its first two games (8-for-42, a .186 team batting average), much lower than the .440 they had slapped coming in. No player poked more than one hit in either game, and Andy Paul contributed the sole homer. The boys had only scored 10 runs, far below their pre-Williamsport clip for the equivalent time at the plate.

Taiwan, however, enjoyed a robust .347 (17 for 49), outscoring their opponents 22 to 4. Their five round-trippers have powered the offense. Of course, who could forget Taiwan's performance over the last three years while winning three Little League World Series championships? They outscored the best teams from the US by a combined score of 42 to 1, hence *Bridgeport Post-Telegram* sports writer Elsberry's *"Mission Impossible"* story opening.

Without Trumbull's rock-steady pitching, allowing just eight hits in two games, and steady defense – only *two* errors, the fewest of any team so far – these kids would have long since returned to Connecticut. Instead, they sat poised to play for the Little League World Championship. In fact, many believed if they stood a shot at winning, it would rest upon their defense.

"We've had the defense whether we've really needed it or didn't, it's always been there and it's been rock solid. Hopefully, it's going to be rock solid for one more game. If we had broken down at any time, we wouldn't be here today, no question about it," Tom Galla proclaimed.

Galla continued, "One more game. We go on the field and we either win it or we lose it, but we're going to play it the best we can. We're not intimidated." It sounded like the Trumbull version of the "The Taiwanese put their pants on the same way we do, one leg at a time" speech.

Tom Galla cautioned that his kids had never seen a submariner like Lee before, so "...that look might give us some trouble. Hitting that kind of pitcher is more mental than anything else. He looks like he going to hit you, but maybe we're tough enough now that that won't make a difference." They may have not swung at a submariner's offerings before, but Tom Galla certainly had seen his share of those pitches; he caught Major League submariner Kent Tekulve when the two played at Marietta College.

Asked how he felt Drury would handle the pressure of pitching in the big game, Galla reminded everyone that Chris had played on a junior hockey team in Bridgeport that had won the national title earlier that year. The pressure shouldn't pose the problem it might for many other pitchers, Galla reckoned.

"[Drury]'s a gamer," Galla affirmed. "He can throw heat and he can throw junk. The way those Taiwanese kids hit fastballs, you've *got* to throw junk to win. We hope he can keep them off balance. He has a good curve and change-up and then can pop that fastball in on you. He's also a real smart pitcher. He'll keep Taiwan on their toes."

Drury's teammate Andy Paul called him "...the smoothest player I've ever seen, even at that age. He had the savvy, the competitiveness, and the confidence of a major league veteran trapped in a 12-year-old body. He was in control the entire game."

"I wouldn't expect that they will make too many mistakes," said Galla. "We can't overrun any bases and we can't give them more than three outs in an inning. We have to make the routine plays. Eighteen outs, that's all we need."

The pre-game ceremonies began about two hours before the first pitch left the mound. Pomp and circumstance must play their parts as well...on a very tight schedule:

- 2:00 PM – Welcoming remarks by Little League officials
- 2:10 PM – Presentation of donation from Nabisco for 50th anniversary sponsorship
- 2:15 PM – Performance by Wilkes-Barre GAR High School band
- 2:39 PM – Parade of champions begins
- 2:46 PM – The Little League pledge is recited in English, Spanish and Chinese
- 2:50 PM – The West Point paratroopers, the Black Knights, land at Lamade Stadium
- 2:59 PM – Presentation of the grand prize winner of the Little League 50th Anniversary photo contest by Minolta Corp.
- 3:02 PM – Presentation by Pizza Hut, including a taped welcoming message from Los Angeles Dodger pitcher, Orel Hershiser
- 3:04 PM – Warm-up for visiting team – Taiwan (11 minutes)
- 3:17 PM – Warm up for home team – Trumbull, Connecticut (11 minutes)
- 3:28 PM – Field is groomed and dressed
- 3:32 PM – ABC-TV announcers are introduced
- 3:34 PM – Presentation of Little League Good Sport Awards
- 3:37 PM – Presentation of Little League Parents of the Year Award to Carl Yastrzemski Sr.
- 3:39 PM – Presentation of Peter J. McGovern Little League Museum Hall of Excellence inductee, U.S. Senator Bill Bradley
- 3:42 PM – Presentation of Little League Volunteer of the Year Ward to Ed Janser of Terryville, Connecticut, by Senator Bradley (first presentation of this award)

UNLIKELY CHAMPIONS: A MIRACLE IN WILLIAMSPORT

3:44 PM – Marine Corps League detachments from Williamsport and Susquehanna unfurl a 50-foot flag on the field for the National Anthem
3:45 PM – Invocation by Rev. Steven Stavoy, chaplain of the U.S. Naval Reserve in Stafford, Virginia
3:47 PM – Singing of the National Anthem by Barry Craig
3:52 PM – Introduction of umpires
3:56 PM – Introduction of visiting team
3:58 PM – Introduction of home team
4:00 PM – Introduction of Bill Shea, president of the Little League Foundation; Dr. Bobby Brown, president of the American League; Senator Bradley; and Al Haynes, pilot of United Airlines Flight 232 for ceremonial first pitch [Haynes, who lives in Seattle, is a Little League umpire and the airline captain who was forced to crash-land a fast-failing DC-10 in Sioux City, Iowa, in July 2989]
4:04 PM – Al Haynes throws ceremonial first pitch to Dr. Bobby Brown
4:08 PM – *Play Ball!*

A local Cub Scout pack inflated more than 7,000 helium-filled balloons and just before the game began, released them, a beautiful splash of colorful dots disappearing into a deep blue Pennsylvanian summer sky.

Senator Bill Bradley eloquently described the impact of Little League on its players and their families when, during his brief remarks, he said, "I want to dedicate this to my mother and father, who, for four years, didn't miss [one of my] game[s] ... there's an old African saying, 'It takes a village to raise a child.' Little League baseball gives the most important thing an adult can give a kid - time."

Amazingly, several members from the original Little League teams from 1939, the year Carl Stotz founded Little League, attended the opening ceremonies to celebrate Little League's 50th Anniversary.

While the opening ceremonies' festivities, lasting nearly two hours, may have entertained the crowd as they took their seats, the players about to take the field just wanted to "Play Ball!"

Andy Paul's memories of the long opening ceremonies were not pleasant. "I hated that pre-game ceremony. We had to parade all the way around the field with the other teams as they had speakers and all this other nonsense. Meanwhile, we are trying to get focused on the game while standing out on the field for what seemed like an eternity. It was very poorly planned."

While fans can attend any Little League game free of charge, they needed to arrive hours before the championship game started in order to grab a seat in the grandstand or even a seat on the hillside surrounding the outfield fence. So, all the pre-game hoopla and anticipation served to whip the crowd into a lather by the time the first pitch was delivered.

The Trumbull faithful sat on the first-base side, decked out in their yellow shirts, waving American flags and banners supporting their kids. On the third-base side, the Taiwanese contingent proved just as pumped, waving Taiwan's flag and banners. No one sat on their hands.

The crowd anticipated the moment...

Ten minutes to game time, with the grandstand seats packed. Did any seats remain? Where?

After a five-hour drive from Shelton [author's hometown], no one wanted "Standing Room Only" for two hours. Fans, friends, and family packed the lower level of the double-tiered hillside, stretching from the left-field foul pole all the way to the right field pole. But the upper level of the hillside held not people who will watch the game but rather kids of all ages, sledding down its steep slope on flattened-out corrugated cardboard boxes, providing unwitting pre-game entertainment to the thousands taking their seats.

Ultimately, the box-sledders would relinquish their slope to the thousands of spectators seeking a vantage point for the championship game. Whereas Fenway Park, the "Most Beloved Ballpark in America," can only shoe-horn about 38,000 at its most crowded, the Lamade Stadium crowd reached 40,000, maybe 45,000. What a venue to take in a sport in perhaps its purest form...Little League Baseball.

Finally the National Anthem echoed around the grounds, the announcer introduced the combatants, and moments later, the home team trotted to their nine positions on the field amidst rousing cheers and screams.

The umpire sounded the call to arms: "Play Ball!" Anticipation quickly became expectation; the thrill of the game flowed by osmosis from the field to the crowd. Energy became tension. In a couple of hours, one team will walk off the field champions, while the other would remember what could have been. For these 12-year-olds, today held no tomorrow.

The crowd comprised a mix of all ages from many places. Kids from Williamsport who loved to watch baseball; elderly couples cheering on a friend's grandchild on one of the teams or the local team from Anywhere USA; young couples with young ball players who wish *they* could play instead of watch; fathers with their eight-year-old sons cheering on their "local team" and who fully expected, in four years' time, to take this same field of their dreams; and folks from wherever who just loved to take in a good baseball game. They mostly stayed the week, all true fans, Williamsport faithful for years just because "...if you build it, they will come."

As morning arrived on Championship Saturday, Tom Galla became a de facto media star across the United States, simply because the two Little League World Series head coaches became natural targets of media attention prior to the title game. At the same time, the media loved him because he spoke his mind. He made it clear that even though most considered his kids the underdogs, and Team Taiwan carried a history of almost never losing in Williamsport, he liked Trumbull's chances.

Galla announced, somewhat unabashedly, "Guess what, we're the team that they have to beat to be the world champions. And we're going to go after them, because we want to be world champions real bad." And although his team had easily earned its nickname of "The Electric Company" for its high-powered offense on the road to Williamsport, Trumbull's defense had in fact keyed its two wins in Williamsport.

How about the Trumbull kids? Did the Taiwanese team intimidate them?

Well, here's a story about the first skirmish in this matchup, one that occurred two nights before Taiwan and Trumbull faced one another on the diamond.

Bill Bloxsom, writing for *The Trumbull Times*, related what happened that evening while the kids relaxed in the game room at The Grove.

Carrying the flag for Trumbull was their spirited leader Cody Lee. The 12-year-old explained, "I was playing ping pong when one of the bigger players from Taiwan came over and put both his hands on the table. Because we couldn't understand each other, I gestured with the paddle for him to move back a bit. He did for a minute, then came back and put his hands on the table again. I again moved my paddle to show him where he should move and he refused. I didn't want to give in so I touched my paddle and then touched my head. This he understood. After staring at me for a minute he backed off."

Lee had fought off the first try at intimidation [for which] the Taiwanese players are legendary…in Little League circles. However, he was tested again later that night.

"A different player from Taiwan asked me to umpire his ping pong game. When I ruled against him on one point he started screaming. By his actions I knew he wanted me to go away. It was his game so that didn't bother me a bit. A few minutes later, I was sitting on a bench waiting to play in a tournament game of my own when he spotted me. He picked up a rock and faked like he was going to throw it at me. It didn't bother me at first, but then I saw he was serious. He was about five feet away and chucked the thing at my head. I ducked out of the way, but it hit the kid next to me. Now, we didn't have an all-out fight, but they did have to separate us. After that, there was no more trouble. Later on, in fact, through an interpreter, he apologized."

While Lee admitted he would have preferred things to have run a little smoother, he did relate a happier ending. "They had an interpreter that I used to begin with. But later on, I got to be friendly with a couple of the players from Taiwan. We just played games together and stuff. It wasn't a big deal."

No chance the Taiwanese intimidated the Trumbull kids. Nevertheless, nerves still play a role...

Miracles don't start with a splash, and this day would prove no different.

Just before 2:00 PM, both teams emerged from their barracks and assembled at the top of the hill, looking down onto the Lamade Stadium field, where, in two hours, "the game" to determine the champion would unfold on what would be one team's field of dreams. For the other, it would be the end of a long road that fell one win short. Both teams would momentarily take their first steps toward whatever the day would ultimately bring.

As the crowd stared at the stairway leading down the hill, they immediately recognized the Trumbull team by their distinctive forest green jerseys with EAST emblazoned across the chest, white pants, and green hats.

What thoughts fought for space in the minds of those 12-year-olds about to step onto a ball field wrapped by a stadium packed with 40,000 people?

Many of the Trumbull players shared the emotions they dealt with that afternoon before that first pitch.

Dan Brown didn't think it was a big deal "...until the [championship game], when there was that insane amount of people watching us. I don't remember much about what was going on [before the game], except feeling extraordinarily nervous. But I snapped right back when the second batter smashed one at me. After that, I didn't even notice the crowd. Now, when I talk to parents, all they talk about is Williamsport, which is not how I remember it."

David Galla recalled how smoothly Dan Brown played that first ground ball.

"I remember watching that hard-hit ground ball going to Dan, he picked it up like he had a thousand times that summer, fired it over to first, and Kenny [Martin] made it look easy, like he did that day and every day until he stopped playing baseball. Now we're rolling. That's when I relaxed a bit."

Andy Paul remembered a personal sense of "nervousness" when he took the field. "It was loud in the park. Everything was just so amplified and it felt very surreal, like you were playing in an alternate dream world."

As only Dan McGrath could put it... "Ha! You must think I felt nothing, but this would have been the first time I was a bit anxious. I can remember walking to the stadium, the people, hugging my folks. There was a massive amount of pregame activity. Then, during the game, my father came down the line to say 'Hi!' to check in and wish me luck. It had a calming effect on me. I also chewed gum before and during games and that was how I would have been prior."

After the game, the media would pursue the angle of Dan McGrath hailing from Australia.

"I remember being asked later on about being an Aussie – the first Aussie to play in the Little League World Series, and until this year [2013], the *only* one to play in the Little League World Series..."

David Galla: "On the day of the championship game, I remember we were on the field for some time. It's different now, but as a 12-year-old kid back then, it was cool. Then we went back to the compound right before the game, and came back down."

What happened next would stay with David Galla forever. "Coming back down the stairs just before the championship game, I remember walking with Danny Brown and Chris Kelly; we were coming down the hill, coming down the stairs and I looked to my right and there was this sea of some 40,000 people. I said to [Brown and Kelly], 'Look at all the people here. This is *amazing*!'

"Hearing the crowd chanting...'U-S-A! U-S-A!' That was awesome. It was at that point you know that you've got the entire country behind you. Seeing all of those people and seeing the magnitude of the moment was awesome.

"Just before the game started was an anxious moment," David continued. "I'm not sure I could verbalize it when I was 12 any more than I can verbalize it today, but it was an anxious moment...

"Just to feel the energy of the crowd, how they were reacting to us coming out, it certainly doesn't relax you. It makes you nervous, anxious. Even if you've done something your whole life and even if you are confident in your abilities, you're nervous. I just wanted to get the game started, get on the field and play. Get that first pitch out of the way. At that point, that's what we had known for so long. Get on the field, play, win, go. I remember looking around during the first inning and thinking to myself, there are a lot of people here, and we've got a lot riding on this game."

On that day and at that moment, Dan McGrath recalled that when he saw Chris Drury on the mound, it really calmed him down. "Chris had a calming effect – he was so far advanced in terms of approach, ability to deal with pressure – it felt like this was all just another game for him...big stage, right kid for the game...couldn't have asked for a more grounded, confident and natural leader to take center stage."

Trumbull might have been nervous, but they were as prepared as they would ever be. The moment had arrived. *Let's play ball*!

CHAPTER SIXTEEN

THE CHAMPIONSHIP GAME

In his opening remarks for ABC's *Wide World of Sports* telecast, Al Trautwig called the Little League World Series "A celebration of family, youth, and dreams."

As Little League celebrated its 50th year in 1989, nearly 7,000 teams in 33 countries competed in the tournament that would end with eight teams fighting it out for the championship in South Williamsport, Pennsylvania. [Author's note: Lamade Stadium actually stands in *South* Williamsport, across the Susquehanna River from Williamsport.]

Now, after more than 12,000 games played worldwide, it all came down to two teams, 28 kids from opposite ends of the earth in a winner-take-all contest: 14 boys from Kaohsiung, Taiwan and 14 boys from Trumbull, Connecticut.

To paraphrase W. P. Kinsella's character John Kinsella in his book *Shoeless Joe*, which served as the basis for the movie *Field of Dreams*, Williamsport may not be heaven, but to these two culturally diverse squads of 11- and 12-year-olds, it came pretty close. The sad part was that only half of these youngsters would return home champions.

Prior to the game, Tom Galla made two changes to his final lineup that he hoped would wake-up the sleepy Trumbull bats. First, he moved Matt Basztura from the #3 hole in the batting order to the #2 hole, sliding each batter after him up one spot in the batting order. Second, he started Cody Lee as catcher, replacing Todd Halky, who had caught every other game that Drury pitched.

Galla explained it thus: "We always had trouble with the #2 spot in the order. We never liked who we had batting number 2. And I wish I had paid attention to Taiwan the year before, because maybe then we would have realized what they were doing where they loaded up the front end of their batting order. I don't know why we were trying to be traditional. We had

Drury leading off and he made a terrible leadoff hitter except that he got a hit almost every single time. I wish I had used the lineup we used against Taiwan all the time. I finally got it right against Taiwan."

Galla continued, "When we picked the team, I thought Cody Lee was one of our best players, but he had some struggles early on. We just weren't sure where to play him. Then we get to Williamsport and I don't know what happened. We thought it looked like he changed, like he matured. He was ready to go out there and play. He got his opportunity because Todd Halky had a tough game against [Davenport] Iowa, lots of passed balls, so we put Cody in to catch the last couple of innings of that game. He did okay, so we made the decision that Cody would catch the final game if we made it that far."

Years later, Todd Halky seemed a bit reluctant to talk about not starting that final game. Not a complainer, he just wanted to play baseball. In the normal rotation of the Trumbull line up, he had always caught Chris Drury's games.

"The night before the game against Taiwan," Todd recalled, "I was visiting with my parents, and I was in a pretty dark place because I knew I wasn't playing the next day. I remember telling them I wasn't going to play. It was tough."

The only strategy Tom discussed with the kids before the game was how to bat against a submarine pitcher [a pitcher who throws it underhand, like former major leaguer Kent Tekulve]. Luckily for the Trumbull kids, Galla's college experience with Tekulve came in handy.

"Before the Taiwan game, I told the kids to move up in the box to catch the ball before it dove down," Galla said. "[I'm] not sure that worked, but it got their mind off of any negative thoughts. I didn't want them thinking 'I can't hit this crazy pitch.'"

Galla finally clarified what he meant in saying he "...caught Tekulve once..."

"By the way, I only caught Tekulve one time in college, and I had a horrible game, with lots of passed balls, because his ball exploded as it approached the plate," Galla noted, traveling down memory lane. "Luckily for me, I got four line drive hits in that game and became an infielder from that game forward. I also could not hit Tekulve in batting practice or simulated games. No wonder he did so well with the Pirates."

So what did the coaches tell Chris Drury before he took the mound to face Taiwan? What did they tell him to throw…how did they advise him to handle their big hitters? Simply put: Not much...

Drury pretty much called all the pitches, whether he stood on the mound or hunched behind the plate. Ed Wheeler "...told Chris to throw whatever he wanted. He was way ahead of his time as far as baseball smarts are concerned."

Jim Palmer didn't give Trumbull much of a chance. "Fodder for the

UNLIKELY CHAMPIONS: A MIRACLE IN WILLIAMSPORT

Taiwanese," he labeled them at one point during the telecast.

After visiting with the Trumbull boys prior to the game, Palmer wished them luck. "You're going to need it today," Jason Hairston remembered Palmer telling them. "It certainly motivated those of us who heard him say that," Hairston recounted. "It really pissed *me* off."

Then moments before the first pitch, in a pre-game interview with Jim Palmer, Tom Galla expressed the hope that his boys' bats would finally come back to life. Galla also said he wanted his team to work hard, play as a team, and, most important, enjoy the moment and have fun.

Tom recalled his brief conversation with the future Hall of Famer…"I didn't meet Jim Palmer until just before the Taiwan game. He asked me if I thought we had a chance to win, and I said, sure we have a chance to win, of course we do. What did he think I was going to say? Nah, they're going to kill us just like last year. *Bulls**t!* *Sure* we have a chance."

Tom reflected further on that moment, "At the time, his question really pissed me off. But, now, in retrospect, when I see how dominant Taiwan had been over the last few years, I understand. I shouldn't have been surprised he might say something like that, but at the time it motivated me."

But despite what the statistics indicate, baseball also remains a game of breaks… and Trumbull got its first break when Taiwan Coach Chin-Ming Wu used his best pitcher and biggest player, Ming-Lan Hsu, in the International Championship game against Maracaibo two days earlier. Under Little League rules, Hsu cannot pitch today.

Fearing the South American representative would prove a tougher opponent than either of the two US teams his team might have to play for the title, Wu gave Hsu the start on Thursday instead.

Technology clocked Ming-Lan Hsu's fastball at 73 MPH, the equivalent of a 98 MPH Major League fastball…nearly unhittable. Yet Wu chose Chieh-Chin Lee, a slight (5-feet, 1½-inches, 86-pounds) 12-year-old submariner, whose pitches would suddenly appear from an unusual direction and arrived at the plate at around 55 MPH, again, the equivalent of an 80-MPH pitch in the big leagues. Lee's only other appearance as a starting pitcher in the entire post-season tournament was in Taiwan's 12-1 win over the People's Republic of China in a Far Eastern Regional game.

Trumbull's second break took the form of the partisan crowd of 40,000 clearly favoring the kids from Connecticut, so much so that the Trumbull team considered it a home game…how could they not? They took the field in front of a crowd larger than the size of their entire town's population…and they heard virtually *everyone* cheering for them…

Taking the mound for Trumbull…Chris Drury, who was unbeaten in his seven tournament games. At 5-feet, 1½-inches, 126 pounds, Drury stood the same height as Lee, but boasted a hockey-tough physique, providing the physical and mental makeup a game of this significance demanded. Drury's ice time clearly helped develop this toughness.

The stocky right-hander didn't bring a lot of heat, but he threw strikes and kept batters off balance with lots of off-speed junk. He also knew how to zoom in from different arm angles – overhead, three-quarters, and even sidearm. Most of his pitches were around 55 MPH, with an occasional fastball hitting the low 60s.

Just before the game, Coach Ed Wheeler, the team's pitching coach, worked with Drury on "...all the junk..." he could...changeups, knuckleballs, sidearm deliveries, and...the "dart pitch." The coaches knew Taiwan could hit the fastball. They didn't think they could hit the junk.

When asked about his pitcher before the game, Galla said, "He'll bend a little, but he's never broken." Sandy Galla, who had watched Chris play for several years now, said, "He was cool under fire."

Today would provide a real test of those words.

In the top of the first, Drury easily retired the first two batters on just three pitches. Leadoff batter, Ming-Lan Hsu, Taiwan's "big man", popped to right. Number two batter, Hsin-Lung Tseng, grounded to short. But Taiwan's number three hitter, starting pitcher Chien-Chih Lee, smacked a 2-and-1 pitch to the left field wall for a double.

Taiwan's cleanup batter, second baseman Chin-Lung Yeh, followed with a 2-and-2 frozen rope that glanced off leftfielder Danny McGrath's glove, scoring Lee. The scorer charged McGrath with an error. With two out, and a man at second, Taiwan quickly took a 1-0 lead.

"Things can get out of control, quickly," Palmer noted.

Drury hung tough and got catcher Chih-Hao Hsu to swing and miss on an 0-2 pitch, retiring the side.

Between innings, Dan McGrath remembered his father visiting the dugout to check on him after his "error." "[My dad] encouraged me to give it a go and that was it. His message remains the same today, get in, have fun and enjoy it. I still laugh about it now because I teach my kids about proper outfield mechanics," Dan McGrath recounted.

Looking at the video, charging McGrath with an error appeared a bit harsh, but remained the official record.

Drury smashed a line-drive directly at the shortstop for the first out in the bottom of the first inning, but centerfielder Matt Basztura "picked up" his teammate with a line-drive double to center, and Trumbull had its first base runner.

The next hitter, first baseman Ken Martin, bounced a 1-0 pitch up the middle. But shortstop Chi-Yi Chang made a great play, nabbing Martin at first. Basztura moved to third on the play but now Trumbull had two outs. Cleanup hitter, Andy Paul then chased a 1-2 pitch off the plate, stranding Basztura at third. Taiwan held their 1-0 lead after one inning.

UNLIKELY CHAMPIONS: A MIRACLE IN WILLIAMSPORT

"When Matt Basztura hit his line drive to the centerfield wall in the first inning," Tom Galla remembered, "I thought, this isn't so bad, we can play with these guys. I really felt that way when he hit it. Now if Chris had done that, I probably wouldn't have felt as strongly as I did when Matt did it. Matt was a good hitter but he wasn't Chris Drury. That's what I was hoping, that we could play with these guys. I didn't want to be humiliated [by Taiwan] like the other teams had been."

Still, when Trumbull trailed by one run after the first inning, Tom Galla started growling. Literally.

"We started 'growling' in the dugout. For some reason I just thought about growling, 'graaaahhh,'" he demonstrated. "We did it about six or seven times on a couple of different situations and it made the kids feel good so we growled," he explained.

David Galla explained the origin of the growl: "My dad played college baseball for Don Schaly, who was a tough guy; he was old-school baseball, very quiet, well organized and incredibly intense. Apparently, one day the team had been losing, but was making a nice comeback late in the game. Coach Schaly told everyone in the dugout, in his gravelly voice, to give him a growl, and everybody did. It was a team thing that got everybody pumped up. They came back to win the game. It stuck with my father. So, when my dad got a little nervous and needed to calm himself down, he yelled out to everyone, he wanted us to give him a growl. At the time, none of us knew what he was talking about, but we growled. It made him happy. You can even see Kenny Martin on TV strapping on his chin strap on his helmet going, 'What is he talking about?' and then growling right back at him. That's what we did; we did things as a team. When coach told us to do something, we did it."

Dan McGrath thought Galla's growl "out of character, but again, relaxing." Between innings, McGrath said the coaches were "…reassuring us…'pay attention to the signs [numbers on the card], get ready to hit early, you have a chance – you have a great chance!'" They sure did. Evidently, whatever magic formula the coaches had to keep the boys focused and relaxed seemed to work. "We weren't intimidated," said Andy Paul.

While no one noticed at the time, Taiwan had scored 13 of its 22 runs so far in Williamsport in the second inning. So when Drury easily retired their 6, 7, and 8 hitters in the second inning, he clearly sent Taiwan a message, even if they didn't get it.

As Trumbull came to bat in the second, those near home plate heard Galla telling his players to "…move up in the batter's box!" so they had a better chance to hit Lee's submarine pitches. The advice didn't seem to work, however, as Taiwan put away Trumbull in order in the bottom half of the second.

Leading off the third inning, Taiwan's number nine hitter, Chin-Chih Huang, laid down a beautiful bunt, but Drury turned an even nicer play and nailed him at first. The leadoff batter, Ming-Lan Hsu, popped up to second baseman Dave Galla for the second out, then Hsin-Lung Tseng bounced back to Drury, who tossed to first to end the inning.

"All week people have said if Trumbull can just stay with them for a couple of innings, they've done a major thing," Palmer told the TV viewers. Palmer and many others didn't realize that the Trumbull kids did not know they weren't supposed to win. They were 11 and 12 years old. They played because they loved to play. Baseball is fun.

Catcher Cody Lee led off the home third with a grounder that scooted under first baseman Ming-Lan Hsu's glove for an error. Third baseman Jason Hairston, at 4-feet, 7-inches, the smallest player on the field, tapped a soft liner to shortstop Wang for the first out, keeping Lee at first. Drury then laced a first-pitch single up the middle, putting runners at first and second with one out and the heart of Trumbull's batting order coming up.

An attempted pick-off of Drury failed when the throw from the catcher sailed high, and first baseman Ming-Lan Hsu appeared to push Drury off the bag. Drury lost his balance and fell, and it looked like Hsu tried to step on his hand. Drury got up and pushed Hsu back. Chris, a tough kid, does not intimidate easily. David Galla called it another example of Drury's "…quiet leadership. He let them know we're not backing down."

Tom Galla charged out of the dugout, fuming. "I thought it was a dirty play. When I watch that play on video now, it doesn't look as bad, but from the dugout, it just looked like Taiwan's first baseman was trying to kill Chris. I was pissed. First, I said something to the first base umpire; then to home plate umpire, Mario Garrido, who was probably the crew chief. He came out and I told him, 'This kid's trying to hurt my pitcher [to get him out of the game].' Garrido said he felt they had control of the game, which was good, but boy, it looked bad to me, and to Bob. What was I going to do? Luckily, Chris didn't get hurt. Obviously, he's not a fragile kid. You'd have to do a lot to hurt Chris." *Hockey tough.*

After a few minutes, play resumed.

Basztura followed with a weak grounder to the mound, which Chien-Chih Lee fielded cleanly, throwing out Basztura at first, but the runners, Lee and Drury, each moved up a base to second and third, respectively, with two out.

Ken Martin stepped in and worked the count full, fouling off several pitches before finally drilling a low outside pitch to right field, scoring Cody Lee as well as Chris Drury when right-fielder Chin-Chih Huang's throw to the plate rode up the first base line. The partisan crowd roared, cheering loudly. Trumbull now led, 2-1.

What so many said no one could do, what so many thought impossible, had transpired. Yes, Mr. Galla, it *was* possible. Taiwan's veil of invincibility had been pierced. Ken Martin's smile as he stood on first base said it all; the Trumbull kids knew they could play with these guys. A strike out ended the inning, but after three innings, Trumbull achieved the unexpected, taking a 2-1 lead over heavily-favored Taiwan.

In the top of the fourth, Tom Galla replaced Andy Paul in right field with Chris Kelly, after Paul struck out for the second time to end the third. "He [Paul] broke down emotionally. We put Chris Kelly in and he did a good job. We were thinking we might put Andy back in to pinch-hit, but the opportunity didn't present itself," Galla told reporters after the game. "He had done such a beautiful job for us Thursday [pitching the 6-3 semi-final win over San Pedro] and we told him, 'Look, your pitching is what matters to us.' But the kid had hit eight home runs going into the World Series, was batting .560 coming to Williamsport and he wanted to hit the ball. He was very disappointed. But he's fine now."

"I got really emotional and couldn't hold it together," Andy Paul remembered. He had left it all on the field against San Pedro. If he hadn't, then Trumbull might not be playing Taiwan for the Little League title.

Though Taiwan put two runners aboard in the top of the fourth off Drury, some sparkling defensive plays smothered the threat.

Jason Hairston made the first one, moving quickly to his left to field a slow bouncer, picking it cleanly and completing a nice throw to Martin, just beating the speedy Chieh-Chih Lee for the first out. Chen-Lung Yeh followed with a grounder that just sneaked under Dan Brown's glove at shortstop into left.

The second sparkler came when Chih-Hao Hsu's attempted bunt for a hit backfired as Drury flew off the mound to field it and nailed Hsu at first, Ken Martin's long stretch making it work.

A wild pitch moved Chen-Lung Yeh to third. When Drury walked Chi-Yi Chang on a 3-2 pitch, Taiwan had runners at first and third. With the tying run at third, Trumbull's defense felt the pressure weigh heavily. But Drury got tough, getting third baseman Kun-Yao Wang to hit a hard bouncer right to Jason Hairston at third. Hairston made the grab and threw across the diamond to Martin at first, easily retiring Wang for the third out.

With one out in the bottom of the fourth, Dan McGrath walked on four pitches, the only walk Chieh-Chih Lee gave up in the game. After Paul Coniglio came in to pinch-run for McGrath, David Galla smashed Lee's next pitch to right-center for a single. Trumbull's crowd roared, as John Coniglio's trumpet echoed around Lamade Stadium. The pressure sat squarely on Taiwan as Manager Wu made the trip to the mound to talk to his pitcher.

After their chat, Cody Lee hit an easy bouncer to third baseman Kun-Yao Wang, but Wang booted it to load the bases for Trumbull. It's Taiwan's second error of the game.

"Trumbull knew it would take some rare circumstances for them to win, and this [a second error by Taiwan] is a rare circumstance," noted Al Trautwig.

Taiwan Manager Chin-Ming Wu, in a move eschewing the spirit of Little League baseball, immediately pulled his third baseman, replacing him with Ming-Chieh Hsu.

Pinch-hitter Harlen Marks' slow bouncer to pitcher Chieh-Chih Lee forced Coniglio at home for the second out. Hairston came back in to run for Marks. Trumbull runners occupied every base as Drury stepped into the batter's box. He hit a looping fly ball off the end of the bat that fell just in front of a diving Hsin-Lung Tseng in short left. The fans in the stands erupted once more as David Galla and Cody Lee cross the plate, increasing Trumbull's lead to 4-1.

Now, with Drury at first and Hairston at third, Trumbull has a chance to steal a run and pad their three-run lead. Opportunity stared Tom Galla in the face.

Jason Hairston knew it immediately, a situation they had practiced many times. For a double steal to work, you need speed at third, a smart base-runner on first, and a patient hitter at the plate. Galla recalled the situation.

"Hairston's standing on third base going like this [both hands up and then arms crossed over the chest] to me, the signal for the double steal," Galla said. "Jason wanted it. So I have speed [Jason Hairston] on third base, and a smart runner, Chris Drury, standing on first with Matt Basztura at bat. And now I've got 'this long' to think about it [Galla snaps his fingers], and I should have said 'yes,' but I don't. It would have put the icing on the cake. I blew it, I didn't pull the trigger. What I should have done was just called time out and asked Bob, what would you think if we do this? I should have called that…oh man! That would have been beautiful, to beat them at their own game."

Instead, Basztura hit a comebacker to the pitcher for the final out.

"They have a startling lead at 4-1," Al Trautwig reported, as the game moved into its fifth inning.

Between innings, ABC's Mike Adamle half-told, half-asked Chris Drury's parents, John and Marcia, "This has got to be a tough experience?"

"It sure is," John responded. "We have six more outs. We're waiting." Adamle asked Marcia how she felt "…at a time like this?" "Very nervous," she replied. Adamle concluded the brief interview with, "At the risk of putting the kiss of death on you, hang in there, keep your fingers crossed, and good luck!"

After faking a bunt, Kuan-Lung Chen hit a soft liner toward right that fell just beyond the reach of a diving David Galla to open the fifth. Chieh-Hao Lai pinch-hit for Taiwan's No. 9 batter and promptly shot a single through the hole between short and third, putting two men on base.

Galla immediately called 'time,' jumping out of the dugout to talk to Drury and Cody Lee.

"Let's get this kid out. We got him out twice with that junk. Don't think you can't throw him a fastball, but you have to keep it in his eyes," Galla instructed his battery. Then, looking at Cody Lee, Galla affirmed "You have to go up there to get it." He ended the meeting with more encouragement, "You've got to work them smart. OK, come on guys."

Palmer reacted to Galla's meeting, "It was the classic advice, 'don't walk 'em, but don't give them anything good to hit.'"

When Galla returned to the bench, he put up a sign for "2," indicating to his outfielders that they need to throw the ball to second base if anything is hit to them. It was good advice, Palmer confirmed, because the tying run now stood at the plate.

Taiwan's lead-off hitter Ming-Lan Hsu once again swung at Drury's first pitch, hitting a chest-high curve high and deep to Chris Kelly in right, allowing Chen at second to tag up and move to third.

Palmer reinforced what John Drury had said between innings, "You're counting outs now. Only five outs to go. You don't want to do anything risky, so you give up the runner at third if necessary since you have a three-run lead."

With runners now at the corners, Taiwan's number-two hitter, Hsin-Lung Tseng, entered the batter's box. Galla clearly wanted him intentionally walked, but Cody Lee doesn't seem to know what he has to do, so Galla ran out to the mound to instruct him. It provides a good moment to relax the youngster, who hasn't caught much.

Jim Palmer immediately second-guessed the strategy. "My question is, with one out and a three-run lead, why would you want to walk the batter and bring the winning run to the plate?"

Al Trautwig chimed in with "We're seeing some strategy that I don't understand." Palmer clarified the situation, adding "So what they're doing is walking somebody who made two outs [in his previous at bats] to get to a guy [Taiwan's best hitter, pitcher Chien-Chih Lee] who's hit two home runs [in the Series] with a hit today."

Palmer further called Galla's strategy into question. "We'll see what this strategy is all about. Maybe you set up the force or turn the double play, but in Little League you don't turn many double plays. Maybe this is how Tom Galla has gotten this far. Usually you see this when you're trailing by a run or two…not when you are leading." A camera focused on Galla, clearly worried, as was Zullo.

Chien-Chih Lee stepped to the plate with the bases loaded as Galla and Zullo repositioned their outfield defense to play deep, with the infield in at the corners to cut the run off at the plate. They told the middle infield [Brown and Galla] to "…turn two," then put up a "4" sign, meaning that the outfielders should throw home with any ball hit to them.

Lee took the first pitch, a beautiful curve, but Drury missed low and away with the next two pitches, falling behind in the count, 2 balls and 1 strike. Lee swung at ball three, a helmet-high fastball. There's no way he could hit that, and he didn't. Chris's mom and dad clap nervously in the grandstand, cheering for their son to get out of the inning.

Lee ripped Drury's 2-2 pitch, pulling it hard down the left field line...*just* foul. The battle continued.

Drury tried to get Lee to chase a curve that broke outside, but Lee didn't bite. With the count full, a walk would bring in a run and Taiwan's clean-up hitter to the plate. Galla was running out of options.

You could feel the tension in the crowd as the "barn door" creaked... Can Trumbull close it before disaster, i.e., anything hit into the gap, struck?

David Galla turned to his double-play partner Dan Brown at shortstop and said, "What are we doing here? We knew who was coming up, we knew their lineup. We knew their power was coming up. We had done some unusual stuff in other games, but nothing like this, especially with the talent that we knew was coming up, to load up the bases. So then Danny and I looked at each other and said, 'I guess we're turning a double play...'"

"We had turned lots of double plays," David Galla noted, "but this was a little different. Sure, we were still 12 years old, but now we were playing in front of 40,000 people. There was a lot more pressure in that situation. Obviously, there was also a lot of pressure on my father for having done this. There was an expectation of execution of every player. So, what they were saying to us was that, look, we're going to put this guy on, because we know you can make the play, whatever it is. That's a cool message to send to kids, that we have faith in you to make this play. All the hard work we had put in was basically on the line at this moment."

Dan McGrath didn't question the decision. "During the game, the coaches coach, we play. In hindsight, it was a gutsy call. He [Tom Galla] was the kind of guy that made hard decisions and was willing to live by them."

Drury's 3-2 fastball was eye-high, and Lee drove it deep beyond McGrath's reach, where it short-hopped the left-field wall. It's the hit in the gap that no one wanted to see, least of all Tom Galla, who had implemented the unusual strategy that had loaded the bases. The first runner scored easily from third. As the second runner rounded third, Cody Lee set himself up for the play...

Dan McGrath fielded the ball cleanly and rifled a one-hopper to Cody Lee at home. Cody grabbed the ball and lunged at the runner, Cheih-Hao Lai, while also trying to block the plate with his leg. Home plate umpire Mario Garrido's right arm shot up like fireworks on the Fourth of July, signaling his call to the 40,000 faithful: "OUT!"

UNLIKELY CHAMPIONS: A MIRACLE IN WILLIAMSPORT

"What a throw from left field!" Trautwig shouted into the microphone over the roar of the cheering crowd. It proved a crucial play at a crucial moment, perfect execution by Dan McGrath and Cody Lee. Coach Galla's strategy had worked.

"A dramatic moment in this game for sure," Trautwig continued while Cody Lee stumbled away, writhing in pain, as Lai had slid into the catcher's right leg. As he fell to the ground, Cody rolled the ball – still in play – toward Drury. Drury kept his cool, rushing in to pick it up. Dan McGrath called it "a smart play." In the heat of the moment, Chris Drury's calm demeanor prevented the remaining runners from advancing.

The crowd chanted "Co-DEE, Co-DEE" as Tom Galla, Bob Zullo, and a doctor walked onto the field to check on Cody Lee's leg. He stayed in the game, but the bruise would take several weeks to heal.

Tom Galla called it "…the biggest play of the game." When other teams had faced such a moment, they did not get it done.

"These other teams that lost to Taiwan couldn't do that. They cracked and then the flood gates opened. That was such a big play. Such a big play," Galla said of McGrath's peg to the plate. Most people who watched that game remember that play. Andy Paul called it "…the turning point of the game, a momentum changer." Todd Halky labeled it "Just unbelievable! What a great throw by Danny. Cody holding onto that ball was awesome."

Even today, Dan McGrath remembers the moment well. "I just grabbed the ball, turned and tossed. It was a pretty accurate throw in general but I wasn't thinking much and just let it rip. Ha - talk about not hitting the cutoff man! I guess I was fortunate to still be in the game as I overheard the coaches talking about whether or not to pull me following the error in the first inning and another ball that was hit over my head later. I remember Coach Zullo telling Coach Galla to leave me in. It didn't register much then, but it did later on in life…"

"I love watching that replay…great pick up, great slide – still have mates arguing about the call…love every moment of it and can still hear that crowd roar…and roar they did…how awesome was Chris then running in, picking the ball up after Cody got hurt? He was magic, mate, absolute coolness under pressure from a 13-year-old…

"I wasn't a nervous kid," McGrath claimed. "I was pretty confident in my abilities, but I'm not sure there is much thinking going on [at a moment like that]. Having practiced catching [fly balls] so often, the body takes control and the mind shuts down. It happened in a flash, grabbed it…turned and tossed…can remember the play faintly…like something from a story book in a way…can remember watching the flight of the ball…a pause [fairly quiet]…then bedlam! Chills run through me as I think about the play now…not a text book toss and I am sure it would have been a talking point had there not been an out at the end of it."

Standing at second base, David Galla enjoyed a perfect view of the play. "Other than the fact that Danny's throw was nowhere near the cutoff man, it was a perfect play," Galla pointed out. "When the ball was hit, I thought it was gone. I turned to look and thought, 'that's out of here, grand slam.' But Dan makes an absolutely perfect play off the wooden wall. It's tough to judge. The ball bounces right to him; he turns around and fires the ball to the plate, to the perfect place for it to hop right to Cody. Cody gloves it as the runner is bearing down on him, which is a tough play for any catcher, especially someone like Cody who did not play the position all the time. Cody throws the tag down, and goes knee to shin with the runner and somehow held onto the ball to get the out. I have no idea how he did it. It was an awesome play. And I got to watch it; it was cool! Danny just hosed it from 200 feet. If you play that game now with 225 foot fences, the guy scores or Danny makes the catch if he is playing deeper. Maybe all three runners score if it bounces three times to the fence, and it's a different game."

Taiwan has trimmed Trumbull's lead to 4-2, and still has runners on second and third, but now there are two outs.

Again, Galla's unusual strategy with runners at second and third was to load the bases, to intentionally walk the next batter, clean-up hitter Chen-Lung Yeh, who had a hit today and two homers so far in the series.

This time Palmer changed his tune.

"If the strategy worked earlier, I guess you do it again here. It makes sense now with two outs; you have a force at any base, but it puts a little more pressure on the pitcher who has to throw strikes. You have nothing to lose." With the bases loaded again, the go-ahead run occupies first base. Four outs to go...

As Drury threw ball four of the intentional walk, Palmer offered, "It's been a marvelous game, Al, one of the few times in recent years that it's even been a contest, with the Far East so dominant."

Once again Galla put up the "4" sign, telling the outfield to throw it home on anything hit to them.

Taiwan's number five batter, Chih-Hao Hsu, then ripped a one-strike curveball from Drury right at third baseman Jason Hairston. Hairston briefly bobbled the ball but stayed with it and stepped on his bag just ahead of the runner, Lee, for the final out of the fifth.

"He made it," Trautwig confirmed. "They get out of it!"

Pom-poms waved and the crowd roared its approval as Jason spiked the ball on the mound and ran to the dugout, greeted by a slap on the back from Galla, who shouted, "Yes, sir! Yes, sir!" Jason's teammates shared their relief as they ran into the dugout.

Three outs to go.

"Chris made some great pitches in that situation with the bases loaded to get out of a huge jam," said teammate David Galla. "He was facing probably the three best hitters on any team in the tournament, and shut them down with minimal damage."

Tom Galla would later say, "That's the way they are. Taiwan keeps coming at you. They force you to make the plays." To their credit, the Trumbull kids *did* make "the plays" virtually every time.

Looking back, Tom explained the strategic moves: "We reviewed their lineup and what their first four batters looked like and what they had done, and their first four batters were pretty awesome. We thought their No. 2 batter [Hsin-Lung Tseng] was the best hitter on the team, and we walked him first. Then, we walked the fourth batter because from five down they were weak, they weren't strong at all, so that's what we wanted. We didn't want that No. 4 batter to rock one out of there and we didn't think 5, 6, 7, or 8 were going to hit a home run."

Put it another way: Just as luck occurs when opportunity meets preparation, a coach proves a *good* coach when the execution of his players makes his unusual strategy work.

Between innings, ABC broadcast a video of Cody Webster's final pitch of Kirkland, Washington's upset victory over Taiwan in the 1982 Little League World Series. They called it "The biggest upset in Little League World Series history." ABC must have enjoyed showing it with a US team finally leading Taiwan…it had been a long time since it had happened.

As Ken Martin stepped to the plate to open the top of the fifth, the crowd wanted more, and so did Ken's teammates. In sports, no lead is ever truly safe…especially in Little League…especially against Taiwan, who expected their comeback to start at any moment, even with only three outs remaining. There are no clocks in baseball; you just need 18 outs. Trumbull wanted to ice a cake…and make sure no one else brought anything to the table.

After taking a pitch from Chien-Chih Lee that caught the outside corner for strike one, Martin did not disappoint as he slammed Lee's next offering, a chest-high pitch in his wheelhouse, deep over the wall in left. The crowd stood up to roar its approval as the white pill disappeared.

"*Goooood – bye!*" crowed Al Trautwig.

Martin hesitated for a moment to watch the ball fly long and far onto the crowded hillside, where it landed and incited a scramble to lay claim to the souvenir. As he slowly circled the bases, Martin's quiet smile beamed brightly. Taiwan's Lee appeared devastated, as Martin's blast seemed to sound the death knell for the dynasty of the Far East.

As he approached the dugout, Martin's teammates mobbed him to Trautwig's exclamation of "*Holy cow!*"

Trumbull reclaimed its earlier three run lead, 5-2.

Tom Galla: "Beautiful! Whatever momentum they had gained moments earlier, well, Kenny really drove the spike through their heart by hitting that home run."

The stress drained from Tom Galla's face the moment Ken Martin's shot flew over the fence in left field. At the same time, Trumbull's dugout erupted into pandemonium. "We felt then that we were going to win it," said Drury.

As he circled the bases..."Fireworks were going off in my head," Martin later recalled.

Martin's homer "...was a huge emotional lift," Galla affirmed. "It gave us a three-run lead with three outs to go and their 6, 7 and 8 hitters coming up. We felt pretty good about our chances."

Taiwan Coach Chin-Ming Wu replaced pitcher Chien-Chih Lee with Ming-Chieh Hsu. As Hsu walked to the mound to warm up, the camera zoomed in on his catcher, Chih-Hao Hsu, whose face said it all...

The crowd again began chanting "U-S-A! U-S-A! U-S-A!"

"As we've been saying since 1963 on ABC's *Wide World of Sports*, this is really an event where dreams come true," Al Trautwig offered.

His broadcast booth partner Jim Palmer added, "After what has happened over the past few years, indeed, this is a dream to have a lead at this point in the game. They [Taiwan] gambled [with their pitching] and they have lost."

Hsu retired Kelly, Brown, and McGrath to end the fifth.

As the top of the sixth inning began, Al Trautwig told the audience "...in a dramatic fashion and a most startling way, Trumbull leads the heavily-favored Taipei team 5-2. The streets of Trumbull are quiet."

Well, Al, silence blanketed the streets of Trumbull because the entire community went indoors, someplace, somehow, to some way see the game. Fans everywhere watched, prayed, cheered, dreamed, and hoped that the Trumbull kids could hold on for one more inning.

Just one more inning.

Just three more outs.

Bill Mitchell, a well-known clothing retailer in Westport, a wealthy community about 12 miles down Interstate 95 from Trumbull, recalled how hundreds of would-be customers packed his store that Saturday afternoon, all standing around a television, enthralled by the athletic drama unfolding in Williamsport.

No one was buying. They stood and watched each critical moment quietly, and cheered with each key play.

Not only did silence blanket the streets of Trumbull, but similar to Mitchell's would-be customers, fans everywhere in Connecticut and beyond stopped doing what they usually did on a late summer afternoon and watched wherever they could find a television. Sure, lots of people watched the game, but not many of them watched quietly.

Once the game began, seats at The Grille & Bar Restaurant in Trumbull Center grew rare. Larry Buchwald and his wife Sylvia sat quietly at the bar. Then, as *Bridgeport Post-Telegram's* Marian Gail Brown told it, suddenly, Buchwald, who his wife says is a very quiet man, "…leaned forward on his barstool, swung his fist in the air, and broke his hour-long silence, shouting, 'Here we go TRUM - BULL, HERE WE GO!'

"The people gathered behind him took this as their cue to roar. They stomped their feet, clapped their hands, and drowned out the three network reporters." Silence may have blanketed the streets, but bottled-up explosions of triumphant Trumbull joy bubbled, ready to flow.

Drury began the sixth tentatively, walking lead-off hitter Chi-Yi Chang on four pitches…with Taiwan's number 7, 8, and 9 hitters to follow.

With that, Tom Galla is "…thinking, we're going to have another inning like we just had. Luckily we didn't. I never thought about replacing Chris…like I've said before, Chris might bend but he doesn't break.

Drury got No. 7 hitter Ming-Chieh Hsu to fly to McGrath in left. Two outs to go.

Next, Drury struck out No. 8 batter, Kuan-Lung Chen, on a check-swing called third strike. One more out to go.

Cheih-Hao Lei, who had earlier singled to left, stepped to the plate, working the count to 2-2.

A Drury wild pitch moved Chang to second. Jason Hairston made his way to the mound to calm Drury down, the stress of the moment mixed with the anticipation of victory clearly showing on the youngster's face. Lei stepped out of the batter's box, walking back to the dugout for a quick word of advice from his manager, Chin-Ming Wu.

Drury waited.

The camera zoomed in on Tom Galla standing at the dugout door, as Al Trautwig projected, "He can taste it." Trautwig then added, "Just one strike away from one of the greatest upsets in Little League baseball."

The game resumed. The next pitch, high and off-speed, fooled Cheih-Hao Lai, but he still drove it deep to the warning track in left field.

McGrath, solid all day in left, drifted back…and, as the ball settled easily into his glove for the final out, Al Trautwig made the call:

"Fly ball, deep left field, McGrath is there. He grabs it. *It's over! Trumbull wins it!"*

Victory!

Yes, victory!

Reporters and cameras immediately swarmed the field.

Todd Halky emerged first from the dugout, and, similar to his teammates, piled onto Drury in jubilation. Their parents hugged and slapped high-fives. The Trumbull coaches hugged in joy. "We got it, we got it," Galla shouted to everyone and anyone.

"We did it!"

Andy Paul, in the dugout, remembered "…getting ready to run out to the mound to congratulate my teammates and celebrate as that ball lifted into the air."

"It was my favorite moment of the game," said Aussie Dan McGrath about his catch to end the game. "I had a busy day in left field. As I ran in to celebrate, Coach Z gave me a bear hug I can still feel this day. I am thankful for that hug. He told me he had confidence in me and that the hug meant more than just celebrating the last catch, it was a sign of support."

"It was chaos," remembered Halky, as the crowd went "...absolutely wild." The roar of the 40,000 fans drowned out conversation with its chant of "U-S-A! U-S-A! U-S-A!"

A replay depicts Drury after the pitch. He turned toward left, crouched as the ball flew toward McGrath, and flung his glove into the air. Mere moments later, his teammates mobbed him.

"Chris Drury...hoping...praying...and it's over," Trautwig exclaimed. "What an outstanding game for these 12-year-olds."

The moment remains clear to Dan McGrath.

"It was bittersweet to have the foreign kid, the kid who had made an error, and made the throw home, catch the last out [of the game]. In reflection, I thought what was better than all of that was the bear hug I received from Bobby Zullo. It felt *amazing*...no better sporting moment in my life. That moment was just a great experience for a kid to have in a game that seemed to have everything in it...intentional walks, issue with first baseman stepping on Chris, bomb by Kenny, great play by Jason at third, great hits, Cody's tag play at home, Chris Kelly playing clutch in right field ...so many things that could have gone left or right. I only wish I got to keep the ball. The umpire grabbed it off me and the last I hear it was placed in the Little League Museum...[I'm] not sure if it is still around."

As the fly ball settled into McGrath's glove for the last out, David Galla thought, "Danny is there, game over, hysteria. My glove goes high and I'm running for the closest guy in a green shirt. By the time I got in there, it was Chris and Cody and Kenny and Jason. I came in as hard as I could, came flying at the pile. The pile fell over when I got there. That one hurt. I wasn't a big guy but I was moving pretty good. When you've got fifteen guys on top of you, it hurts, but it was a good kind of hurt."

Matt Sewell, watching firsthand every day since his broken arm spoiled his dream, had sat in the stands with his folks.

"The last out of the game was an amazing moment. When the game ended," Matt said, "my dad wanted me to be part of the celebration on the field, but I told my dad, I didn't want to go on the field and embarrass myself because I felt like I wasn't really part of the team at that point." But Matt's dad refused to allow his son to miss the on-field celebration and convinced a security guard "...to let me [Sewell] go on the field. I'll never forget that he did that. It was a special memory for me."

"I think the nerves were all down in my gut," said Tom Galla. "In anticipating the last out, praying for that last out, expecting it but never knowing...I don't think I ever had the feeling it was out, I don't think I did, but it was far enough, and Danny had had so much action out there in left field, that one more time, just make that catch. He did okay. He made it look pretty easy. You know, you're doing that in front of 40,000 people, under those conditions, in a close game, the last inning. Phew! That's all she wrote!"

When Mike Adamle of ABC asked him how he felt, Galla praised his kids.

"I knew this was a team of destiny," Galla asserted. "We had to win this game." Then Adamle asked Galla, "What makes these kids so special?"

"You saw it on the field," Galla replied. "They don't know how to lose. They didn't care who they were playing today. They didn't care that it was Taiwan."

"Chris pitched the game of his life," Galla continued, "and we were much more aggressive at the plate. We only got six hits but that was two more than we got in the last two games. Drury's a gamer. He'll do whatever it takes to win."

When asked if he considered Drury his number two pitcher, Galla said, "I don't have a number two pitcher, I have two number ones."

Galla held high praise for Ed Wheeler, the team's pitching coach, who had worked so hard with Drury all year, teaching him how to throw the dart pitch and all the other junk.

"He's thrown that stuff throughout this tournament," Galla noted. "It was perfect. He came at them with everything. He pulled out the stops. We knew if anybody could beat them it was going to be him [Drury]. He kept them off-balance. He was phenomenal."

Adamle then spoke with hitting star Ken Martin, telling him, "You looked pretty cool out there. You went into the home run trot pretty quick."

"It was great," said Martin.

"The thrill of a life time?" asked Adamle.

"Oh, yeah!" Martin smiled.

Then Adamle spoke with Chris Drury.

"I was up with your parents in the stands earlier and they were on the edge of their seats, but you were a picture of calm and collected on the mound," Adamle related to the youngster.

"I don't know, I just try to keep cool," Drury said. "I couldn't give them something to hit, because they would hit it."

Adamle then asked the team, "What are you going to do to celebrate?" They shouted together, "Go swimming!" *Now* they could use the pool!

Discussing his team's performance after the game, losing Manager Chin-Ming Wu said, "They didn't show their real ability. The big crowd made them nervous. His [starting pitcher Chien-Chi Lee] performances before were good, but today I guess he wasn't ready."

When Wu and Galla shook hands after the game, Wu never spoke a word to his counterpart. Obviously, the loss held too much disappointment for Wu.

Later, when reporters surrounded Tom Galla, he continued praising his team and his coaches.

"These kids know how to play baseball," Galla asserted. "They know how to catch a ground ball and make a throw and try for a double play and hit the ball… but the mental game is so crucial…

"Ed Wheeler, who is our third coach and, unfortunately, unable to go into the dugout, meant so much to us from the mental standpoint, too. He'd sit with the kids in the back of the bus and be into their heads and be their friend and the whole bit. I think between him being their friend and me being the bad guy, because I was always the tough guy most of the time, and Bob Zullo being both ways, I think the kids realized that we were all in it together."

As the broadcast closed, Al Trautwig said, "They say that Little League is supposed to teach you many things: how to play the game, how to take instructions, how to lose, and in some instances, how to win. Such is the lesson learned today by Trumbull, Connecticut, pulling one of the greatest upsets in the history of Little League. As Jim McKay said in 1982 when Kirkland, Washington won, it was an amazing day, just as amazing a day as it is today for Trumbull, Connecticut."

Trautwig concluded… "A historic victory for Trumbull; the drought is over. The Far East has been beaten."

CHAPTER SEVENTEEN

THE WINNING REACTION

Tom Galla knew his defense answered the call, playing tough all day.
"The defense held up," Galla noted. "Yeah, we made the error, if that's what you want to call it. We weren't happy with it, but you understand it's a big game and those things are going to happen. But other than that, we were pretty solid defensively, which is what we expected we would be.

"I had watched so many of those Little League championship games in prior years when the US team had that big, strong right-hander, who could throw fastballs at Taiwan, and Taiwan would just be hitting one line drive after another," Galla recalled.

"So, Chris didn't do that," Galla explained. "Chris threw slow, slower, and slowest. Side-arm curve, over-hand curve, dart pitch, every once in a while a fastball up high, out of the strike zone; it was never going to be right down the middle. Still, they did hit the ball hard that game. Luckily they hit a bunch of balls at shortstop Danny Brown and they also hit a bunch of balls at Danny McGrath in left field. Danny [McGrath] had trouble with the first one, missed it, but he handled every other one throughout the game, including that throw to the plate, which was just unbelievable. That play was a back-breaker."

"I don't blame people for thinking we were going to lose," Galla added. "We didn't look very devastating in the first two games. We had a lot of luck going and we thought all along that you needed a lot of luck to get this thing done. But I felt good because of who was on the mound and I knew the kids were ready. I know the kids weren't intimidated. I knew we could play defense. I was just hoping we were going to get the hits, and we did. We got enough to make it happen."

His son David agreed.

"We weren't intimidated at all," the younger Galla claimed. "When we got here, we knew we had a shot to win it."

When asked 25 years later about the unusual strategy he executed in the fifth inning, Tom Galla said, "Sometimes you make decisions that are questioned, like what I did in the Taiwan game to walk the bases loaded [twice, with good batters due up], or like what happened to Westport this year [2013] in Williamsport. If it works and you win, you look smart, look like a hero. If it doesn't work and you lose, then you come home the goat. It's all about the outcome. And with all the games on television, you've got these pros in the booth second-guessing every move you make. It's all about the outcome."

The goal remains simple: to win.

In a single elimination tournament, you must win today, and you cannot turn your attention to that next game until you hold today's game tightly in your pocket.

Later, Tom Galla confided to *Bridgeport Post-Telegram's* Chris Elsberry, "It hasn't quite sunk in yet. I felt like we just won a game and I want to cry. I'm just relaxed it's finally over. I didn't want to come here and finish eighth. We came here to win three games."

Years later, Danny Brown reflected upon a few moments from the Taiwan game…

"After we beat San Pedro, we all thought we would go out against Taiwan and get crushed," Brown admitted.

"I was surprised by their choice of pitchers," Brown commented. "I thought the kid who came in as relief against us was a better pitcher than the guy who started. I think we got a little lucky with their choice of starting pitcher that game. Then, I remember Tom Galla making us growl once in a while. It was what he did to get us fired up. I thought it was a little hokey at the time. But he was really into it and wanted us to be passionate. When we were losing, he always told us to cut it in half, getting a few runs. When we were winning, he always wanted us to put a couple more runs on the board."

"I think when they made a couple of errors, and when Kenny hit his home run, were big moments," Brown recounted. "And the fact that Chris got that 'big dude' at first base to pop up every time he was up was also big. As the game progressed, it finally dawned on people that we might win and I think Taiwan kind of tightened up a little."

When Dan McGrath made his huge play in the fifth inning nailing the runner at the plate, Dan Brown remembered that "…on that play, I'm the cutoff man and Danny [McGrath] moon-balls it right over my head. I thought it was ridiculous when it happened. He was supposed to throw it to me, but instead he skies it over my head…usually that isn't a good thing, but it turned out to be the perfect play at the moment. The runner was called out and that was awesome."

Dan McGrath felt that the baseball gods were with him at that moment. He knew he had air-balled it over Brown's head, but it provided a big break. If McGrath had hit the cutoff man, the runner probably would have scored, and who knows what would have followed.

"Yeah, I toss it through the cutoff man and we get the guy out at home!" McGrath laughed.

"When we got to the sixth inning," Dan Brown remembered, "I was thinking '…we're up three runs and we only need three more outs.' I was as nervous as anyone else, probably in disbelief that we were even in that position. At the moment Danny caught the ball [for the final out] I didn't know whether to turn around and tackle him or dive into the dog-pile on the mound. I mean…you just can't believe it. In the end, we won because we certainly had a lot of talent, and a fair amount of moxie. We weren't about to go out and get beat by anybody. We had enough of a swagger that we never gave up."

"Oh yeah, luck, catching a break, plays a major role in everything that happens, and everything that happened that summer, well, we got lucky more times that summer than we should have," Jason Hairston rationalized. "It wasn't like we got all these calls that went our way or huge breaks in games, but the ball bounced our way more often than it bounced the other way…

"And because of that we were very successful," Hairston noted. "Sometimes we would get lucky during a game. But, more often what happened was the other team didn't think we were very good and threw their better pitcher the day before we played them… Even though we had won games big going into the World Series, we didn't get too many hits once we got there. So, the scouting report on us probably said, 'these guys can't hit.'"

With the game over and the stress broken, the kids' excitement erupted.

And why not? Why wouldn't they flip out after what they had just accomplished?

They sat on top of the world, the Little League world. And yet they seemed grounded as well.

This wasn't the Super Bowl, and they weren't going to Disney World…just yet.

At 12 years old, you don't know otherwise – you're a kid. Enjoy the moment. And that would prove their coaches' and parents' toughest task over the coming months, keeping them grounded, reminding them to enjoy being 12-year-old boys.

David Galla remembered that "…no one picked us to win that game. We knew it; we knew we were the underdogs. We knew we had nothing to lose. And you know why we knew? Before the game, my dad was interviewed by Jim Palmer, who basically asked him, 'How much do you think you're going to lose by?' Palmer also said, do you think you have a chance to win? He was looking for my dad to say something like we just hope to stay with them for couple of innings...

"My father very confidently said to him that we can beat these guys, if we play our type of baseball, play strong defense and get good hits," David Galla recalled. "When he came back to the dugout after that interview, I could tell he was fuming about something. I didn't know what. As I grew up, we are able to talk about these kinds of things. He told me, 'You know, Jim Palmer really got me mad.' If we had lost to them [Taiwan] 20-0, people would have chalked it up. They would have said that that is what was supposed to happen. But instead we went out and showed them what we could do."

Dan McGrath looked back at the team and how they won the game this way: "We were sound in every facet, except we had an X-factor, and sadly, a low expectation from the television commentators... but a firm belief by our coaches, families, friends, and supporters. History will say many things, but the result speaks for itself...Trumbull National was a team of gamers...kids who had been told they would never have a chance, and as my 10-year-old says in jest some times, 'cop it sweet' [Aussie slang]. We were better than they were on that day – and you get one shot at it – we made the most. I think our coaches out-planned them and we executed the plan perfectly."

The size of the crowd and the desire to win the big trophy put tremendous pressure on the Trumbull kids. It's the human condition.

But Chris Drury carried the experience of the national stage, having won a Pee Wee Hockey national championship earlier in the year. Later, when asked which win he found more rewarding, his Pee Wee hockey championship or his Little League title, Chris Drury replied, "In the winter I like hockey, in the summer I like baseball. But this is a bigger deal, you know? Baseball's, like, our national pastime."

In Little League baseball, as in Major League baseball, we focus most of our attention on the pitcher. It's where all the action starts.

The parents of Little League pitchers carry the stress. Just watch a game sometime, and focus on the parent of a pitcher. You'll see.

Chris Drury's parents did not stray from the norm. During the game, whenever a TV camera focused on them, their eyes told the tale.

John and Marcia had plenty of experience with "the baseball butterflies" each and every time their son took the mound. In some ways, the Taiwan game seemed quite similar to every other game they watched in the past, but, of course, in reality, the game took on a very different aura because that day they awoke knowing Chris would toe the rubber as the starting pitcher for his team in the World Little League Championship.

After all, all anyone from Trumbull heard in those weeks leading up to their town team's appearance in Williamsport concerned "The Taiwan Talent" – the odds against any team hanging in with the Taiwanese for even a few innings, let alone having any chance of emerging victorious. No one wanted to see their kid – or their neighbor's kid – embarrassed on the international stage.

In fact, every parent sitting in the Williamsport stands or watching the game on TV who had a child who played in Little League that summer watched with that certain anxiety that only a parent can feel, regardless of whether their child had made it to "The Game." As their boys grew into adults and had children of their own who played sports, they experienced the same anxieties that their parents awoke to on Championship Saturday morning, and so many other mornings before and since.

John Drury expressed his fears so well that morning when he told *Bridgeport Post-Telegram* staff writer, Carole Burns, "Oh, I hope Chris is alright today." Carole Burns described what John really felt when she wrote, "John Drury's concern was not as much about his son's performance as his son's welfare." No one wants their son or any kid to suffer embarrassment or psychological scarring.

Years later, John Drury told Jeff Brantley of *ESPN Magazine* that while driving to Williamsport for the title game, he began to think of what he'd say to his son "…if he gave up 20 runs in the first inning, which seemed like a possibility," John said. "I could make up something really dramatic, but, in truth, I have no idea what I would have said to him." Instead, the John Drury advised his wife, "He's going to get shelled, so let's be prepared to support him."

Not against Taiwan, with its array of 175-pound, five o'clock-shadowed mashers.

No one knew what to expect. Not everyone believed the dart pitch could work against Taiwan's sluggers. No one considered Trumbull's chances good. Taiwan appeared a "sure thing" to most everyone, seemingly arriving in Williamsport already adorned with their crowns….

But "sure things," in fact, aren't always "sure." They must play the game. Just ask the 1969 Baltimore Colts, upset by "Broadway Joe" Namath's upstart New York Jets, or the "World's Best-Ever" Russian hockey team who fell to the young, unheralded Team USA in the 1980 Olympics.

Andy Paul put it quite simply when, years later, he said that while luck may have played a part in the win, "I think that any other 12-year-old boy besides Chris Drury loses that game because of the pressure and level of competition. And we kept our cool under a lot of pressure."

After the game, Martin said he knew his fifth-inning home run would leave the park as soon as he hit it. "It was a fastball, right in my wheelhouse," he remembered. "After I saw [Taiwan's pitcher] once, I knew I could hit him. I felt I could have a big day."

Martin's big day couldn't have come at a better time or a bigger moment. As the *Bridgeport Post-Telegram* headline shouted the next morning, "Martin's homer added the finishing touch" to the game and to the championship.

Jim Fuller, Sports Editor for *The Trumbull Reporter*, summed up the situation nicely, "Taiwan had earned a well-deserved reputation as a team who pressured their opponents into mistakes, using clutch hitting, airtight defense, and solid pitching to emerge victorious. But this time Trumbull stole the script, the one no writer in Hollywood would have dared touch for fear of ridicule."

After a summer of long hours of practice, Ken Martin realized the hard work that makes a good team a winner had paid off. He commented, "We played our game. We did what we had to do to win it. We deserved it. We worked our butts off to get here. Teams have gotten out in front of us early and we've always come back. We knew we would come right back. Our coach got us psyched up."

Indeed, they *had* come back each time, and, except for the Taiwan game, come right back each time an opponent had taken an early lead on them throughout the post season.

Jason Hairston summed up the win with a single word: "Awesome." Owen Canfield, writing for *The Hartford Courant*, labeled Hairston's reaction: "…eloquent."

Later, Tom would add, "I don't think Taiwan ever thought they were going to lose that game. Every game I saw them play, whenever they had runners on first and third, they always pulled the double steal. They never even tried it against us. I think they were just waiting for the big inning to come against us. They knew it was going to come; they didn't have to waste any time trying to steal second base. We were the weak team from the East. I guess I couldn't blame them for thinking that way. We didn't look really good against Iowa, and we didn't look really good against California."

This lack of respect by Taiwan's coach ultimately became a huge break for Trumbull.

You look for signs, little things to give you hope in near-hopeless situations. When Trumbull National held Taiwan to but one run in the first inning, and then hitless in the second and third innings, hope sprang, well, not eternal, but it sprang. After Trumbull scored two runs in the third inning, hope became the Little Engine That Could: "I think we can, I think we can...."

Third baseman Jason Hairston's mom, Indira Hairston, said, "Once we finished that first inning and we knew we were able to get some runs, I knew we could win."

Ken Martin, father of first baseman Kenny Martin, said, "You can't understand the emotions…" He spoke of exhilaration, joy, and… exhaustion.

Centerfielder Matt Basztura's mom, Cheryl Basztura, offered her words for what she had just witnessed: "I'm never going to have an experience like this again. I don't know if I could take it again."

Andy Paul's dad, Ken Paul, reacted to the win: "We've seen these kids grow up. A few years ago these kids weren't even very good Wiffle Ball players." Andy's mom, Holly, followed up: "When I think of how fortunate we were to win all those games, it's amazing."

"Not another minute. I want a vacation. It was brutal here, let me tell you," exclaimed Sandy Galla, wife of coach Tom Galla and mother of second baseman Dave Galla.

"With that final out, car horns began blaring in Trumbull," said Genevieve Molgard, co-owner of the Kimberly Inn. "It was great. There were tears. The emotion was unbelievable," she shared.

When the game ended, Grille & Bar owner Jamie Rose began the celebration by uncorking 10 bottles of champagne for the crowd.

"Business is business, but you don't get a chance like this to show off too often," he said.

Meanwhile, celebrations broke out all over town. *Bridgeport Post-Telegram* staff writer, Marian Gail Brown, described one such celebration. "Outside the [Grille & Bar] restaurant, an informal tailgate party was forming on White Plains Road. One thing was clear. The celebration was just starting." Twenty-four hours later, the Grille & Bar would become Celebration Central, where the homecoming party would really get rolling.

So, what did the team do that evening after the big win? As David Galla remembered, after celebrating on the field, "we finally headed… back to our cabin [in The Grove]. The room is no bigger than a postage stamp, and there were like 400 people in the room. They let everybody in because the tournament was over, so they didn't care who came in. It was nice."

First item on the agenda concerned the matter of Mr. Thomas Galla's hair-do…someone had ordered a shearing if (or when) Trumbull National accomplished its goal to win the Little League title. Tom Galla walked in and his players immediately engulfed him, after which he shouted, "Hey, let's cut someone's hair. I've had this hairstyle for a while, I need a new one."

Tom Galla recalled the promise he made after Ed Wheeler got his head shaved at the Regionals: "After we won [the Regional], I figured if he can do it, I guess I can do it, too."

With the deal done…once again, Dan McGrath, Sr. had come prepared with the electric clippers.

Guess who cut the first swath? Of course, son David accepted the honors. So, as their parents, siblings, and friends looked on, each kid took his turn snipping off a swath of Galla's hair.

"Dad, you're going to lose some clients," quipped David.

"I think I'm going to wear a hat for a while," Tom responded. When the shearing ended, someone handed Tom a mirror so he could admire his new "doo."

As David Galla sat on his bunk, he watched as his father sat patiently allowing each kid to take their turn cutting a little chunk off. "The first cut was right down the middle. I remember my mother sitting there watching, and saying, 'I can't believe he's doing this!' After that I don't remember anything else, except that we did talk to a lot of press, newspapers, television. Guys would get called out to talk to some TV station. That was a blur."

"That night after we won the [championship] game, we stayed in there [The Grove] and Cody and I stole a golf cart and we drag-raced down the main street," Todd Halky remembered with a grin. "Luckily we never got in any trouble." [Read: "Caught."]

Jason Hairston and a few of his teammates jumped (finally) into the pool.

"We went swimming. We hadn't been swimming all summer, so…and we also spent some time signing a lot of autographs. There were people leaning over the gates [at The Grove] asking for our autographs, which was a little strange. We also spent time saying good bye to other teams who were leaving."

Andy Paul didn't remember much, except "…spending time with my family and teammates that night. I don't remember doing anything out of the norm, because we were all tired… and relieved."

Dan McGrath remembered that they "…let it rip, partied!"

"After the final game, [Team Uncle] George Girio took Bob and me [and the other Team Uncle, Ed Claudius] back to his house to watch the game on video tape," remembered Tom Galla.

Ed Wheeler stayed with the boys, allowing them to let off some steam and have some fun.

"The kids just tore the place apart," Wheeler recollected. "I stayed with the team when Tom and Bob went over to the Team Uncles' home for a few beers. I kind of let them do what they wanted to do… Tore the bunks apart, there was shaving cream, and a few of the kids were driving golf carts all around. They had a little fun that night. It was a real party."

UNLIKELY CHAMPIONS: A MIRACLE IN WILLIAMSPORT

The next-day's newspaper headlines told Trumbull's story:

The Trumbull Times **"HOW SWEET IT IS!"**

The Trumbull Reporter **"WORLD CHAMPIONS"**

Bridgeport Post-Telegram "Trumbull Wins!" and "All-Stars overpower Taiwan team, 5-2"

The Hartford Courant read "Big Win for Trumbull's Little Guys" and "The boys of Trumbull are winners"

The Boston Globe "Trumbull captures Series"

The Williamsport Sun-Gazette "Trumbull Ends Far East's Five-Year Reign with 5-2 Win"

The Waterbury Republican-American "Trumbull team fulfills dream" and "Triumph a shocker to locals"

The New York Daily News "Trumbull brings LL crown to U.S."

Newsday "Nutmeggers Bring Title Home" and "A Victory for U.S."

Palm Beach Post "U.S. Team flying high after win"

The Florida Times-Union "Born-in-USA team wins LL World Series"

While Trumbull's triumph shocked many Little League followers, Trumbull's victory in Williamsport did not surprise Oakville (CT) Little League President John Putetti, who watched the team's run to the Eastern Regional tournament championship. He considered Trumbull a team not to be denied.
"I watched their game against Brandywine (Delaware) and I could tell this team was better than a lot of the other Little League teams you see," said Putetti. "They're very aggressive, confident players – all the players. None of the kids look to walk. They can really hit. They go up to the plate swinging at the first or second pitch. That's very important in Little League baseball. That stuff about a walk is as good as a hit is a lot of baloney in Little League, believe me.
"And they make all the plays in the field, too," Putetti continued. "Like today, Taiwan had the bases loaded and two outs and one of their

players hit a shot to the Trumbull third baseman. He knocked it down and still beat the Taiwan kid to the bag. He did what he had to do, and their whole team did. It was quite a thrill."

CHAPTER EIGHTEEN

OUR CHAMPIONS RETURN HOME

While most people would normally say Trumbull sits 10 miles north of Bridgeport, on this day, Bridgeport now sat 10 miles south of Trumbull.

If *New Yorker* magazine had put a map of Trumbull's view of the world on its cover the day after Trumbull National's victory in the Little League World Series, it would place Trumbull at the center of the universe...or maybe on top of the world. Trumbull was now "on the map," regardless of who drew that map.

Thanks to Andy Paul's dad, Ken Paul, a pilot for Trump Shuttle, 96 people enjoyed a chartered Trump Shuttle jet flight the next day from Lycoming County Airport in Williamsport to New York's LaGuardia Airport, where they landed at 2:00 PM.

Ken Paul related how it all happened. "Some of my fellow pilots got so excited about what was going on that they said they would try to work with the company and Donald Trump to see if they could fly the kids home if they won. So after they won, I got a call from the COO of Trump Airline, Dick Cozzi, who also happened to be a resident of Trumbull. He said OK.

"So on Sunday, some of my friends flew down an empty, old-version 727 to Williamsport, which luckily had a runway that was long enough," Ken Paul explained. "We were able to bring back all of the kids, their siblings and lots of their friends, as well as few adults. I had my uniform with me so I put it on and flew the plane back. It was a beautiful and glorious day. I was so thrilled to be able to do that. Then, as we approached the landing in LaGuardia, I started thinking to myself, boy, if I don't make a good landing here, all the kids and their parents will remember. So I was lucky and made a really safe landing. Then we taxied up to the Eastern Shuttle Terminal., where everyone got off the plane. As we walked up the ramp into the terminal, there was this huge burst of press, photographers, and television cameras. There must have been 20 photographers. It was like being on the red carpet. Then one of the reporters said to me, 'So, how was your landing?' Before I could even respond, one of the parents answered, 'It was terrific!'"

The next day, *The New York Post* had a photo of Andy with his pilot dad, Ken. "I really loved it," Andy said.

David Galla remembered the flight. "I think we were in the air for a total of 37 minutes. It was awesome." Andy Paul noted that "we were the only team that took a bus to Williamsport due to our close proximity but we flew back. We all wore our championship tee shirts. It was a really special end to our week in Williamsport."

"When we landed at LaGuardia Airport, yeah, that's when the whirlwind started," Todd Halky recalled.

David Galla described it as "…our first taste of the lifestyle that we were going to experience for the next year, and especially over the next few months. There was a bank of cameras taking pictures of us getting off the airplane. That was actually really cool. It was our first experience with paparazzi."

The scene in the terminal proved totally chaotic. The media folks wanted "…to talk to everybody, get some interviews, and take some pictures," remembered David Galla. "They were looking for certain people. My dad did a nice job to usher us through. They wanted a group picture of us all holding up our two fingers in the V for victory sign. None of us understood why they wanted us to do that. We had won. We were number one, not number two. So we held up our Number One finger instead. It's a great picture, because we were together after all we had done."

From there, they boarded buses, really nice coaches, donated by Joel Schiavone of Connecticut Limousine, for the trip home. Luckily for Connecticut Limousine, a few parents also rode the vehicles, otherwise, David Galla, said, "We might have torn the bus apart."

"I was on the flight back to New York, and my parents were also," Matt Sewell recollected. "I don't remember much about the plane, it was cool flying on a Trump plane, but the bus ride back [to Trumbull] was absolutely fantastic."

While the boys had not expected the crush of the New York press corps at LaGuardia, they found it exciting.

It was just the beginning. For a few days after they returned home, Ken Paul remembered the press almost living outside the front door of their home. "People would come to the house who wanted to film you. We got calls from *The New York Times*. It was just amazing!"

On the ride home they expected that the bus would take them to Unity Field, where they would meet their parents for the rest of the ride home. So when a police and fire escort greeted them as they exited Interstate 95 in Bridgeport and took the loop onto Route 25 north for the final leg of their victory journey, something seemed different…

UNLIKELY CHAMPIONS: A MIRACLE IN WILLIAMSPORT

Then, as the buses exited Route 25 into town, sirens blared on the fire trucks, announcing the arrival of the champions. The boys found the hometown reception totally unexpected, almost shocking. After two weeks of living in near isolation, first in Bristol, and then in Williamsport, the kids and their parents had no idea. They knew nothing of the planning that had gone into the reception into which they arrived. Andy Paul called it "startling..."

When the buses approached the commercial center of town, the crowd grew. Just after passing under a banner that hung across White Plains Road, a huge crowd at the always-busy corner of White Plains Road and Daniels Farm Road had gathered, standing 10...15...even 20 deep, spilling into the roadway right in front of The Grille & Bar Restaurant, where the party had begun the previous evening. The motorcade stopped, with the players taking it all in through the vehicle windows. As the crowd chanted, waved, sung, screamed, and yelled, the players waved back and raised one finger for "No. 1." Someone passed a microphone around the bus. Chris Drury grabbed it. "Thank you, Trumbull!" he exclaimed.

Thank YOU, Little Leaguers! World Champions!

Eventually the motorcade wound its way around town, up Church Hill Road, left onto Edison Road, then north on Main Street all the way up to Town Hall, then back down Church Hill Road.

What First Selectwoman, Morag Vance, had thought would be a 20-minute ride around town turned into an hour-and-a-half event. The Town had come out to see their young heroes; they just went crazy for them, and wouldn't let go for months. As Morag Vance put it, "People in town couldn't get enough of them. Trumbull had become Little League World Central." It was only the beginning of what would be a months-long magic carpet ride for the kids and their coaches.

Kids sat on their dads' shoulders, while moms held little ones' hands. Well-wishers held high their signs greeting the champs, nearly everyone gave them the "No. 1" sign, index fingers proudly pointed high. Car horns honked. One small banner hung on a car, read, simply "WOW."

Other signs bore messages such as "Trumbull, We Are th World" and "Thank You, 1989 Boys of Summer," or noted that "Cody Lee Shovels Our Driveway" and even paraphrased signs common throughout New England regarding George Washington's nocturnal stops around the region in the early years of our nation: "Ken Martin Slept Here."

Matt Sewell considered the ride around town one of his "fondest memories."

"What an amazing crowd!" Todd Halky said.

"It was quite a scene with the streets full of people screaming," Ed Wheeler recalled. "I was a little shocked by the crowd to be honest. It was a bigger deal than even I thought it was. It was quite a turnout. For miles and miles, there were people stacked everywhere, yelling and screaming. I guess everybody knew what a big deal it was. The parade and everything was every impressive."

Yellow streamers hung from homes; plastic bats adorned mailboxes as flags. Bunting hung everywhere hailing the new champions. There were signs everywhere. One of them carried the message of the day: "TRUMBULL WORLD CHAMPS #1."

Crowds lined the streets, often spilling over the sidewalks onto the roadway, cheering the champions as they drove by. One estimate put the crowd size cheering them on at more than 15,000 as the motorcade wound around town.

They all cheered for their hometown heroes on a homecoming day no one there would ever forget. Trumbull had never seen such excitement as when their champions returned home.

"When we got back to Trumbull it was surreal seeing all the people," Jason Hairston said. "We couldn't understand why [the fire trucks] were there. Then we realized they were there to escort us into town. When we got into the center of town, it was crazy to see how many people there were celebrating us. The roads were filled with people. It was great! Then we drove around town and everywhere there were people outside their homes cheering us on as we drove by. There are a lot of good memories from that day. For instance, they renamed the street I lived on, Teeter Rock, as Jason Way. I think at that point it may have hit us that this was a big, big deal."

Danny Brown also used the term "surreal" in describing his recollections. "I didn't know that many people lived there," he said. "It was really bizarre. I remember sitting on the bus and saying 'What is going on?' It was just an insane thing."

"When we drove into the center of town, basically every single person who lived in Trumbull was standing on White Plains Road," David Galla remembered. "They were there to see a bunch of 12-year old kids. We didn't realize how big it was to Trumbull until that moment. I remember sitting there on this big bus, seeing friends along the road and turning to Chris Kelly saying that I wish I wasn't on the bus so I could say 'hi' to my friends. They took the coaches off the bus and put them onto the back of a convertible. Then Chris turned to me and said, 'I want to be out there in a convertible. That would be really cool.'"

Cody Lee called it, "The best."

The kids all wanted to be in convertibles, just like the coaches. They wanted to be with their friends, not hidden on a big, fancy bus where no one could see them. This wasn't fun.

Andy Paul remembered the welcome the team received when they got back to Trumbull.

"It was easily the most amazing experience of the whole summer for me. I can't believe what it looked like and how many people came out to see us in Trumbull that day. We had no idea at the time what was in store when we arrived home. I remember we were in a very nice coach bus and remember seeing a few people with signs and waving to us as we got off the highway. I thought it was so crazy that a couple of families went through the trouble of meeting the bus at the exit. Little did we know the streets were lined with thousands of people holding signs, waving, cheering for us we rode around town on the bus; watching it from inside was mind-blowing...

"I couldn't believe the outpouring of support from Trumbull and Connecticut as a whole that day," Andy Paul continued. "It was essentially our homecoming and the people made us feel so welcome. You could tell they really appreciated our success and how we represented them to the world. It wasn't until we got back to Trumbull that I realized the extent of how much we accomplished that summer, even with all the media and television, coming home really opened my eyes to how important it all was."

Tom Galla called it "...the most unbelievable thing I have ever seen. Even more so than winning the World Series was coming back and seeing the reception we got."

Finally, after the long ride around town, the motorcade arrived at Unity Park, their home field. From there, a short ride from Unity Field up White Plains Road to Daniels Farm Road, then up the hill to Trumbull High School, where, later in the evening, the town would gather on the football field for a rally to celebrate the victory at 8:00 PM.

One week later, the boys returned to the classroom for the start of a new school year.

In between the hometown championship celebration and the start of school, the Trumbull teammates enjoyed a whirlwind of amazing experiences...

They appeared on ABC's "Good Morning America," lunched at Mickey Mantle's Restaurant, where the Hall of Famer himself personally greeted them, met Connecticut's Governor William O'Neill at the State Capitol in Hartford and enjoyed a media-free picnic and pool party at his home, and went to Yankee Stadium to watch the Yankees play the Angels as the guests of legendary New York Yankees owner George Steinbrenner.

On the seventh day, Saturday, they rested. Coach Ed Wheeler hosted a pool party for the team. "They're really looking forward to that," Galla said.

Even after school began, the events and celebrations continued. In October, they traveled to the White House for a Rose Garden reception with President George H.W. Bush, and a week later, Mickey Herbert, a local businessman and sports enthusiast, flew the boys and coaches to Oakland where they attended the first two games of the 1989 World Series between the Athletics and the San Francisco Giants. Chris Drury and Andy Paul *both* threw out the first pitch of Game 2 at Oakland-Alameda County Coliseum.

Herbert remembered the afternoon Trumbull State Senator Angelina "Lee" Scarpetti called asking for some help. She needed 10 local businesses in Trumbull to pony up $1,000 each so that the entire Little League team could attend the World Series in Oakland. She was stunned when Mickey responded with a quick, "No." Then after a pause, he added, "But I'll do the whole $10,000." He offered to sponsor the entire cost of sending the Trumbull kids to the World Series. Mickey would later say, "It was worth a half-million dollars in publicity" for his company.

Everywhere the boys went, they were surrounded by people seeking their autographs. They were heroes.

Here's the rest of this story...

A rally for the hometown heroes

Tom Galla recalled that as the bus took the loop off Interstate 95 onto Route 25 and home to the waiting crowd, his emotions once again overwhelmed him, the same emotions he felt the previous afternoon in Williamsport when tears trickled down his face after Danny McGrath squeezed the final out deep in his glove and the crowd began chanting "U-S-A! U-S-A! U-S-A!"

Most men have trouble showing such emotions. But clearly Tom Galla had demonstrated he did not fit into the category of "most men." He had just led 15 extraordinary 11- and 12-year-old boys in attaining something so special, so unexpected, and so unlikely, that he simply could not contain the moment.

As dusk approached on Sunday evening, thousands of people gathered at Trumbull High School's football field, waiting patiently for the team to arrive. Many wore the now-famous yellow T-shirts with "World Champions 1989" emblazoned in green on the back, and "Trumbull National" on the front. The Connecticut Hurricanes Drum and Bugle Corps and the Trumbull Rangers football cheerleaders entertained the throng.

A few minutes after 8:00 PM, a roar traveled like a wave through the crowd as they realized the motorcade approached, and the moment they anticipated had indeed arrived. Twelve convertibles, loaded with the kids and their coaches, drove a lap around the football field as the crowd cheered loudly, many in the crowd shouting out to their favorite player. Two of the boys rode with an American flag draped over their shoulders. The kids, clearly exhausted from their long day of celebrating and traveling, not to mention the six weeks of intense ball games, politely acknowledged their accolades.

Dan Brown remembered..."driving around the track in some old convertible. The whole thing was very, very strange. I didn't realize that many people would think it was such a big deal and take part in it."

State Representatives Dale Radcliffe and Lee Scarpetti, who organized the rally along with First Selectwoman Morag Vance, Trumbull

UNLIKELY CHAMPIONS: A MIRACLE IN WILLIAMSPORT

Little League President John DelVecchio, and many others, served as host and hostess, and led the crowd in reciting the Pledge of Allegiance. Then, reacting to the size of the crowd and its outpouring of support, Radcliffe commented, "I'm really not surprised...I think the town has rallied behind the team and caught the spirit of the event."

Paul Coniglio's father, John, ever present with his trumpet, performed the National Anthem to open the ceremony. After an invocation, First Selectwoman Morag Vance welcomed everyone to the celebration, calling the occasion "...a joyful and proud night, a night to say thank you." She thanked the team, the coaches, and the parents, then declared the coming week as *Trumbull Little League Week*.

Trumbull Board of Education Chairwoman Clare "Tee" Hampford then stepped to the dais. A true baseball fan, according to her daughter, Kate Hampford Donahue, she had followed the locals all summer, usually scoring each game herself. It was a ritual she developed watching her three sons play Little League baseball. The pressure she felt as a Little League mom had carried over into the summer of 1989 as the Trumbull kids marched through the tournament. "During the [final] game, I had a dry throat, wet eyes, a lump in my chest, and I breathed about every half-inning," she told the crowd.

After watching Trumbull's final victory on TV, she composed a tribute to the team that parodies Ernest Thayer's legendary poem, *"Casey at the Bat: A Ballad of the Republic Sung in the Year 1888."* She read *"A Ballad to the Town of Trumbull Sung in the Year 1989"* to the crowd, which is reprinted with permission of Mrs. Hampford's family. [Mrs. Hampford's composition is reproduced as it appeared in the November 29, 1989 *Bridgeport Post-Telegram*.]

> The summer was a grand one for the Trumbull team this year.
> To Williamsport they ventured with a dream they held most dear.
> Just how did Trumbull gain this trip? How did they do so well?
> The story warrants once again their glorious deeds to tell.
>
> This team of Little Leaguers from the east side of our town
> Met District opposition and of course they mowed 'em down.
> They beat both teams from Stratford and the Fairfield nine as well.
> They rolled right over North End East (but Park City rang their bell!)
>
> They bounced right back, however, when next they took the field;

And blanked those Bridgeport upstarts. District championship was sealed.
Connecticut's best ball teams they met, and conquered all.
The state crown sat on Trumbull's head. "Hey guys, this is a ball!"

They traveled north to Bristol next, with bats and gloves and fans,
And took on every comer from the East Coast of our land.
Goodbye Vermont, New Hampshire New Jersey, Delaware.
This is the Team from Trumbull. Williamsport, beware!

They're Todd and Paul and Cody, and three Chrises and two Dans.
They're Jason, Dave and Andy, two Matts, Ken and Harlen.
The Manager's Fantastic (Sir Galla, Tom Terrific).
Coaches Zullo and Ed Wheeler are simply beatific.

Now board those buses, players. Bring Mom and Dad, et al.
It's off to Pennsylvania. It's off to play more ball.
So proudly wearing jerseys with EAST upon the chest
To show the world where Trumbull is; and do it with great zest!

First up, the team from Iowa who bowed out 4-3.
The underdogs from Trumbull were really on a spree.
Next came the boys (and one lone girl) from favored San Pedro
Who also fell along the way, a tough test but vanquished foe.

They did it! Trumbull's Number 1, the champions of the land!
But Trumbull National Little League had one last final stand
Against a team from Taiwan, billed the Greatest of the Great,
Before whom all must falter; the rest are second rate.

That Saturday in August blazed a perfect day to play
And, as they came upon the field they heard it "USA."
Not only from the faithful those yellow-shirted hordes,
But from the throats of thousands, those changed, awesome words.

"USA, USA" was cheered and cried and roared.
"Let's go Trumbull, we're with you," hearts stopped and spirits soared.
They played the national pastime. They checked their flashcard cues.

They did all things as they were taught; they knew they'd paid their dues.

And when the game was over, and the winner was declared
Where were the boys from Trumbull? How had the National fared?
The scoreboard hailed it 5-2 as the final out was made
And the Little League from Trumbull left Taiwan in the shade.

Oh, somewhere in this favored land the sun is shining bright;
The band is playing somewhere, and somewhere hearts are light,
And somewhere men are laughing, and somewhere children shout;
And "Somewhere" is in Trumbull - mighty Trumbull had the clout!

A few months later, "Tee" penned these final two stanzas:

The days and weeks have flown since then, the team has come back home
But the celebration carries on; across the land they roam
From TV show to White House to Yankee and to Shea
To Oakland for the Series, to school? 'Most every day.

The tournament's memory; the banners will be furled
The Little League from Trumbull is Champion of the World.
But the magic never pass, we're all forever young
Because the Boys from Trumbull made '89 such fun.

After John DelVecchio congratulated the team, he brought State Representative Dale Radcliffe back to the podium for the presentation of citations from the Connecticut General Assembly to Tom Galla and his coaches, Bob Zullo and Ed Wheeler.

Several other elected officials and dignitaries followed, including United States Senator Joseph Lieberman, who enthusiastically congratulated the team, saying "while the Capitol of the United States is in Washington, DC...tonight the Capitol of the world is in Trumbull, Connecticut. You made us proud to be an American." He made it clear that he considered the team's achievement nothing short of remarkable. "They worked hard and went out and did it," Lieberman said. "This makes all of us in Connecticut about three feet taller."

After congratulatory letters from Governor William O'Neill, and Congressmen Christopher Shays and John Rowland were read, Little League

District Administrator John Heher, who also coached in Trumbull, shared his thoughts. Following Heher, State Senator Lee Scarpetti presented citations to each player.

All the speakers expressed how totally thrilled they were with what the Trumbull team and their coaches had accomplished. They focused their comments on praise for this feat and actually forgot about politics for one night...or at least didn't discuss any.

Finally, the host and hostess introduced Tom Galla, freshly shaven head gleaming, to the estimated 7,000 in attendance. As he stepped to the podium and took the microphone, the crowd stood and roared.

In his remarks to the crowd, Tom described his emotions at the end of the championship game when the Lamade Stadium crowd chanted, "U-S-A! U-S-A!" Then, as if on cue, the Trumbull crowd spontaneously launched a "U-S-A!" chant of their own.

Galla admitted to a slight case of nerves, sharing "I've never spoken to more than five or six people at one time before." He then asked the crowd to "growl" along with him, which really solidified the entire crowd, and served to help Galla relax as he spoke of the pride he had for his players, coaches, and the town. The butterflies he had experienced only moments earlier as he stepped to the microphone now scattered.

Galla explained how the Taiwanese Little Leaguers are "...taught to perform; they live in military fashion, and are *expected to win*." While not being critical of their opponents, he noted that "...they were crushed when they lost."

Tom Galla then asked the townspeople for their help in getting the Trumbull youngsters through the hoopla en route to a return to normalcy. He cared deeply for these kids and for what they had done. He still does, 25 years later...he's that kind of guy.

"Please be kind to them. Help them get back down to Earth. Because it won't be easy," Galla said.

Clearly, Galla worried that the impact of what they had accomplished – the instant celebrity bestowed upon them – might prove difficult for the boys to process. Galla also feared that the kids would encounter some resentment from peers jealous of the attention they had received.

"Everybody is not happy for us," he said. The road back to normal will not be easy.

Once again, Tom didn't have to worry. These kids had strong parenting, great coaching, and a community that has never stopped loving them, even now. You can expect strong parenting and a loving community, but you never really know about the coaches. Just as no one goes through a college curriculum to teach them how to be a parent, there are no classes that teach you how to coach a team of 12-year-olds. In the end, one thing remained clear above all else: Tom, Bob, and Ed had proven masterful.

UNLIKELY CHAMPIONS: A MIRACLE IN WILLIAMSPORT

Galla told Tom McCormack of *The New Haven Register*, "As it turned out, I needn't have worried."

Galla also announced that he would not coach the following year. Instead, he hoped to try his hand at umpiring. [Author's note: Tom tried it for a while, but eventually decided to stop.]

Tom confirmed the strength of all the players' families: "All the kids on the championship team had one thing in common. They came from the most stable families you could find. This is why they were so easy to handle."

Galla knew he needed to have one final talk with the kids to put the victory into perspective. "I think we have to tell them they have to get back to their normal routine," he said. "This [championship] isn't going to pay their bills or put them into the Major Leagues. We have to tell them not to be cocky, to be kids again. This doesn't mean a darned thing come a week from now (when school starts)," he said.

Police Captain Ray Baldwin, a long-time friend, assistant coach with Tom during the regular season, and former Little League teammate of Galla's, then presented Tom with a wig of long locks to cover his shaved head. [Author's note: Unfortunately, I have not been able to find any photos of Tom wearing his wig.]

Galla then introduced each of these "great kids." As he called their names, the crowd cheered loudly for each of them as they took to the stage and waved to the crowd.

Colin Koenig, writing for *The Trumbull Times* noted, "Watching them up close, they really do look like kids, much smaller and younger than they do on television." He continued, "The Trumbull Nationals hugged, shook hands, high- and low-fived, and stood together for all to appreciate. For one pleasantly cool August night, a whole town was together, kids, grownups alike, just happy to be a part of young people's and sports history."

First Selectwoman Morag Vance then closed the event, thanking the crowd for their enthusiasm, and the team for bringing the town together.

Afterward, John DelVecchio, who helped organize the homecoming, said, "It was *fantastic*. It really sent a shiver through you."

Third baseman Jason Hairston reacted to the fanfare and rally, saying simply "It's exciting!"

When asked how he felt about the day's events, shortstop Dan Brown could barely speak. "Fine," he said, "except I lost my voice from all the screaming. This is great."

"Winning a world series was a dream since I was a little kid," said Todd Halky. "It's amazing what this town has done. I didn't think this would be this big."

Matt Sewell remembered "Tom Galla giving that speech at the high school, 'Let them be kids,' to help everyone understand the complexities of the situation.

The homecoming clearly overwhelmed Galla. "This is almost as awesome as winning the game itself," he said. "I'll never forget this."

CHAPTER NINETEEN

...AND WE CELEBRATE THEM

After the hometown party on Sunday, the next days, weeks, and months included a torrent of offers for appearances and invitations. To see them, one would agree with Tom Galla's frequently stated appraisal: a bunch of ordinary kids, who had accomplished something extraordinary. Now these 12-year-old kids found themselves "stars" wherever they went, every day yet another magical experience.

"When we got back to Trumbull and saw the outpouring from the community, the people in the streets, and the parade they put on, wow, we saw how it had touched so many people's lives," Todd Halky reflected. "Then it went into a whirlwind, a world tour, meeting the president, so many other things. We had to grow up, and with all that, we had to learn humility quickly or we could lose our friends."

After losing his spot on the team, Matt Sewell appreciated that "...after the tournament was over, Trumbull Little League did a fantastic job making sure we were one team. I got to participate in each event."

A visit to "Good Morning America" then lunch at Mickey Mantle's Restaurant (Monday, August 28, 1989)
Dawn arrived early that morning after the rally at the high school. Rising before the sun did, the team was already well on its way to the ABC television studios and "Good Morning America" in New York City as the dark sky brightened into morning.

Tom Galla looked back on that day. "I was exhausted, we were all exhausted. They picked us up at 5:30 in the morning on Monday at Unity Field, then, drove us down to New York in limousines. Everybody's pumped up because of where we're going. It was great. Spencer Christian did the interview. He was terrific."

Matt Sewell recalled that "...they asked Chris [Drury] a question, but then they saw my cast and asked me a question. That was interesting, on live TV, answering a question. I thought I was just there to smile, so I was kind of surprised."

"It was fun to see the studio, the bright lights, and the people getting their makeup. We had to go down to New York ridiculously early that day, but it was fun stuff," added Andy Paul.

Their next stop was at Manhattan's world-famous FAO Schwartz toy store. Before they knew it, lunchtime had arrived.

"John Coniglio had arranged for us to have lunch at Mickey Mantle's Restaurant," Tom Galla said, "and we meet Mickey Mantle and sit at his table with him. He's signing autographs and taking pictures. It was *terrific*!" Galla beamed. The players gave "The Mick" a souvenir "World Champions" T-shirt.

Andy Paul recalled "...sitting with Mickey Mantle as he signed autographs, watching him. He looked very old but I know I was in the presence of greatness." Dan Brown, a Yankees fan, also reflected upon meeting Mickey Mantle, agreeing, "He was real old."

"When we were at Mickey Mantle's Restaurant, WFAN was also there broadcasting their afternoon show. So we got to be on the radio," Todd Halky commented.

David Galla cited his favorite "Meeting Mickey Mantle" moment: "Seeing how thrilled my dad was to meet Mickey Mantle. That was cool. We knew Mickey Mantle was a big deal. Mickey Mantle was my dad's hero. He was the biggest thing back then."

Matt Sewell noted "Mickey kept calling me Mack and I kept telling him, no it's Matt. After a while, I finally gave up. Anyway, that's how he signed the autograph for me, 'To Mack.'"

"Having lunch at Mickey Mantle's Restaurant and meeting 'The Mick' was the best," remembered Dan McGrath. "I still have my signed Mick cards and a great picture with him at the restaurant. Guys here still don't believe I met the man."

A barbecue and a swim with the governor

A few days later on Thursday, August 31st, the cameras once again followed the team as they traveled to Hartford for a meeting with Governor William O'Neill in his office in the Capitol Building. During the press conference, O'Neill designated the day as one for Connecticut residents to honor the team: *Trumbull Little League World Champions Day*.

"The team from Trumbull was poised, determined, gutsy, and skillful," said O'Neill, flanked by the players and coaches. "In victory, the Trumbull players were joyous, exuberant, sportsmanlike, and generous. They won with style and class in the best Little League tradition. The people of Connecticut share a great and well-deserved sense of pride in the achievements, performance, and integrity of the Trumbull Little League team in emerging victorious."

Tom Galla presented the governor with a team-autographed baseball.

During the ceremony, the Governor unveiled new blue-and-white signs that would eventually appear along Route 25 and the Merritt Parkway [Route 15] in Trumbull declaring "Trumbull – Home of the 1989 Little League World Series Champions." After the signs came down years later, they found a new home hanging on the side of the press box at Unity Park, Trumbull Little League's home field, where they stayed for many more years.

During the press conference, Tom shared the enormity of the experience. "The cards and the letters and the phone calls have just been overwhelming," he said. "I tried to go to work yesterday and it was just a waste of time. I might as well have stayed home and answered the phone calls."

"Our kids are pretty relieved it's all over," Galla continued. "We worked real hard for a couple of months. Now we just have to get them back to normal. They start school next Tuesday."

In less than a week, the team received myriad invitations to numerous events and opportunities, including an offer to do a television commercial and a rap song video, which drew groans from the kids. The team turned down both offers. "We're not doing anything that is going to exploit the boys in any way. We're just going to do fun things we think they would enjoy," Galla insisted.

When it came time for the youngsters to step up to the microphone, most of the team suddenly grew very quiet. However, the team's jokester and "unofficial" spokesman, Cody Lee, didn't hesitate to take the microphone. "We knew how good our team was, but didn't know anything about the competition. Even before it all started, we thought it was going to be a lot harder than it was," he maintained.

Lee further said he found it "weird" to play youngsters from another country who couldn't speak English, but that he made friends regardless. "The pitcher [on Taiwan] gave me his hat. I guess if they win the game they get college scholarships and if they lose, then they are dishonored." Lee finished by saying he wanted to play professional baseball because "…baseball's fun and you make a lot of money."

Afterward, the boys' busy day continued when the entire team headed over to the governor's mansion in Hartford for a barbecue and swimming without the intrusion of television cameras. For the first time in several days, they would enjoy a short respite out of the spotlight.

"I remember the barbecue at the governor's mansion," Todd Halky said. "It was real nice. Cody and I snuck upstairs; it was pretty cool."

Matt Sewell remembers, "It was the last day I had my cast on, so I couldn't swim in the pool. The next day the cast came off, so that's why I remember the pool party so well. I vaguely remember the governor, because we took a picture with him which I have."

Afterward, Tom Galla would call the meeting with the governor "Terrific. The kids had a great time. They went swimming in the pool and they had a cookout. It was a great day, a lot of fun."

Dan McGrath summed up the day concisely and eloquently: "Pool, volleyball, free eats and treats!"

Visits to Yankee Stadium - Shea Stadium - Fenway Park

The team ended the week with a Friday night visit to Yankee Stadium, where New York Yankees owner George Steinbrenner hosted the boys during a game against the California Angels. Commissioner of Baseball, Bart Giamatti, had died earlier that day, making the mood at Yankee Stadium somewhat somber. Tom Galla remembered that he, Chris Drury, and Ken Martin visited the television booth for interviews with George Grande and Phil Rizzuto. The passing of Giamatti served to downplay Trumbull's triumph.

"Still, it was pretty cool," Galla remembered. "We got to meet Mel Allen and shake hands with Don Mattingly, Steve Sax, and Wade Boggs."

According to Galla, only about 5,000 people made it to the game that night. "Can you imagine that?" asked Galla. "The Yankees weren't too good in 1989. It would have been nicer if there had been 40,000, but it was still nice, a great memory."

"Going to Yankee Stadium and meeting George Steinbrenner is one of my biggest thrills," recalled the younger Galla. "He treated us like no one else had up until then. I played catch with Don Mattingly, which was awesome. We sat in the Yankees' dugout before the game, sat in George Steinbrenner's box, Kenny Martin got to meet Phil Rizzuto, who was his hero, and Mel Allen came down to see us. The Yankees did it right!"

"The best part was we got really cool Mets, Yankees, and Red Sox team jackets," Andy Paul remembered from their visits to the respective teams. "It was lots of fun to attend those games. I had a catch on the field with Yankees players and met Don Mattingly, who was a childhood hero for almost our entire team. I was just awestruck by Mattingly."

Jason Hairston thought "...seeing the Mets, the Yankees, teams that we followed, was more memorable" than the World Series trip to Oakland, because it "...was special for us to meet guys like Darryl Strawberry and Don Mattingly. We also got Mets jackets and Yankees jackets. That was pretty cool. Back then I was a Mets fan, really liked Lenny Dykstra, and Mookie Wilson was my favorite. Now I'm a Red Sox fan; had some real good experiences with the Red Sox while in college."

UNLIKELY CHAMPIONS: A MIRACLE IN WILLIAMSPORT

Bob Zullo remembered a remark that Mets General Manager Frank Cashen made during their visit to Shea Stadium: "If the Mets had your cohesiveness, gentlemen, we'd be in the World Series." Quite the compliment!

Though he favored the Red Sox, Matt Sewell declared the "...best event was the visit to Yankee Stadium. The Yankees treated us with so much class; it was so awesome. I remember talking to Jesse Barfield in the dugout. The way they handled it was great; they're just a top-notch organization, whereas the Mets were a bit discombobulated. The Red Sox were nice, and being a Red Sox fan, being on the grounds at Fenway Park was just awesome."

Dan McGrath met his childhood hero at Yankee Stadium. "My passion for the game – watching it – was based around Don Mattingly, who was my childhood hero, so meeting him because of the Little League World Series was pretty cool. I also met Craig Shipley [at Shea Stadium] who played for the Mets. He was an Aussie playing MLB. I still have the jackets [we got]; my kids will wear them.

A few days later, at Fenway, "Boston was playing Oakland, and they ask me to throw out the first pitch," Tom Galla recalled. "I don't know why. So, the whole team was standing on the mound with me, and in the Oakland dugout, one of the guys stands up with a number, just like what Sandy had made for us in Williamsport. We start laughing, and they're laughing. It was great."

"At Fenway, they took us around, we met and talked to the players in the dugout, and got to go on the field," remembers Ed Wheeler. "We sat up in left field toward the top. They gave all the kids Boston jackets. They took us all around the ballpark and behind the scoreboard to the batting cages. It was quite the tour. We got to meet lots of players. They were great with the kids. I even got to talk to Ricky Henderson."

In the midst of this flurry of Major League activity, the kids finally caught a break when Ed Wheeler hosted another one of his famous pool parties at his home on Saturday, September 2nd. After all the "formal" appearances, the pool party provided welcome relief and a day of real fun for everyone.

The first day of school...
Tuesday, September 5th arrived, another special day; the first day of school. After the whirlwind of the last 10 days, how does a 12-year-old sit still in a classroom?

"Actually, we were pretty good students, pretty smart kids, so it wasn't really an issue when school started," Todd Halky remembered. "Being a 12-year-old 'celebrity' helped with the girls. We were all into girls at that point."

According to Jason Hairston, "It was hard [getting back to being a kid again] because we had to leave school a lot the whole first part of the year so that we could go to all these events. On the first day of school, I think we were in middle school, and everybody was out in the hallway celebrating as we entered together. At the beginning of school, our teachers may have treated us a bit different but after a while, we were still the same kids causing [the] problems [that 12-year-olds cause] in the classroom. Regarding my studies, it was not an option for me to not do well. My parents wouldn't let me play sports if my grades weren't good, so I got back to the books pretty quickly."

The way Todd Halky saw it, "Ultimately, reality set in when we went back to school, but to the other kids in school, we were just who we had always been. What we had done didn't matter anymore. I still had to work hard to get the grades. And after that, [anytime any one of us stepped onto a baseball diamond, there] was always someone gunning for us on the field."

When school started, Andy Paul found himself attending a new school, Hopkins, in New Haven.

"It was the first time I was ever in school with girls," Andy noted. "I had gone to Fairfield Country Day before that, which was an all-male school. So I was really distracted from academics because of that (I had just turned 13) and having to do all the Little League things that fall. It was a lot, and my grades suffered, plus it was a very challenging school. When school started, some of my classmates were into it while others were jealous. I didn't understand the jealousy piece at the time but it makes sense looking back."

"Going back to school kind of forced us to get back to real life," Dan Brown agreed. "Life was basically 'normal' when we went back to school; no one treated me any differently. Getting back to school was a little tough because I felt a bit self-conscious [about all the attention we got]. I just wanted to fit back in; I wasn't into standing out."

The way David Galla remembered it, "Life was different. People treated us differently. They wanted to know about what had happened, be a part of it. For the most part, people were really happy for us. But I remember one day leaving school early for one of the many unbelievable things we got to do, and there was some jealousy around that, and some [classmates] were not happy that we were treated differently. So, in the end, it wasn't easy getting back to being a kid again because we kept getting pulled out of school to do things. There wasn't a week that went by where we weren't doing something amazing. How many kids show up late for school because they were on "Good Morning America" that morning?

"We did a lot of stuff," Galla related. "Looking back, I'm sure it was draining for the parents and coaches, but the kids were having a good time."

UNLIKELY CHAMPIONS: A MIRACLE IN WILLIAMSPORT

"At first, to our teachers, it was a point of conversation," Galla continued. "After a while, we were just middle school kids trying to get into trouble, trying to see how far we can push, and the teachers were trying to not let us get into trouble. They treated us like they treated everyone else. We were just like the other kids in their classroom. In the end, I don't think all this stuff had any effect on my studies."

A Nets-Bulls game at the Meadowlands

"I remember meeting Michael Jordan at the Nets game, where we were honored," said Jason Hairston. "He came up to me, and I remember he had the same exact shoes on that I did, *his* shoes, so I said to him, 'Nice shoes!'"

Andy Paul remembered that "Cody went up and high-fived Michael Jordan. Seeing Jordan up close was special." As a Bulls fan, Dan McGrath enjoyed seeing Michael Jordan "...up close...nothing better!"

"We went to the Meadowlands to see the Bulls play the Nets," Tom Galla related. "Phil Jackson, whose wife at the time was a Trumbull girl, introduced himself to me; I actually went to high school with her."

A White House Rose Garden party (October 10, 1989)

On Tuesday, October 10th, the team traveled to Washington DC, along with nearly 100 family members and friends to meet with President George H.W. Bush [#41], who continued a long-established tradition of honoring and toasting the nation's Little League champions in a Rose Garden ceremony.

According to Ed Wheeler, "There was a lot of standing around that day as we waited for the president, a lot of standing." As the team and their parents waited for the president, who is a self-proclaimed "baseball nut," to join them in the Rose Garden, the kids fidgeted, joked amongst themselves, and gently pounded their fists into their gloves. Were they actually nervous?

"They don't get overly excited," said their coach, Tom Galla, *himself* quite excited. "I don't think a 12-year-old can fully appreciate what they're going through."

Finally, the long-awaited announcement: "Ladies and gentlemen, the President of the United States." As the president entered the Rose Garden, Washington Bureau Chief David Lightman of *The Courant* noted Bush stood "...tall and lean in his dark-blue suit, somehow looking not like the commander-in-chief, but a slightly older version of the neighborhood father who hasn't changed out of his work clothes yet."

President Bush, who played college baseball at Yale University, spoke to the uniformed youngsters, their entourage, and the mass of reporters, photographers, and television camera crews. He urged the 12-year-olds to emulate his "boyhood hero," the late Hall of Famer and Yankee great, Lou Gehrig. "He showed, like Little League, that what matters is how we conduct ourselves off, as well as on, the field," the president advised the youths.

A former Little League coach himself, President Bush continued his pep talk to the boys. "What memories you have given us, and what memories you'll cherish of great heart and great plays, or that crowd cheering 'U-S-A! U-S-A!' there at Williamsport, and of the spirit which says that nothing is impossible, in Little League or in the bigger fields of life."

He informed the youngsters that they had learned "...the lessons of Little League: lessons like friendship and generosity; like 'do-unto-others' and doing your best; lessons which go beyond balls and strikes and which have made Little League a global institution."

The president then heaped praise on manager Tom Galla and his staff for a fine job of leadership, adding that while Frank Robinson and Roger Craig may be leading the vote for Manager of the Year, "...there should be a recount if Tom Galla is not right up there in contention."

After shaking hands with Coach Tom Galla and the entire squad, the president said, "You truly are Number One." After his comments about sportsmanship, President Bush then had individual accolades for several players. Seeking Chris Drury, he said, "Beating Taiwan to win the championship game – which is Chris? There he is, modestly in the back row there." Then he addressed Dan McGrath: "Squeezing that final out as 40,000 people roared in disbelief."

And big Andy Paul – "I called Cape Canaveral about this guy, about the homer he hit against Davenport, Iowa, and then they tell me it's somewhere in orbit between...Williamsport and Harrisburg." He also mentioned the key plays made by Ken Martin, Andy Paul, David Galla, Cody Lee, and Jason Hairston.

Each mom and dad beamed brightly with parental pride.

Afterwards, *The Hartford Courant*'s David Lightman noted the kids "...seemed blasé about their 15-minute journey to the center of world power. Some played catch on the White House grounds while others were interviewed in the same spots where world leaders had been surrounded by the White House press corps. The kids were just as polite as the heads of state, and just as nonchalant about the scene."

How do 12-year-olds react to meeting the President of the United States? Their visit with the leader of the free world certainly impressed them, but perhaps not quite as much as meeting one of their major league baseball heroes. Even the president's own grandchildren may not place the same import on the stature of grandpa's office as do most of his constituents. When asked about that, the president admitted that one of his grandchildren wanted to be a baseball player "...because politicians don't get their pictures on bubblegum cards" and ballplayers do.

"The president was pretty unbelievable," Andy Paul marveled. "Being mentioned in the president's speech by name was one of the highlights of my life. It was a great experience going to the White House with my family and teammates."

Ken Martin evaluated his experience: "Nice. It was great."

"You know, we did stuff that people will never do in their entire lives," David Galla commented, "and we did it at 12 years old. All because a group of 12-year-old kids accomplished something in sports that is still being talked about, and gained some notoriety from it, but really, throughout that whole process got to have experiences that have helped us in life, and will continue to help us in life. No one gets to meet the president, and *we* got to go to the Rose Garden to meet the president. That was awesome."

"The visit to the White House was awesome," Todd Halky echoed. "My parents and brother and sister were all with me there in the Rose Garden. Even as a 12-year-old, we got it. It was a big thing to meet the president of the United States. We also got to meet First Lady Barbara Bush."

Perhaps no one in fact counseled the boys on presidential protocol, but apparently President Bush had no problem with Jason Hairston addressing him simply as "George."

"I was young enough and naïve enough to call him George," Jason admitted. "Chris immediately hit me in the arm and said, 'It's *President* Bush.' President Bush then said to my younger brother, 'You must be Jason's brother?' and Charles replied, 'No, he's *my* brother.' Those were fun times. Seeing the president was pretty cool."

"It was fantastic; it was crazy," said Matt Sewell. "To get an autograph and shake the president's hand, it was very cool meeting George H.W. He was a classy guy. The connection, that he went to Yale and he was a lefty first baseman, it was a great event."

Meeting President Bush seemed "surreal" to Dan McGrath. "I gave him an Aussie pin and asked him to give it to his wife…"

"We were having fun with the Secret Service guys at the White House," recalled Dan Brown. "But I wasn't that impressed meeting the President. I wasn't all that into it. He wasn't a sports guy, so what did I care. I would have rather met Don Mattingly, and I was a huge Knicks fan – Pat Ewing, John Starks, those guys. Charles Barkley. Those were my sports idols back then."

"I think the kids thought they were going to be able to play catch with him," Tom Galla laughed.

Congressmen Christopher Shays and John Rowland, who each represented parts of Trumbull in Washington, DC, had set up the two-day trip to the nation's capital. After the ceremony, Shays and Rowland led the group on a tour of the U.S Capitol building, followed by a visit to the FBI's J. Edgar Hoover Building. While viewing an exhibit of guns at the Hoover Building, several of the kids asked FBI staffers if they had ever been shot. "No," came the stern reply.

T.R. Rowe, a Trumbull resident and Little League umpire during summer breaks, interned in Congressman Rowland's office that fall while a sophomore at Catholic University in Washington DC. "As perhaps the lowest-level person on Capitol Hill, chances of going to the White House were slim to none," Rowe recalled. "That is, until Trumbull won the World Series and was invited to the White House. Since I worked in Congressman Rowland's office, I also got an invitation to the Rose Garden ceremony, no less! I was so very proud of the team and coaches. I had been watching most of these kids for a couple of years and knew there were more than a few talented players."

Bridgeport Post-Telegram Washington Bureau reporter, Anna Maria Virzi, noted that after a long day, "The entourage was hungry, tired, and more than ready to go home. So, while munching on burgers and fries in a House office building cafeteria, they chatted up their upcoming weekend adventure to the opening game of the 1989 Major League World Series in California between the San Francisco Giants and the Oakland Athletics."

CHAPTER TWENTY

GO WEST, YOUNG MEN – THROWING OUT THE WORLD SERIES' FIRST PITCH

On Sunday, October 15th, the entire team, attired in their championship uniforms, received recognition as 1989 Little League Champions prior to the start of the second game of the 1989 World Series in Oakland, California, between the San Francisco Giants and the Oakland Athletics. Andy Paul and Chris Drury both threw out the ceremonial first pitch.

Upon his return home, trip sponsor Mickey Herbert, president and CEO of Physicians' Health Services, wrote a firsthand account of the trip to the World Series in Oakland, California. Mickey, an avid sports fan, played fast-pitch softball for many years, winning a national championship with the 1983 Raybestos Cardinals and leading the United States team in hitting in the 1984 World Softball Championship. He is a member of the Connecticut Fast-Pitch Softball Hall of Fame. Mickey's 10-year-old son, Chris, accompanied his dad on the trip.

Mickey granted the author permission to include the following excerpts from his story, which first appeared in *The Trumbull Times* on October 19, 1989...

> The trip to the real World Series in California begins in the pre-dawn hours of Saturday, October 14th. It's a 75-mile ride to Bradley International Airport in Windsor Locks (20 miles north of Hartford). After gathering in the dark at Unity Field at 4:00 AM, where their journey started three-and-one-half months earlier, the players and escorting parents jump on a bus donated by Fairfield Transportation Group. A few have to "suffer" the one-and-a-half hour ride in a luxurious stretch limo donated by Mario D'Addario's Limo Service. Thanks to Mark and Elaine Pericas of Pericas Travel for making these travel arrangements.

The Little Leaguers arrive at Bradley at 5:30 AM, mostly all attired in New York Mets jackets. They don't even check any luggage, but simply carry on what they've packed.

Shortly after 6:00 AM, they board a mostly empty Chicago-bound 727. The kids are disappointed they're not on a "big bird" and won't have a movie to watch.

As I am introduced to each boy, I am struck by how courteous every one of them is. I remember hearing Tom Galla say at a Trumbull Chamber of Commerce breakfast something to the effect that these are not special kids. They are simply ordinary kids who have accomplished something special.

A huge sign greets the kids as they take their seats. "United Airlines Welcomes the Trumbull Little League World Champions, from the Second Shift Cleaning Crew."

Before long, the kids are all over the plane and fortunately the flight attendants are more forgiving than I've ever seen. Breakfast arrives and the kids want to know why the silverware comes in a sealed plastic bag. Halfway through the flight, the flight attendants present the three coaches with a bottle of champagne which they have filched from first class.

The plane lands at Chicago's O'Hare International Airport at 7:30 AM (Central Daylight Time). The huge, new United Airlines terminal overwhelms all of us, as does the interminable walk to our connecting flight on a full 737 jet to Oakland. This is a frustrating flight because the plane is full, it's a longer flight and we are mostly split up in lots of middle seats. The flight attendants give each Little Leaguer a deck of cards and they mount on the bulkhead a large sign proclaiming Trumbull the "World Little 'Leauge' (sic) Champions." No one corrects the spelling.

A guy in front of me asks five of the kids, "Who's the best player on your team?" At least three kids answer in unison, "No one!"

As we get ready to land, Cody Lee yells out to no one in particular, "Does anyone have any gum?"

It has taken a while to get to the hotel because we first have to go to another hotel to get the World Series game tickets [paid for by Trumbull Little League]. The boys are starved by the time we arrive at the lovely San Ramon Marriott at 12:45 p.m. (Western Daylight Time) where Trumbull Marriott General Manager Bob Andrews has arranged for rooms for all of us. The boys descend on the restaurant where they devour a meal and head for the pool. Most of the adults head for the room for a quick nap. Tom and Sandy Galla head for the supermarket to stock up our bus with lots of snacks.

At 3:00 PM, we're on another bus headed for the Oakland-Alameda Stadium. Our bus driver has put a large banner on the side of the bus to tell the world who we are. He has even gotten a local disc jockey to ask, on the air, for drivers to honk and wave when they see our bus. It's a sunny and warm day in the valley where we are staying, but as soon as we get near Oakland, it becomes cool and cloudy, with a light shower. We packed all the wrong clothes as we were told it's 90 degrees this time of year. No one cares. We're too excited at just being here.

When we arrive at the stadium, I get my first real appreciation of how these kids have captured the hearts of America. The parking lot is full of "tailgaters" who break out into applause when we begin getting off the bus.

As we walk to the Stadium with our bright yellow World Champion T-shirts, many people approach us and congratulate us. Someone asks, "Where's your spitting pitcher? A couple of fans spot Ken Martin and say, "That was a terrific home run you hit against Taiwan."

What amazes me is how complete strangers 3,000 miles away, seven weeks after the "big game," remember the Little League Championship so well. It not only indicates what a special event this was but also of the unbelievable influence of national television.

Our seats are upper deck behind third base, a long way from home plate. But we can see everything. It has stopped raining, and with a little hot chocolate, we're in great shape.

Before the ceremonial first pitch, the Yale Whiffenpoofs sing the Star Spangled Banner and there is a moment of silence for the late Bart Giamatti, former commissioner of baseball. Giamatti's son throws out the ceremonial first pitch and we're all pretty proud to be from Connecticut.

I thought most of the Little Leaguers were cheering for Oakland because we were in Oakland, because their uniforms were the same colors as Trumbull's, or because of former Yankee Ricky Henderson of the A's. Or maybe it's because Danny McGrath, Harlen Marks, and Matt Sewell, all Oakland fans, were sitting near me. I didn't find out until the plane ride home that most of the kids were actually cheering for the Giants.

Final score: Oakland won 5-0.

At 9:30 PM, we arrive back at the hotel. I am exhausted, having been up almost 23 straight hours. By 10 PM, my son and I are sleeping. I find out the next morning that most of the Little Leaguers went for a swim, ordered pizza, and some even watched a movie before calling it a night.

On Sunday morning, I meet Tom Galla. He tells me he has made a firm decision not to coach next year, either at the Little League level, or at the Babe Ruth level, where almost all of the players will be playing next year (except Paul Coniglio who has a year of Little League eligibility left). That's a great loss for Trumbull's Little League, except that Tom says he hopes to come back as a Little League umpire. That's a great gain for Little League! He would even like to be able to return to Williamsport as an umpire.

My son and I do some sightseeing while the Little Leaguers set off for the stadium, in full uniform, to be photographed by ABC in preparation for the opening ceremonies of Game Two. That means going right out on that gorgeous field.

After the picture taking, the bus takes off for San Francisco, where the team is given a whirlwind tour of the City by the Bay. The Little Leaguers invade the tourist shops at Fisherman's Wharf where everyone wants a T-shirt or sweatshirt proclaiming the World Series as "The Battle of the Bay." It seems strange to me that the kids want Major League memorabilia while we adults want souvenirs that say "Trumbull World Champions."

At 4 PM, we arrive at the stadium for Game Two and receive the same warm reception by the fans. At 4:45 PM, pitchers Andy Paul and Chris Drury, Tom Galla, Ed Wheeler, and Bob Zullo head for the playing field because Andy and Chris will be throwing out the first balls to start the game. From the upper deck, we proudly watch Andy and Chris warm up, while Tom, Ed, and Bob talk to reporters.

Oakland A's manager Tony LaRussa comes out of the dugout to chat and kid Tom Galla about having his head shaved. Tom tells him that the kids have been treated to five major league games this year and the home team has won every time.

Meanwhile, up in the stands, we have been discovered by the press corps including Hartford's Channel 3. It's neat to watch each kid being interviewed while the cameraman hovers over him, no more than three feet away.

Finally, it's time for the big moment. It all happens so quickly but what a kick! At 5:25 PM, the announcer directs the crowd to watch Andy and Chris while the huge Diamondvision screen in centerfield shows the team and the celebration against Taiwan. The scoreboard welcomes "Chris Drury and Andy Paul of the Trumbull Little League World Champions" and then it's game time. No more than 45 seconds, but then again this game is being broadcast to 100 million people all over the world. What did Andy Warhol say about being famous?

The game seems truly anticlimactic, especially since the Little Leaguers have now been discovered in the stands. The kids busy themselves signing autographs and posing for pictures with the fans.

I have little trouble convincing my son Chris that he and I are only fans ourselves. But it's great fun just to be able to be here and bask in the reflected glory that these kids have brought to all of us. And let it be said once again that these coaches and managers and parents have done a great job convincing these kids that they are not special, just ordinary kids who have accomplished something truly special.

Oh, by the way, the final score is Oakland 5, San Francisco 1.

We have a fancy bus with a television mounted in the front. The driver pops in a videotape and we watch a movie all the way back to the hotel. The kids complain when we arrive because the movie isn't over yet. But they quickly recover and head for the pool for a vigorous game of water football.

Monday morning at 5:15 AM, we are back on the bus. It's time to go home. On the ride to the airport, Bob Zullo and Ed Wheeler recount all the tricks the kids have played on them the past couple days. Like tying Bob's shoestrings together while he slept on the plane. Or emptying his can of shaving cream on every door knob and light switch he touched in the room. When you hear these stories, you think how these kids could be yours or mine. This is the only relatively quiet bus ride we take, as the kids seem temporarily to have run out of gas.

At 7:30 AM, we take off for Dulles Airport in Washington, DC. This time, it's a "big bird," and we get a movie ("*Jackknife*"). But the best part of this flight is the ABC "short" that preceded the movie. It's none other than a feature on, you guessed it, the Little League World Championship, and it's only being shown by sheer coincidence. What a thrill to see highlights of the Taiwan game all over again, especially after you've gotten to know the team. It gave me chills all over again, and everyone on this full 747 clapped when "our" team won. Once again, the kids were set in motion signing autographs as they became instant celebrities, and once again, the coaches received champagne from United Airlines.

The last plane ride to Hartford is short and sweet. And as we get off the plane at 4:15 PM, there are [camera crews from local television] Channels 3 and 8 to film the kids, and a few parents to meet them. As Chris and I say goodbye to each of them, it's almost like saying goodbye to family. That's how nice these people are.

Chris and I arrive back in Trumbull at 7:00 PM, with very special memories of the world famous Little League team we've had the privilege of getting to know over the past exhausting 66 hours. Thanks to each of you: Matt Basztura, Dan Brown, Paul Coniglio, Chris Drury, Chris Fasano, David Galla, Jason Hairston, Todd Halky, Chris Kelly, Cody Lee,

UNLIKELY CHAMPIONS: A MIRACLE IN WILLIAMSPORT

Harlen Marks, Ken Martin, Dan McGrath, Andy Paul, and Matt Sewell.

Andy Paul recalled the trip to the West Coast: "The flight out there, missing a day or two of my new school, was cool. They gave us per diem money so we could buy souvenirs and food. Funny, how I remember that. It was a big deal having your own cash on a mini-vacation with your buddies to the other side of the country. Also, we left a day before the earthquake, which I always thought was just good fortune. Throwing out the first pitch to game two and meeting Mark McGuire and Jose Canseco in the dugout was exciting."

"The trip to The World Series in Oakland was very cool," Todd Halky concurred. "I wished we could have stayed for a game at Candlestick Park, but after the earthquake hit, I guess we made the right decision [to come home]."

"Going to the World Series was awesome," Jason Hairston said. "Being on that field, being recognized in front of the baseball community, was sweet." David Galla agreed. "Going to the World Series game in Oakland was great. Not getting trapped in the earthquake that hit the day after we left was pretty good."

Going to the World Series in Oakland provided a brand-new experience to Matt Sewell. "I don't remember too much from that trip, except I watched *Major League* on the bus ride over [to Oakland] and we sat way up high in the stadium. It was the first one I have ever been to, so it was cool."

"*Fantastic* – living the life!" Dan McGrath labeled the trip. "I would later meet a guy who played in that Series (Terry Steinbach) who was an alumnus of my college (University of Minnesota). I would later meet him regularly as his son played on a junior team I coached in Minnesota."

"We ran into Manute Bol [a 7-foot, 6-inch NBA player who played his college ball at the University of Bridgeport], who was with Chris Mullen [they played together on the Golden State Warriors in 1989], just before we walked into the World Series game in Oakland," recalled Tom Galla. "Jason Hairston, standing next to him, was about up to his knee. He was a monster."

Ed Wheeler cited "...all the parents telling me to take care of their kid, so I was worried. It was really incredible that the earthquake happened after we came back. Imagine what would have happened if we had been there? I'm glad we didn't get caught in that. I guess our luck followed us to Oakland."

November 3, 1989

More than 500 people turned out at the Fireside Inn in Newtown, Connecticut, on November 3rd to honor the Trumbull National Little League World Champions. Master of Ceremonies Tim Quinn had a little fun with the boys when he addressed the team and said, "Would we all be here if you had lost? Well, no. So what you guys have done is screw up another Friday night for us."

Bobby Valentine presented the commemorative watches to the players.

Macy's Thanksgiving Parade (Thursday, November 23, 1989)

When you get an invitation to participate in the Macy's Thanksgiving Day Parade, you of course say "yes" without hesitation. But then the night before, reality sets in when you realize that your day will start very early. You need to *leave* Trumbull at 5:30 AM in order to arrive in New York City by 7:00 AM. Then you have to wait until the parade actually starts at 9:00 AM.

As 1989 Little League World Champions, the Trumbull Nationals received that special invitation. In one sense, it was just another event in the whirlwind of events in which the boys participated since winning the Little League title. But it is also a very special event, televised nationally.

Ed Wheeler remembers that Thanksgiving Day, November 23rd, "…was snowy and freezing." The team rode on a float festooned with a 16-foot-high red apple and the New York skyline as a backdrop. The pop music group "New Kids on the Block" joined them on the float, as did a few Major League baseball players, like Tommy John, who had just retired as a New York Yankee during the 1989 season. [Author's note: Tommy John would later become manager of an independent minor league baseball team, the Bridgeport Bluefish; Trumbull is a suburb of Bridgeport. Mickey Herbert, who hosted the team's trip to the World Series in Oakland, would one day be majority owner of the Bluefish.]

Andy Paul remembered the ride on the float: "I was already pretty cool in my new school coming off the Championship but when news spread to the girls down the hallway that I would be sharing a Macy's Day Parade float with the New Kids on the Block, my reputation hit sterling level. Really, it was a lot of fun. They lip synched at the end of the route, the part that was on television, but all in all it was memorable."

"I don't think I knew at the time when we were in the Macy's Thanksgiving Parade what a large event that was," Dan Brown recalled. "I went there last year with my kids and, wow, there were just so many people there."

David Galla remembered "…my wife Traci, who was a good friend of mine back then, said to me before we left, 'Whatever you do, you have to get me an autograph of Joey McIntyre, you have to get me autographs from New Kids on the Block...'

"We weren't asking for anyone's autograph when we were down there, and certainly not New Kids on the Block because she might have been into them, but for a 12-year-old guy it wasn't cool to ask," David declared. David Cone and Darryl Strawberry, and maybe Keith Hernandez, were also on the float with us, as well as other New York Mets. It was a big deal for us to meet them. They were all real nice to us. Everybody wanted to be around us, were interested in what we had done and wanted to talk about it."

Dan McGrath was the only team member who did not go to the Macy's Parade. "The girls in my class were devastated as I could have met the boys from NKOTB, but my folks felt enough was enough and that it was getting out of hand. Also, we were due to leave the country and return to Australia, so we used the break as a chance to visit family friends in Washington DC. No parade for me."

Controversy over a commemorative uniform

After the stunning upset of Taiwan, Williamsport broke with its tradition and decided to give the Trumbull kids their uniforms. Previously, Little League would reuse the uniforms in the following year.

"Because it was the 50th anniversary, because there was so much attention given them and they were such underdogs, we felt we could break tradition," Steve Keener, a Little League spokesman said in a 1990 story in *The Hartford Courant* by staff writer Greg Garber. In December, Little League sent 14 commemorative uniforms, one for each boy except Matt Sewell. Little League *had* provided Matt a jersey to wear for their meeting with President Bush, but he had to return it.

From Little League's point of view, once Matt got hurt and Chris Fasano replaced him on the roster, Matt was no longer entitled to a uniform, nor would they allow him to travel with the team, eat with the team, or sit on the bench with the team during games.

A year later, in August 1990, Matt Sewell had still not received a uniform, despite the call for Little League to do the right thing for the boy. "Rules are rules..." was the word out of Williamsport. This understandably upset Matt and his coach, Tom Galla.

In Garber's story, Mr. Keener indicated "...that there were 20 green-and-gold jerseys bearing the **EAST** legend." After accounting for the 14 given to the players and the jerseys that hang in the Baseball Hall of Fame in Cooperstown and in the Little League Museum in Williamsport, "...that leaves three or four that are gathering dust," according to Tom Galla's math.

After speaking several times with Dr. Creighton Hale, President of Little League, Tom's frustration and anger clearly showed.

"Little League is supposed to be for the boys and girls who play ball," Galla argued. "A person who gets injured should not become a non-person. To exclude someone who had been part of the team is silly, really...

"So WFAN radio in New York called me about it," Tom Galla continued, "and I spoke with them about Matt Sewell not getting his uniform. This was after *The Hartford Courant* ran [Greg Garber's] story. Eventually, it went viral. People were talking about how Little League wouldn't give this kid his uniform. People were calling WFAN from all around the country to talk about it, *big* names, like Wayne Gretsky and others...

"Finally, Little League gave Matt a uniform."

Letting the kids be kids

After months of public appearances, dinners, celebrations, and other promotions, Little League Baseball, Inc. President Creighton Hale "benched" the Trumbull kids in January 1990 when he told them to cut down on the publicity or they could lose the team's membership in the league.

"These are 11- and 12-year-old youngsters," Hale said. "They are not grown men and they aren't great athletes."

The "pitch" that ended it all…an advertisement in a national sports collectibles magazine for baseballs autographed by the Trumbull champs, brought to the attention of officials at Little League headquarters in Williamsport.

The team had received other offers for commercial endorsements, which Little League rules strictly prohibit, and which the team turned down. However, the ad for the autographed baseball [selling price $99.95] by Big Bob's Baseball Cards Inc. in nearby Milford, Connecticut, proved the proverbial last straw, even though the owner of Bob's and Trumbull Little League officials said all sale proceeds would be used to purchase equipment for the League. Little League officials told Bob's that it could not use the balls carrying the Little League trademark because they had not authorized the promotion.

While many parents and some Trumbull Little League officials unhappily disagreed with the decision, Tom Galla put it all into perspective. "Everybody's relieved and happy that Little League took the action they did, so we could get back to normal without some of us being the bad guys saying it was over," Galla explained. "I felt like Miss America, so when we got the letter, it was a blessing."

After things settled down to the new normal, Ed Dzitko, a sports reporter for *The Brookfield Journal* posed the obvious question: "How does one readjust after such an emotional high?" Then he asked a few even tougher questions:

• How are the kids' friends going to treat them?

UNLIKELY CHAMPIONS: A MIRACLE IN WILLIAMSPORT

- What kind of expectations are going to be placed on them?
- Is everybody going to be shooting for them, trying to knock off the Little League champs?

Tom Galla held a clear concern, and rightfully so; remember, these were 12-year-old kids, after all. But after reflecting on what they had experienced and how well they had handled *everything* so far - the ball game itself and a national television audience, the reputation of the team in the other dugout, the many moments during the game when it could have all come crashing down with victory slipping through your fingers, the international media coverage that followed, the overwhelming notoriety accompanying every television, newspaper, or radio interview, the immediate recognition from nearly everyone who met them, and finally returning home to their family, friends, and neighbors as the newly crowned Little League World Champions, Galla didn't need to worry.

He told reporter Dzitko, "You may be right. The kids have been pretty level-headed through this whole thing."

A good example that "getting back to normal" might not prove too tough for the kids appeared in a report on "Eyewitness News Sunday" wherein one of the players said, "I have to go home and get some sleep. School starts next week."

When it all finally ended months later, the Trumbull team certainly savored what they had done and enjoyed the aftermath, but as Joe Burris of *The Boston Globe* wrote, "They not only tasted the thrill of victory, they were consumed by it."

Sports columnists around the country wrote tributes following Trumbull's unlikely championship game victory. [Author's note: See *Epilogue 4 – the Sports Writing Community Celebrates the Victors.*]

No one doubted that the Trumbull victory had caught the attention of sports fans in every corner of our sports-crazed nation. Even two decades later, few could forget what these kids had done.

In 2010, Marc Tambor, writing for Internet blog *Bleacher Report* authored an article entitled "Little League World Series 2010: The 10 Best U.S. Teams Ever" in which he ranked the 1989 Little League champions as No.5. He wrote:

> Trumbull, Connecticut, won the 1989 Little League World Series with a 5-2 victory over Kaohsiung, Taiwan. They couldn't have done it, though, without 1989 Little League World Series MVP Chris Drury, center for the New York Rangers. This marked the first time in Little League World Series history where these kids were called upon to bring attention to the dying sport of American hockey. If nothing else, those kids learned a lot about sportsmanship. A big enough moment to earn fifth on the list.

CHAPTER TWENTY-ONE

REMEMBERING THE EXPERIENCE AND SHARING LIFE LESSONS LEARNED

"There are moments in a boy's life that are seared into his memory."
"One Shot at Forever" by Chris Ballard

    To complete the circle comparing Trumbull National's miracle in Williamsport in 1989 to the 1980 Miracle on Ice, the late Herb Brooks, who coached the 1980 US hockey team, told his players before they took the ice that day against the vaunted Soviets, "You were born to be players, you were meant to be here, this moment is yours." [From the film "A Day that Changed the Game (February 22, 1980)"]
    Recently I spent time with many of Trumbull's "Boys of Summer" reminiscing, one-on-one, about what they accomplished and experienced during that magical summer of 1989, what has transpired since, and the life lessons they learned that made them who they are today. While their memories of certain moments have long since vanished, their recollections of the many key moments that occurred on the road they took to the title in 1989, as well as often untold details about what went on behind the scenes, remain vivid.
    We spent many hours talking about the "what happened" and the "how did you feel about this moment or that moment," as well as how their experiences that summer affected their lives, guiding them to where they are and who they are today, teaching them life lessons that still remain.
    We also focused on what they learned about teamwork, the importance of having a good attitude, self-confidence and self-motivation, and how self-esteem can affect performance. They are much better equipped to answer these questions today than they likely would have when they were 12 or 13 years old. Isn't hindsight great?

At the same time, several members of the team chose *not* to talk about what they did 25 years ago, or even to discuss what has happened since. As one might imagine, I was disappointed. After reflecting on why they might have chosen to remain silent, I can understand their decision. Then, while speaking with Ken Paul one day, he helped put it all into perspective for me.

"Like any other human being, they don't want to be frozen in time as 12- or 13-year-olds," Ken shared.

"It's a burden they carry today," he continued. "Maybe they are tired of the reactions they got from their peers or the questions they get as adults about why they never played professional baseball. It takes a while to detox from the experience. While some have assimilated it into their lives and enjoy talking about it, others just don't want to talk about it anymore. How many adults in their late 30s want to talk about what they did when they were 12 years old?"

What follows comprises their thoughts and recollections of the experience as well as the life lessons they learned a quarter century ago. Thoughts, recollections, and lessons they agreed to share with today's youth who dream of someday traveling the same road that Trumbull did some 25 years ago.

Andy Paul remembers…
"The experience [of playing in the Little League World Series] made me squarely face success and fame but also failures and insecurities at a very impressionable age; the kind that most don't experience in a lifetime. For example, in the same week, I pitched two winning games on ESPN, then struck out twice in front of 40,000 people and a national television audience in the Championship game and was benched.

"Really, it was a whole spectrum of emotions during and after the experience that I think shaped the way I see things to this day; the way I see sports and life. I wouldn't trade that experience for anything but it was a lot to deal with, especially the fame and what comes along with fame at such a young age, as well as dealing with expectations – not only your own expectations and the way you see yourself, but also those of your peers, coaches, teachers, and loved ones.

"Yes, [I enjoyed that summer] very much. It sounds clichéd but it seemed like the summer went on forever. From practices to tournaments, to spending time with your neighborhood baseball buddies, to all the pool parties, and traveling and just everything about being a boy in the summertime was exhilarating and exciting. Plus all the families got along and it was like one big traveling road show once we got out of the District Tournament. Some say the parents, friends and siblings had a better time that summer than the team and coaches.

"The fondest memory of my entire childhood was playing and

practicing at Unity Park in Trumbull. The nostalgia will consume me when I drive through there when I'm home at Christmas break or stop by every couple years. Not to mention my sister ran the concession stand there with the help of my old man, so it seemed like my family lived on the grounds. Chris Drury's house was one street away and he was always there, too. I like to think that Unity Park is a kind of sports sanctuary and we were blessed to have that recreational space as our playground. Trumbull has one of the best park systems in the state and Unity is the jewel. After we won, the 'Trumbull CT Home of the LL World Series Champion' sign that was on the Merritt Parkway was eventually hung on the side of the press box at Unity.

"Looking back on the whole thing now, I'm most proud of winning that championship for the Town of Trumbull. It was where our families were from, where we played, where we learned and where we grew up. It was a tight community. No matter what your hometown, I think people in general are proud of their roots and where they came from and the championship was a way for us to put the town on the map and say I'm from here and it is a special place.

"It was a crazy ride, and we were in so much demand for appearances and interviews and other stuff that it all got to be too much, especially with going back to school and [returning to] real life. All the extra events were so much fun but after a while we decided to get back to normal. I think Coach Galla and the other parents put their foot down.

"As a parent with kids who are just starting to play baseball, I would tell a kid playing in the Little League World Series to '…enjoy every second. Don't worry about getting caught up in all the extracurricular stuff off the field. Just play and have fun with your coaches and teammates. Remember what got you there.'

"As a father with kids starting youth sports, playing in the Little League World Series helped me appreciate more about the coaching, counseling, and encouragement of all our kids through sports and really helped shape my view on winning/losing and competition in general. This is especially so as I get older and now find myself behind the fence looking in. Little League, as well as any youth sports organization, is really about the basic principles of teamwork, personal growth, confidence, and, above all else, adolescent enjoyment. And it is very easy to get away from that mission if people have the wrong intentions or if parents or coaches try to live vicariously through the kids. Luckily, for me and my friends from Trumbull, we had a lot of love and guidance from some special mentors along the way which created the perfect environment for us to grow and believe that we could achieve great things."

Todd Halky remembers…
"I am proud of what we did that summer. The experience made a

UNLIKELY CHAMPIONS: A MIRACLE IN WILLIAMSPORT

bunch of young kids grow up fast. All of us loved to play baseball. The reality was that as we got further [along in the playoffs], to the many people who followed what we did, it was more than just a game. Still, to us, it was just baseball. Certainly, there were points in time when it got tough, but it was a great summer.

"This experience helped me progress throughout life. As I grew up, I realized I could accomplish anything I wanted to. After that, I never again looked back and said I couldn't do something or become somebody. It's a life lesson I have tried to instill in my children today.

"I don't want to make it any bigger than it was but it was a special moment for the country. Even now, when I meet people and they know I'm from Trumbull and played baseball, they know the story about us. I remember the week I went to college they did a story about us. So when I got to the University of Richmond, the baseball coach asked me to come out because he knew I had played baseball in high school. But I chose to focus on academics once I got to college. I didn't want to be distracted.

"The memories from that summer are just tremendous. The bond that I have with these guys is something you just can't replicate. Even if we're not keeping in touch, when we get back together it's just awesome.

"Looking back today at that moment, when we are sprinting around the field carrying the championship banner, I get a tremendous sense of national pride, patriotism. I really feel like we were representing our country. I knew what we had done was a pretty big thing.

"One life lesson I learned was humility. Building upon some difficult moments is also important. After not playing in that final game, I had to deal with that situation, had to hide my emotions. I didn't really want to deal with it, I had had enough, was upset about what had happened to me. But I didn't want to be a detriment to the group. From my perspective, that last game really changed me. It was tough. I'm not going to sugar-coat it; it's still tough. After that, I set a new path. It motivated me to become a better player, it pushed me. I wasn't going to allow myself to be in that position again. After that, I never felt like anybody could beat me at anything. It was how I was raised...my father was always very competitive and still is today.

"I also learned throughout the summer that no one person can do it all by themselves, you're a team. The team concept is really important. You have to stay even-keeled, control your emotions, because of what's going on around you. It's something you can take with you throughout your life.

"How much did luck play in our win, a lot; did we win some games that maybe we shouldn't have, sure. Was California a better team than us? Was Taiwan better? Sure they were. Maybe if we played them in a best-of-five series, we don't win it. But we did get some breaks which you need no matter what, especially in a single-elimination tournament.

"There are so many ways to exhibit leadership. Chris Drury was our leader. We looked up to him, because he was superman. He always kept a level head, never had an ego, never showed it or made us feel that he was more important than any one of us. He didn't carry himself like a 12-year-old. He never said a lot, but let what he was doing on the field speak for itself. No one thought it was his team; we were a cohesive unit; Coach Galla made sure we were a team.

"I actually had a chance to text with the catcher on the Westport Little League team, which went to Williamsport this summer [2013], and told him 'One, don't let anybody tell you that you guys can't do this. You can do anything you put your mind to. You're there for a reason. Two, be focused as a team. Play as a team. Win as a team.'

"I know that lots of people think baseball is a boring game, but they're missing the whole point of the game. Baseball is a crazy mental game. You constantly have to be thinking on every play. It's an individual sport tied into a team sport. What I mean by that is, if you make an error, everybody knows that you made the error. What young kids learn from that is how to be a team and pick people up. Say to that kid, 'that's OK, get 'em the next time.' You can't hide when you make a mistake in baseball, like you can in other sports.

"The beauty of it is that kids learn how to fail miserably and still be successful. A good hitter fails more than 60 percent of the time, but he still succeeds more than 30 percent of the time, which is incredible. It's the most unbelievable sport not only in what it can teach people but how it teaches you to grow up."

Jason Hairston remembers…

"The experience was a little surreal. The experience set a foundation for my life and has contributed to everything I've done in life since. It taught us hard work, perseverance, commitment, believing you can reach high goals, believing in your teammates, and coming together as a team and a family. We did all of that. It also taught me how important it is to enjoy the game, to love the game, but also to play the game hard.

"I sure did have fun, but at the same time there were so many things we sacrificed that summer, things that kids would normally do during the summer, besides playing baseball. I gave up playing on an Olympics development team for soccer. The coaches spoke with my parents and then, my parents and I talked through it. They thought this might be a special team, and the team needed me. They said I should commit to baseball and could always play soccer next year. Anyway, I was 12 and this would be the last year I could play Little League, so…I played.

"The first game against Stratford National when we scored 23 runs, I think was a wake-up call to our parents that this was a special team. We hit a bunch of home runs. Then as we moved through Districts, people would come early to watch us hit batting practice, because guys were just launching them out of the ballpark. I wasn't one of them, but I distinctly remember adults pitching batting practice and watching Ken Martin, Chris Drury, Dan Brown, Andy Paul just launching shots into the woods beyond the outfield fences.

"Life eventually did get back to normal, of course, but so many people knew what we had done. I've had a couple of experiences where I was shocked that people recognized me years later; for example, when I was in college, I was in a restaurant, when this guy came up to me when he saw my name and asked if I was on that team. I just didn't expect that. It gave us something to share, to talk about.

"I would tell a kid today, don't get caught up, have fun and play your game."

Dan Brown remembers...

"My overall perception of the experience has changed over time. While I was living in Trumbull, I was really uncomfortable with it as a middle school and early high school kid who just wanted to fit in. Then I forgot about it as I went on with my life. Now as I look back on it, this was an amazing thing.

"But now I find people I meet constantly want to talk about it. It's amazing how many times when I tell people I'm from Trumbull, Connecticut, or when they're in my office, I have this thing hanging in my office that people see, and then they say that they remember watching the game on TV. They tell me where they were or who they were with. And these are people who aren't from Trumbull. For some reason this game has some importance to people far outside the local circle. It seems to have stuck in their minds, far more than I thought it ever would. Then they want to talk to me about their kids who are playing Little League.

"I had no conception of the Little League World Series when we showed up in Williamsport. I had never before watched a Little League game that I wasn't playing in. So I had no idea what to expect. We had played in local baseball tournaments before, and lost. Yeah, we had won some also, but all I know is that that one year we kept winning and kept going places to play baseball. Even in the Regionals, all the games were in Connecticut, so we weren't too far from home...

"It wasn't until we got to Williamsport that we were pretty far from home. It was a different time, because there weren't too many Little League games on television. And part of that experience is the way that Tom Galla managed the team. He kept it that we were just going to play baseball. And for whatever reason I never felt like we were going to go out and lose. For me it was no big deal, we were just playing baseball, playing another team, we would just keep winning.

"Looking back at that final game, we weren't one of those teams that had a pitcher like the teams today who have that monster guy on the mound, who's like six-five, throwing at some incredible speed and no one can hit him. Even in that final game, and Chris was a great pitcher, but it's not what our team was. I'm not sure how we won because we were not out there dominating anybody.

"The whole experience, it's a big event in my family's history, certainly. My whole family was there, my five brothers and sisters, my parents, and my extended family. They were all at the game. We still talk about it all the time.

"However, I don't think what we did influenced my life too much. I was a little bit uncomfortable with all the attention. I wasn't into wearing the gear like the other guys were. I went another way socially. I was running with a different group of people the next few years.

"At the time, I'm not sure I learned any life lessons, but looking back I can probably derive a few. I was a smart-alecky kid, thought I was cool; thought all that hoopla got to be too much.

"We came to every game with the right attitude and were never scared of anybody. We never thought we shouldn't be on the field. Being able to play a game we played every day without backing down was important.

"In that last game, I wasn't too involved in any key plays but in baseball, you need everybody to be there when they are needed; teamwork is important. In the end, everyone experiences the joy. It's everybody's victory. Anyone who plays baseball learns that you have to rely on each other to make the play. You need a full nine players to have a team, and more, a good bench.

"The coaches instilled a lot of confidence in us. They were always motivating us in that way. But also, the player-leaders on the team, Chris, Kenny, and Andy, all had that attitude and we kind of followed along. On the sports side, the experience certainly increased my self-confidence, but I had always felt that I could play wherever I went. I'm just not sure this experience translated into other areas of my life.

"We had all those events afterwards, for I don't know how long they went on, and I'm not sure I even remember all of them, but then life goes on. You're a thirteen-year-old kid, and other things become more important to you, like girls and just being a 13-year-old kid.

"Then the next season comes along and all of us became 13-year-olds in a Babe Ruth League, where the field is all of a sudden enormous. Then everybody is targeting us the rest of our baseball careers. We're the Little League champions that everyone wants to beat. It's pretty tough.

"After things got back to normal, there was certainly a letdown unless you're like Chris Drury and win championships at every level. I never felt as good at baseball as I did when I played in Little League. Unless you're a professional athlete, as an adult you'll never have the experience of having 10,000 people watching you do anything. It is a memory now that I cherish. I look back and say I had no idea how awesome an experience it was at the time.

"What I would say to a 12-year-old today is 'It's no big deal. It's just another game. It'll probably be the most awesome experience you may ever have, so enjoy it.' It's tough to comprehend a 12-year-old that you could approach with that frame of mind. They're either too caught up and nervous about it or they just don't really understand the scope of [the event]."

David Galla remembers...

"Playing baseball has meant a lot to me as an adult. Baseball is one of the most unique games in that you not only get to play as a team but you also have to produce individually. You rely on your teammates for a lot but your individual production is a must. Playing baseball has given me the ability to translate those same characteristics into my work life. I need to rely on individuals to do what they do but I also have to produce for the team to succeed.

"From the Little League standpoint, it's taught me a great deal, such as how to produce under pressure, how to stay calm in stressful situations, how to not take yourself too seriously, and how to handle adversity. You learn more from your failures than your successes.

"We were so young, I'm not sure it changed us but rather it helped to mold us. For example, while in college I got to play in two World Series. I was ready for the pressure.

"Baseball did teach me to never argue with the umpire, because they make the next call.

"I know the bond we as teammates have with each other is special; we can sit down at any time and talk about what happened, as if it just happened. It's helped us to handle adversity and the problems that we all face in life, knowing that if you just stay the course you'll be fine.

"Winning was important because we were competitive kids, and we wanted to win. We weren't under a microscope. We weren't held to a level of performance. We played at the level we wanted to perform. We never saw newspapers, so we didn't know what was going on.

"Winning that final game was a culmination of everything that had happened during that summer. Our ability, as Coach Zullo had said, to make the routine and not the spectacular play, to swing the bat hard, to play within ourselves, and to try to keep a cool head or an even keel. We were taught pretty early to never get too high and never get too low. You might strike-out but you're going to get another at-bat. You might hit one out but you've got to get up there and face the guy again. You might kick one in the field but the next ball could be hit right at you and you can make a great play.

"In the end, we were just a bunch of kids just playing baseball with our friends. Yeah, we had fun. We were 12-year-old kids playing baseball.

CHRISTOPHER GALLO

It was an amazing summer. Plus we got to do some things that most people never get to do in their lifetime, and we did things that 12-year-olds should do, go to the movies when it rained, did things that built the team and not just practice the plays. As you know, in business it's about building relationships, building a team around you so you can be successful. It's no different in sports. You can teach someone how to play baseball but you can't teach them how to be on a team unless you build that team.

"We learned many life lessons: we learned about persistence, consistency, playing your role but not being afraid to step up when you need to, friendship, trusting your teammates, and most importantly, having fun in what you're doing. If you can't enjoy it, why do it?

"In baseball, like other sports, there is always someone better, who tries harder or who has more ability. It's how hard you want to work that sets you apart. Look at Chris Drury. He was never the biggest guy on the ice, he was never the strongest guy on the ice, but Chris worked hard off the ice to put himself in a position to win. He did that in baseball, too. If you can think and be smarter than the other guy, it doesn't matter if you're not quite as talented, you're going to win.

"What I would tell a 12-year-old today? Well, that's a tough question because it is so different now. I would tell them to do your best to try to relax. I think that is the biggest part about playing ball or doing anything in front of a large audience. People don't want to look silly in front of a large group, so sometimes fear can take over and you lose your ability to perform at the level that you have been prepared to. Whatever coping mechanism you need to relax is important. When you watch the kids today, they play like the pros, they play like adults, they play like they've been playing in front of TV cameras since they were six years old. It's astounding how they're able to do it.

"I get stopped by people to this day who say, 'I remember when you guys came home on the bus and I was standing here, I was doing this when you came home.' I'm not sure how they remember, but they do. It's amazing how many times I introduce myself to people, and they say, 'Galla, Little League?' And I'll say, yeah, that's me. 'You were on that team, played second base, right?' It's amazing how much people still remember about that day, about that team, about that group of kids. Whenever I tell people where I am from, Trumbull, Connecticut, the first thing that comes to their mind is the Little League World Series. I don't go around with a t-shirt on or advertise it in any way, but it is amazing how many times each week I am stopped and asked if I played on that team or if I know anybody who played on that team.

"People remember and people will continue to remember. When people find out that I played on that team, they will tell me what they were doing the moment the game ended. I remember meeting this one guy who told me he was fishing 50 miles off the coast of Cape Cod, and how they were having unbelievable luck catching fish. But they had a portable TV with them and he said they stopped fishing for three-and-a-half hours, 50 miles off Cape Cod, to watch a Little League game. It's one of those things that stick in the mind of people for some reason. As someone who played on that team, I don't get it, but I am glad that people have such positive memories of it, and I am glad I could be a part of it.

"Every group of leaders has a leader. In our case, we had lot of successful guys, but we had a leader in Chris Drury who we looked up to, and his ability to do things for the team was unparalleled. He made plays that 12-year-olds don't make, and got hits that 12-year-olds don't get. He was able to get us going in a quiet manner. There are people in life who are mouthy about their successes, but Chris was the exact opposite of that. He was the kind of guy who would quietly go about his business and quietly lead us to success.

"In sports, superstars are determined by the final game or the game that people remember the most. In our case, people remember the championship game the most because we beat Taiwan which had not lost in a long time; because Chris pitched a phenomenal game, made great plays and had some big hits; because Kenny Martin hit a home run in the final game; because Cody Lee made the great play at the plate; because Dan McGrath caught the last out; Matt Basztura hit the ball like he had never hit it before; Danny Brown made great plays; Jason Hairston smothered the ball like crazy and made great plays at third base; and Andy Paul played very well. They remember Chris spitting on the mound...

"Because of all of those aspects of that particular game, I think that the reason people were deemed superstars is because that is the game that people remember most. It's unfortunate because in the games preceding that game, every single guy on that team had an opportunity and did step up to be a superstar. That's how I would like it to be remembered.

"If you didn't have your moment on national TV in front of 40,000 people, it changed the story."

Matt Sewell remembers...
"I was delivering newspapers [on August 9, 1989], going down a hill on Ironwood Road, when I hit a patch of sand and flipped. It didn't really hurt that bad at first. I didn't understand the implication of what it meant at the time as a 12-year-old kid. I was just playing baseball. As the tournament went on, I realized what it meant – that I couldn't participate as fully as the other kids. It was pretty tough for me, but the coaches and the guys kept me involved as much as they could.

"We had a great team with some real good talent. Looking back, I've come to realize that you don't always get a chance to play with talented kids like Ken Martin and Chris Drury. We went from just playing baseball all the time, which was a ton of fun, to winning games and realizing, oh my god, we're on a trip of a lifetime. But I couldn't play. My identity as a kid was so wrapped up in playing baseball, so it really hurt. You could tell that everyone felt awful for me. The kids felt awful, my friends felt awful, the coaches felt awful, my coach John Heher felt awful for me. I think they went out of their way to make it as good as possible for me. On the other hand, Little League baseball did a very poor job of how they handled it.

"Of course it was fun. It was fun practicing twice a day. I never thought of it as work and never wished I didn't have to go to practice the next day. I even played baseball after I got home from practice. It's fun winning, too. It was a lot of fun killing teams 15-to-5. Some of the guys on our team could really mash the ball.

"Not being part of the team was what I missed the most, not being in the dugout, not being able to wear the uniform, sleeping in the same bunk beds like the other guys, was more of the issue than playing in the game itself. Watching that first game [Forestville] after I broke my arm, I couldn't sit in the dugout. I had to sit in the stands. It was definitely tough to be on the sidelines, to watch the game and not even be in the dugout."

When Little League refused to give him a commemorative uniform in December 1989 like the other 14 boys, Matt told reporters, "I don't understand it, but I try not to think about it – it just gets me mad." Looking back, Matt said, "I felt left out when I didn't get a jersey, like the other guys. Then I was relieved when I finally got it. I guess you could say I was kind of naïve before this.

"I'm a cardiologist today, so the experience is part of the foundation of who I am. When we were in Williamsport, I couldn't sleep in The Grove with the guys, couldn't practice with the guys. Ed Wheeler was there. He took care of me. I may not have realized back then how important the little things he did for me were, but I realize that now. I remember driving around Williamsport with Ed. He just kept talking to me, being there for me, showing empathy. I think that's one of the things I do well now as a doctor, show empathy. I understand what illness and sickness means in patients who truly see themselves one way, but with their illness can't [see their reality]. I think some of those things I may have learned, some of those bittersweet memories have made me who I am today.

"The keys to our success were preparation, attitude, and talent. Kids today are so much more sophisticated because they have personal coaches, but I think we were at that level back then. We also had a lot of talent; there were lots of talented guys on that team. And, I don't think anyone was really nervous. We were just playing baseball and having fun."

Dan McGrath remembers…
"The Little League World Series experience was very special to me in many ways. Baseball at its best, like our own little "*Sandlot*" movie…only we lived it. The fact we still talk about it today, and that it was

UNLIKELY CHAMPIONS: A MIRACLE IN WILLIAMSPORT

a monumental achievement, speaks for itself. The game, the win, and the things that came later allowed us to be kids…very spoiled kids, but it was just good old fun!

"I was unaware at the time of the magnitude, and only having been in Connecticut for a couple years prior, the enormity of the challenge and the fact that we won it did not really register until I was much older. The postgame experience was very different for me, as I left the country by December, moving home to Australia, so the fanfare, chaos, etc. ceased the minute I arrived in Australia. Only a very small community of baseball people knew about the experience, which allowed me to continue my baseball without having the "Little League" experience being hung over my head. I was an unknown person and just another kid interested in playing an American game in a country that loves its Aussie Rules footy and cricket.

"I would later appreciate the experience much more as the magnitude and likelihood of such a dream event sunk in. Moving to Australia soon after really squashed the celebration but over the past two decades I have learned to appreciate grass roots sports more…that so much can be achieved and learned from great coaches and experiences.

"The experience and opportunity has had a positive effect on my life on many levels. I had a keen interest in baseball but played more for fun and to hang out with mates. As I grew older, the novelty of the experience stayed with me and I still think it is one of the best experiences of my life. My parents and sister talk openly about it and as a family it will be something I will pass onto my own boys…that a little Aussie kid, who was pretty lanky and fit the bill of a typical lefty, had been in the right place at the right time…getting goose bumps now just thinking about the experience.

"In short reflection, as a springboard for baseball, the Little League experience drove me to love the game more and having travelled the world playing Junior Baseball for Australia, then college baseball at University of Minnesota, the pivotal event in my life experience, baseball-wise, is and still remains that summer with mates playing a game. I've played semi-pro here, travelled, etc., still…Little League is by far the greatest experience from a sporting point of view.

"I have coached Junior Baseball since I was 16 and still coach today…20 years later, all because of Little League. I am now trying to promote Little League as much as possible here. Only a couple months back I presented a current crop of Little League players from my area with the gear I once wore – all the stuff I had from the experience and the families didn't realize how big it was…and I was talking from the year of 1989! The game and its structure is amazing now…still in awe.

"The experience was a good starting point really to learn about teamwork, the importance of attitude, self-confidence, self-esteem, and self-motivation. I use some of the events and experiences in my coaching of junior players now in a variety of sports.

"Perhaps one area it changed me was I learned how to be humble – that leaving the States allowed me to learn to appreciate just how amazing the feat was and that a handful of Trumbull kids could achieve the ultimate in junior baseball.

"I didn't have a clue what to expect that summer and being naïve at the time probably helped. But it was certainly *FUN*! Plenty of gags, great nights with mates, families getting to hang out and travel together…so many things crammed into the experience, parties, barbecues…was something out of a movie. I have not returned to Williamsport but will one day fly my wife and kids there to see what all the fuss is about.

"I was in awe of Chris Drury – he was a man amongst boys, really, and showed a level of professionalism and determination that obviously assisted him later in life. I wasn't big into team leaders…or at least at 11 or 12 years old, I wasn't thinking too much about leaders…just enjoyed being part of a well-oiled machine really and essentially just played the games because that is what you do.

"I would tell a kid to soak it all up – win or lose, enjoy it because in the blink of an eye it will be 25 years later and you are watching your own kids play the game…and enjoy the friendships you make, they last a lifetime.

"Simply put, my Little League experience has been part of my shaping as a person both with baseball and outside of it. While baseball does not define me as a person it certainly has had a profound impact on who I am today…the people, the experiences and things I have achieved because of baseball have been a positive and will be held dear to my heart…I only wish my boys will one day enjoy baseball and its simplicity the way I have – with respect and utter joy."

Ed Wheeler remembers…
"I thought it was a little silly that I couldn't sit in the dugout in Williamsport, but they had their rules. There were other things that bothered me, like I couldn't be in the team picture that is in the Little League Museum. Same thing with Matt Sewell, he couldn't stay with the team in the barracks, so I always made sure I brought Matt there bright and early so he could be with the team all day. They didn't make it easy with all their little rules. Eventually, a few years later, they changed the rules so there could be three coaches in the dugout.

"I thought Taiwan was real good. I wasn't confident we could win the game. I knew we had to play the best game we could play and they had to not play well for us to beat them. I still don't believe they were all young ball players. They were very mature baseball players. Their first baseman was taller than me, and probably weighed the same as I did. He was a big kid.

"I was just hoping that we could do well. If not win, do well. I was concerned about the kids feeling bad. I was more worried than the kids were but only because I was worried about their feelings. To come all this way; a team like that could kill you. If that had happened I would have felt real bad, but it didn't, so...everything turned out alright.

"I remember walking down the hill to the field as a team, the crowd started yelling, 'U-S-A!' It was quite the scene. It got to you a little bit, you know. We marched around the field. There were a bunch of ceremonies before the game. It was something. I don't remember much because I was occupied with the kids, trying to entertain the kids until the ceremonies were done. We had to just sit there on the side.

"We got a lot of breaks. The main break we got was having an umpire [behind the plate] that gave you a wide strike zone, and Chris was just unbelievable in taking advantage of it. If Chris got a strike an inch outside, his next one would be two inches outside. If he gave him that pitch, the next one would be three inches outside. That was a big part of it. He had that strike zone for both teams, but Chris knew how to take advantage of it.

"We played well. They didn't play as good a game as I had seen them play before. A couple of times, things could have gone a bit differently, then who knows what would have happened? Seeing-eye singles, hit the right way, going through the hole the right way, then they hit the ball right at people. Stuff like that happened throughout the game.

"It was Bobby Zullo who came up with the idea to walk their big guy if he could hurt us. We talked about it the night before, and we agreed if he came up in a situation where he could hurt us, we'd walk him. He was like a major leaguer. He could hit anything and he could hit it hard. So, when he came up, it was a weird decision, but we walked him.

"After we took the lead, well, I figured we had a shot. They were loaded with pitching, four or five kids, who could throw like our two aces. So, when we scored a couple of runs off them, I got a little confident that we could actually beat this team.

"Everything went our way that day. I don't know that there was one spot during the game that was critical. The whole game was tight. It seemed like every time they had a guy on base we made a good play. We never felt like we had a call go against us. Things just seemed to work in our favor. I guess we were supposed [to win]. Danny [McGrath] throwing the kid out at the plate was real big, probably the biggest play. We got lucky in a couple of spots.

"I was actually at the door to the dugout during the whole game. Tom said something to the guy from Little League before that game that it was ridiculous that I couldn't be in the dugout, telling him, 'Look, he's one of our coaches.' So the guy said, okay, but have him just stay in the room next to the dugout. I stood in the doorway, so they wouldn't get mad.

"Between innings, Chris would come up to me by the door to talk about pitching. We'd talk about positioning, where the batter stands, what the batter might be looking for, what to throw at certain times. Chris caught too, so it really made it easy for him to comprehend. In fact, during one of the games in Bristol, I charted the whole game. He'd come up to me after an inning and ask what did I think about the way he was calling the pitches? He was catching, and Andy was pitching. I'd tell him what I would have done differently, but he had called the game perfectly, just like I would have called it.

"Kenny Martin's home run to lead off the fifth inning was a monster. We were used to seeing that. We just knew Kenny got one. There were games he hit two or three like that. In the Districts, he hit some that went over trees. You couldn't put a tape measure on; they would have been out of major league parks. He really peaked as a 12-year-old [that] year. Nobody had a 12-year-old year like he did; nobody could hit a ball farther than him. It was just unbelievable.

"When Kenny hit his home run, I got a little excited, and went into the dugout to hug him. Kenny was good friends with my son, he was always at my house; he was like a son to me.

"I never had any doubts that Chris was going to finish that [last] game, and neither did the other guys. We knew that Chris was our guy. He had the guts and everything to pitch to that team. We were so glad that he got to pitch to them. Chris had the heart. We always felt when he pitched that he was going to win.

"That last out that Danny McGrath caught was back almost to the fence. A little more on that and it's gone. I was relieved that it was over when he caught it. We'd won. All the pressure was off. It was time to smile, relax and celebrate. If we played them 10 times, they would probably beat us most of the time. But we beat them when it counted.

"Winning the championship was the best moment for me. That's why we were there."

Tom Galla remembers...
"The experience was a '*dream come true.*' I really think the adults realized that much more so than the kids at the time. The kids went about it like it was what they were supposed to be doing. They worked hard for it, went on the field, played the game, and won.

"I think it gave them a lot of confidence which they carried forward into their lives. They got to do a lot of things normal kids don't get to do. I guess I just felt it was a positive for the kids.

"I can tell you that I think the experience actually helped them mature, it gave them confidence which carried over as they got older. So, for us, I think it was nothing but positive. Sure there is pressure, but there would be a lot of pressure whether the TVs were there or not. In Little League, kids do cry when things don't go well, but they seem to bounce back pretty quickly. After that Park City loss, the parents were devastated,

UNLIKELY CHAMPIONS: A MIRACLE IN WILLIAMSPORT

the coaches were devastated, and the kids were devastated... for about a half hour; then they were back to normal, being kids, having fun, joking around. I think kids recover quickly, they're resilient. In most cases, they handle it and get over it quickly.

"We got a few breaks against Taiwan that really made a difference.

"One – obviously, it goes without saying, the play at the plate. One bounce off the fence, he turned and he threw...a bullet. It happened so fast that there wasn't a lot of stuff going through my mind at the time, except 'make a good throw.' Never in my wildest imagination did I think he could throw a guy out at home trying to score from second base on a Little League field with these short bases. But it was a perfect throw, and Cody caught the ball and got down, put the tag on the kid, and Mario Garrido called him out. Cody got kicked in the leg, in his calf, by the kid who was trying to score, not intentionally, but he got hit hard enough that he was down on the ground.

"All I could see was Cody on the ground. Bob and I ran out, and asked him if he was okay. The doctor came out. We put some ice on it. Cody stayed in the game. When we came home, he had a hematoma that he needed to have drained. It was a pretty good bump.

"I never even had a chance to think about the play at that moment, because, as Bob and I went back to the dugout, we looked at each other and said, 'We've got to walk this kid, too.' It's a good thing we had talked about all this the night before, because, God only knows, we may not have walked anybody. We might have just stood there and watched them knock four or five runs across. I don't know. You know how I feel about Bob Zullo; I give him credit for that. Just knowing him as I did, I'm pretty sure it was his idea.

"When I looked at that play afterwards, I wonder how he [Cody] made that play. It was a short hop, a tough ball to catch, and he had to be in the right position and somehow get down and make the tag. When I look at it after the fact, it's like, holy cow, how'd he do that? And how did Danny McGrath make that throw? How could Cody possibly put the tag down? It wasn't an easy play on either end, it was a very difficult play, and they both made it.

"If that inning had blown up, Taiwan might have scored six runs, and our fans would have crucified me. But luckily, it ended up the way it did.

"In my opinion, Little League baseball, at that level and under those conditions, is not like playing Major League Baseball, where you can win 60 percent of your games and be the best team in the Major Leagues. We had to win every game. So, you're not going to play every situation identical to the way the Major Leagues might play.

"Jim Palmer saying something like, I don't understand this, why are we loading the bases with one out to bring up the number three hitter?

That's right, Jim, you don't understand that. Even though Jim Palmer thought we were making such a big mistake against Taiwan, we knew going in that any one of those first four hitters could hurt us, and we weren't going to let that happen. We were not going to let those kids get swings against us if we got into a situation like that.

"So, we ended up only pitching to two out of the four, because of what we decided the night before, Bob and I talking about it until one o'clock in the morning. The first kid we pitched to, he popped up. The only kid who got a hit [in the game] was the number three batter. So, one out of four got a hit, two got walked, and one popped out. Luckily it all worked out well. But, of course, it could have back fired, but it didn't.

"But that's why when people say to me, what was that Westport coach thinking about when he took that pitcher out with a big lead in the 2013 Little League World Series, a game they eventually lost, that I say, just like Trumbull in 1989, he got there doing things possibly a little unorthodox that…had it worked…everything would have been fine. Unfortunately, it blew up in his face, and you knew they were not going to get to the final game.

"Don't forget, Chris Drury was on the mound, with a lot of help from his friends, because McGrath and Cody make that play. That's a *big* out. Then, they hit the ball right at Jason, and he traps it *under* his glove, but he had the presence of mind to pick it up and run to the base. He *just* beats the kid to the bag, and the Taiwan kid *doesn't* slide, what's the matter with you, kid? I thought you guys were taught better than that? If he slides, maybe they get the call, he's safe and another run scores.

"Cody did a phenomenal job. I put a lot of pressure on him. He came home a hero.

"Two – the fact that we faced either their number two or number three pitcher was probably the biggest break, because, though I never saw their number one, the big lefty first baseman, throw, I expect that he was probably a fastball pitcher and was probably overpowering. But, you know, we were throwing the ball as hard as we could during batting practice against our kids and they were hitting the ball, hitting it hard. We had high school kids come in early on to pitch against them, and they would hit the ball. So, if we had faced the big kid, I'm not convinced he would have shut us down, but he probably would have slowed us up a little. Certain of our guys probably would have been able to catch up to him, while others might not have been able to catch up to him. Not that we scored that many runs against them, but it would have been tougher to string a couple of hits together and score runs, as we did.

"So, getting to face that second pitcher was the first break of the game, and that wasn't the first time that happened to us, which was a good thing. You can't expect you're going to win the Little League World Series without catching some breaks along the way.

UNLIKELY CHAMPIONS: A MIRACLE IN WILLIAMSPORT

"Three – having Mario Garrido behind the plate was probably a big break. The fact is I will never forget his name because of the wonderful job he did behind the plate. I'm not going to say he was favoring the US team against the foreign team, but he had a big strike zone. He called it the same for both teams. Personally, I believe that Little League instructs these guys to have a big strike zone. And what is big to me might be small to you, so I might call one that far off the plate, and maybe Mario had a different understanding of what a big strike zone was. It favored us because Chris was all over the place, he didn't have pinpoint control. He'd keep it around the plate, and he'd keep it exciting for the batters." [Author's note: Chris Drury walked four, including the two intentional passes, and struck out two, while Taiwan recorded five strike outs and walked only one batter.]

"Four – our guys did not seem to be bothered by the 40,000 people in the stands that day. Still, I'm not sure I ever felt comfortable until the top of the sixth, even when Chris made it exciting when he walked the leadoff guy. Looking back at the fifth inning, you can understand. It was like we were waiting for them to explode. I was just nervous about that.

"I enjoy talking about this experience, and how proud I am of our accomplishment, how proud I am of these kids, and what kind of a miracle I thought it was. For me it was the experience of a lifetime, and I was able to experience it with my son, and with these other kids, who were so close to me, because of all the time we spent together. I knew these kids from a baseball standpoint maybe as well as my son. I'm not sure I can find the right words, but this was special.

"I was the *luckiest guy in the world* to be associated with these kids. What a *treat*. How many guys in Connecticut have done what I have, what, four? I did something that thousands of guys would love to do.

"I'm not saying that I'm anything special. All I'm saying is I was a lucky guy. Holy s**t! Holy cow just doesn't do it.

"It wasn't just me. There was Zullo and Wheeler, too; the three of us. We pitched in, but it's the kids who did it. We helped them, we guided them. Our goal was to put the nine players on the field who gave us the best chance to win.

"I wish I could give you a brilliant answer about strategy.

"However, in thinking back most of what went on did not involve great strategy or advice. The exception was against San Pedro when I went out to talk with Andy after all the home runs they hit. I told him that 'it was no big deal' because we would come back and score plenty of runs for him. I was trying to get him to look forward rather than dwell on the home runs he had just given up. Once he started having success with the dart pitch I think he settled down and gained confidence.

"Everything we did after we won was just so overwhelming. You just couldn't say 'no' because everything was so great. Are you going to say 'no' to going to Yankee Stadium; to meeting Don Mattingly; to the kids playing catch with Steve Sax and then sitting in Steinbrenner's box for food and drinks; and to speaking with Phil Rizzuto and Mel Allen just like we would with friends? Are you not going to the White House and or to the World Series in Oakland? You couldn't say 'no' to these things, they were just so tremendous.

"They were just a bunch of ordinary kids doing something miraculous. That's not taking anything away from them, but it was miraculous. You just can't do what we did, but we did it. We killed Casey Fossum [of Cherry Hill], and he became a major league pitcher.

"I don't recall all the events I spoke at, but I do remember speaking at a Chamber of Commerce meeting in Williamsport. I went to Anthony's Pier 4 Restaurant in Boston to speak to the Boston Red Sox Royal Rooters; there were hundreds of people in the room.

"We got a bronze plaque when we won that said 'Little League Champions – 1989' that was mounted on the press box at Unity Field. [Author's note: It is still there.] Both of my grandsons are playing Little League baseball now. So, I was at one of their games last year that was being played on the main field, the one with the press box, and before the game began, the announcer says, 'We'd like to welcome everybody here to Unity Field, Home of the 1989 Little League World Champions.' I was like, oh my god, I wonder if they do that all the time. That was pretty cool. Can you imagine what other teams feel like when they come to Trumbull, where we won the Little League World Series?

"The stuff that happened back then [after the team won the World Series] was just amazing. It was exhausting, but at the same time, it was so exciting, that you did it. Finally, Little League said, 'That's enough.' They did all of us a favor. We met with two guys from the NCAA because we wanted to be sure that we weren't doing anything that would hurt the kids later on in college.

"I would tell parents to just enjoy whatever happens. The chances of you experiencing what our [team's] parents experienced are very slim. But you're out there, watching your son or daughter grow up, gain confidence, and have fun. They're like sponges when they're young. They're like putty. They're so much fun to be with. They grow up so fast. It goes by so quickly. Before you know it…they're teenagers.

"To me, it's all about the memories. I feel so lucky that I was the guy who got to coach this team. I feel great how it impacted the kids so well. They played so well. I wish everyone could experience something like that just once in their lifetime."

CHAPTER TWENTY-TWO

A FEW FINAL REFLECTIONS

I'll never understand why I didn't make the trip to Williamsport to see that final game ending in Trumbull's triumph over Taiwan. Sitting in front of my television that day, the thought never crossed my mind. Like so many others who watched in the comfort of their Connecticut homes, I thought, why bother take that long five-hour drive to see them get their butts kicked. Then, after they had gotten their butts kicked, I would have to drive another five hours, mostly in the dark, to get home. Oh, and remember, if you don't get to Lamade Stadium by 11 in the morning, you won't get a seat in the grandstands; no, you'll sit on the hill. OK, not bad, you're there, but…why bother. It's easier to watch from home. How many others took the easy road that day, only to later regret their act of omission? "How could you not think that," Tom Galla replied when I shared my regrets. "If I was sitting home, I'd probably be thinking the same thing."

Just as the *"Miracle on Ice"* inspired boys and girls in the US to play hockey, leading to the tremendous growth of the game throughout America and the expansion of professional hockey, so have Trumbull's **Unlikely Champions** inspired Little Leaguers everywhere to dream what they can do and live their dreams. Sure it takes lots of hard work, but when it is over and you actually *do* realize your dreams, I promise - you will never forget it, and who knows, you may even inspire others to dare to dream.

Years later, in an interview in *Hockey Magazine*, Al Trautwig, who called the 1989 Little League Championship game on ABC's *Wide World of Sports*, said he "…remembers that game well. That game was played at a time when Taiwan was considered unbeatable, and there were suspicions that they were playing free and easy with player-eligibility rules. We asked Chris [Drury] before the game if he was nervous. He said, 'Nervous? Why would I be nervous?' I think of that day every time I get to interview him now." [Author's note: Trautwig does pre-game and post-game shows for the New York Rangers; Chris Drury played for the Rangers from 2007 through 2011.]

When you look at what Chris Drury did as a twelve-year-old, it was clear that he stood out as a special and talented kid. He had a tremendous feel for the game of baseball. Who knows what he might have done in baseball if he hadn't broken his wrist in high school and decided to focus on hockey? Maybe the *"Miracle on Ice"* had inspired him to focus on hockey. Chris established himself as a tremendous athlete, though he was never the biggest kid or the fastest kid. But he had heart, that intangible that differentiates the best athletes from everyone else. He had *it*, whatever *it* is. Part of *it* is leadership. Strong leaders have the ability to inspire others around them to rise and perform at levels beyond what they truly believe they can achieve. That is why I believe his story, as well as the stories of his teammates and their coaches, needed to be told. Their stories truly inspire.

Their experiences have had a major positive impact on who they have become, and I am grateful that so many have shared the life lessons they learned and the impact their experiences have had on their lives. Tom Galla may have said it best when he called them "ordinary kids who accomplished extraordinary things." After meeting them, speaking with them, learning about what they have done, I respectfully disagree with Tom. What these 15 men accomplished 25 years ago as 12-year-olds was clearly extraordinary, but they have grown to be extraordinary adults, parents, husbands, businessmen, and community leaders. Bob Zullo knew they would when he said back in 1990, "I believe they will all be decent human beings. What they all have going for them is that they all have solid values and come from good families." Well said, Bob! To me, this is the best part of the story I have had the honor to tell in this book.

My final thought is that I hope the parents of Little Leaguers will put this book down having learned the simple lesson about what Little League baseball *is all about*, and what it is *not* all about. **Little League is all about the kids having fun playing baseball.** It is not about parents living vicariously through their children. It is not about putting pressure on your children so that when tryouts come they are so nervous that they are afraid to fail, or worse, they don't want to play. It is not about winning at all costs. It is not about the fame that comes from winning an important game with a world-wide audience watching. It is not about abusing a volunteer umpire who may have blown a call - for are we not human, subject to making mistakes, those unintentional errors to which anyone can succumb when pressure is applied.

It is about playing the game and having fun, dreaming, working hard to make dreams come true, learning to trust your teammates, and picking up your teammate when he or she is having a bad day. Knowing that you have given your best is a wonderful feeling. It is also about the children learning to trust the adults who teach them the game.

UNLIKELY CHAMPIONS: A MIRACLE IN WILLIAMSPORT

Little League is all about the kids having fun playing baseball.
These are the life lessons that should be taught to a 12-year-old.

However, I also believe that as children grow older, move into high school and then to college, and finally into the working world, there are other life lessons that will become important for those stages of life. For that reason, I have included them here, so that no one thinks I am so naïve to think that what is important to a 12-year-old will be the same when they become adults.

In 2011, Augie Garrido, one of the most successful college baseball coaches in America, wrote a wonderful book titled *"Life Is Yours to Win: Lessons Forged from the Purpose, Passion and Magic of Baseball."* Some of the lessons he says are critical for success in life and that can be learned from baseball include:

- Finding your purpose and pursuing it with passion
- Recognizing your fears and managing them
- Learning from failures and moving forward
- Committing to mastering the skills you need to succeed
- Doing whatever it takes to achieve your goals
- Creating and seizing opportunities and acting upon them
- Being a team player, willing to play whatever role is needed
- Being as good a friend to yourself as you are to others

These are all terrific life lessons, but the most important words he may have put into print in his book are these:

"The greatest lesson the game of baseball teaches you is how to deal with adversity and distracting emotions while continuing to pursue your dreams and goals."

These are a few simple but powerful words to remember, forever. Dream on…

Now that you know the real story and all the tremendous life lessons that can be passed onto future generations of Little Leaguers, you understand that what those 15 Trumbull boys accomplished that summer was something that no one could have expected until it had happened, and even then it was incredible to think that they had done it. Tom Galla put it well when he said, "We did it with talent, hard work and good old-fashioned luck. Our lives had changed but soon returned to normal. We had all shared, in my opinion, the most wonderful summer of our lives, *The Summer of '89!!*"

Coach Ed Wheeler wrote his tribute to these magnificent 15 boys that he called, *"To the Boys of Summer 1989."* It is presented here with his permission.

What would have happened if these boys didn't
have determination, desire, talent and heart?

CHRISTOPHER GALLO

What if Chris Fasano didn't come to every practice as an alternate and keep the team members trying hard to keep their spot on the team?

What if Paul Coniglio wasn't there to run every time we needed a jet on the bases?

What if Jason Hairston wasn't there to cut off all the balls hit between short and third and make them outs?

What if Harlen Marks wasn't there to pinch hit and get a rally going when we needed it?

What if Matt Sewell didn't get clutch hits and lead the team in on-base percentage through the states?

What if Todd Halky didn't hit throughout the state and catch a great game against NJ?

What if Dave Galla didn't get three hits in the Delaware game and start rallies throughout the World Series?

What if Dan Brown didn't go down town in the Forestville game and make great plays in the NJ game?

What if Chris Kelly wasn't there to fill in whenever, and wherever his great defensive talent was needed?

What if Matt Basztura didn't reach over the fence to take away a home run against Iowa and throw a perfect strike to third against California?

What if Andy Paul didn't pitch a great game and shut out NH and change his pitching style completely to beat California?

UNLIKELY CHAMPIONS: A MIRACLE IN WILLIAMSPORT

What if Cody Lee didn't make a great play at home plate and catch a great game with clutch hitting against Taiwan?

What if Dan McGrath didn't make a diving catch in the gap in the Forestville game and make a perfect throw to home plate to stop a Taiwan rally?

What if Ken Martin didn't hit the cover off the ball throughout the All-Stars, and get two key hits against Taiwan while playing excellent defense?

What if Chris Drury didn't have the heart and guts to give one great performance after another as our team leader?

What if you weren't WORLD CHAMPS?

You would still be a special and great bunch of kids and always wanted and welcomed in Wheeler World.

What this team of 15 boys and their three coaches achieved was no small feat. It was *extraordinary*! They had beaten the odds, won the Little League World Series, and captured the nation's heart. I hope you have enjoyed this "trip of a lifetime."

PHOTO GALLERY

UNLIKELY CHAMPIONS: A MIRACLE IN WILLIAMSPORT

Photo courtesy of The Trumbull Times
A TENSE MOMENT FOR TOM GALLA DURING THE STATE CHAMPIONSHIP GAME AGAINST FORESTVILLE

Photo courtesy of The Trumbull Times
DAN BROWN IS GREETED AT HOME PLATE AFTER HITTING A THREE-RUN HOMER IN FIRST INNING AGAINST FORESTVILLE IN STATE CHAMPIONSHIP GAME

CHRISTOPHER GALLO

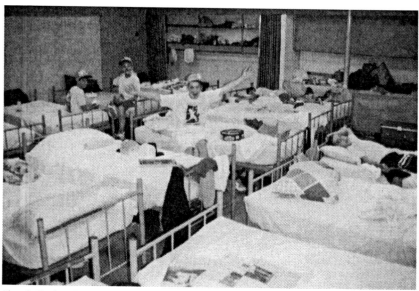

Photo by Sandy Galla
"LIVING IT UP" IN A KINDERGARTEN CLASSROOM DURING EAST REGIONAL IN BRISTOL, CONNECTICUT

Photo by the author
ED WHEELER DEMONSTRATES THE "DART PITCH" GRIP

UNLIKELY CHAMPIONS: A MIRACLE IN WILLIAMSPORT

Photo by Sandy Galla
ANDY PAUL CLOSES OUT BRANDYWINE, DELAWARE, IN EAST REGIONAL CHAMPIONSHIP GAME TO EARN TRUMBULL NATIONAL A BERTH IN THE LITTLE LEAGUE WORLD SERIES

Photo by Sandy Galla
DOGPILE AFTER THE WIN OVER BRANDYWINE

CHRISTOPHER GALLO

Photo by Sandy Galla
THE TEAM GETS READY TO BOARD A BUS FOR THE DRIVE TO WILLIAMSPORT AFTER WINNING THE EAST REGIONAL TOURNAMENT IN BRISTOL, CONNECTICUT.

Photo by Sandy Galla
TEAM PHOTO TAKEN AT UNITY PARK BEFORE LEAVING FOR WILLIAMSPORT

UNLIKELY CHAMPIONS: A MIRACLE IN WILLIAMSPORT

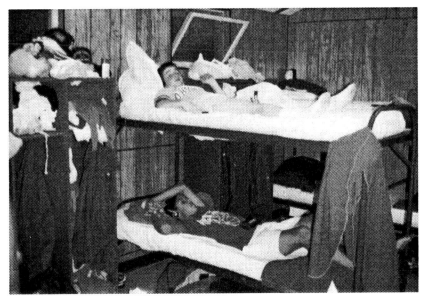

Photo by Sandy Galla
RELAXING IN THE TEAM BARRACKS IN THE GROVE (LITTLE LEAGUE COMPLEX IN WILLIAMSPORT)

Photo by Sandy Galla
THE TEAM WAVES TO THEIR FANS BEFORE BOARDING A TRUMP AIRLINES 727 FOR THE FLIGHT FROM WILLIAMSPORT TO LAGUARDIA AIRPORT IN NEW YORK. STANDING FAR LEFT IS PILOT, KEN PAUL, FATHER OF ANDY PAUL.

CHRISTOPHER GALLO

Photo by Sandy Galla
ON THE SET OF *GOOD MORNING AMERICA* WITH SPENCER CHRISTIAN

Photo by Sandy Galla
THE TEAM IS CELEBRATED AT CAPTAIN'S COVE SEAPORT IN BRIDGEPORT, CONNECTICUT

UNLIKELY CHAMPIONS: A MIRACLE IN WILLIAMSPORT

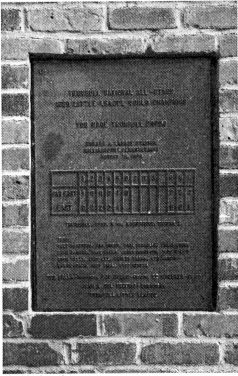

Photo by the author
COMMEMORATIVE PLAQUE AT UNITY PARK IN TRUMBULL, CONNECTICUT

Photo by Sandy Galla
THE LAMADE STADIUM SCOREBOARD TELLS THE STORY

CHRISTOPHER GALLO

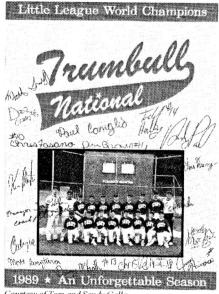

Courtesy of Tom and Sandy Galla
COVER OF COMMEMORATIVE PROGRAM

Photo courtesy of Theo Westenberger Archives, 1974-2008, Autry National Center, Los Angeles.
One of several photos taken during a photo shoot by Theo Westenberger for the December 25, 1989 issue of Sports Illustrated
(TOP ROW, FROM LEFT) MATT SEWELL, PAUL CONIGLIO, JASON HAIRSTON
(MIDDLE ROW) DAN MCGRATH, MATT BASZTURA, CODY LEE, ANDY PAUL, HARLAN MARKS, KEN MARTIN, CHRIS DRURY
(BOTTOM ROW) CHRIS FASANO, DAVID GALLA, DAN BROWN, CHRIS KELLY, TODD HALKY

UNLIKELY CHAMPIONS: A MIRACLE IN WILLIAMSPORT

Courtesy of Tom Galla, photographer unknown
AFTER SPEAKING AT A WILLIAMSPORT CHAMBER OF COMMERCE MEETING, TOM GALLA (FAR RIGHT) MET CARL STOTZ, LITTLE LEAGUE'S FOUNDER.
ALSO WITH TOM ARE: (LEFT TO RIGHT) ED WHEELER, JOHN DELVECCHIO, HANK RYDECKI, CARL STOTZ, AND RAY BALDWIN.

Courtesy of Tom and Sandy Galla
ON THE STEPS OF THE US CAPITOL BUILDING AFTER VISITING THE WHITE HOUSE

CHRISTOPHER GALLO

President Bush greets the Trumbull National All-Stars in the Rose Garden at the White House.

Courtesy of Tom and Sandy Galla

MEETING PRESIDENT GEORGE H. W. BUSH IN THE ROSE GARDEN

"Congratulations and Best Wishes to the Trumbull National All-Stars. The State of Connecticut is proud of you."

Governor William O'Neill

Courtesy of Tom and Sandy Galla

MEETING GOVERNOR WILLIAM O'NEILL AT THE STATE CAPITOL IN HARTFORD

EPILOGUE ONE

THE NEXT 25 YEARS – WHERE ARE THEY NOW?

1990 – The next year...
The following year, Ray Baldwin coached the 1990 edition of the Trumbull National All-Stars, the defending champions in name only.

"We only had one kid on the team, Paul Coniglio, who had been on the team the year before but had seen little playing time," Baldwin affirmed.

"I was pretty excited about the prospect of being identified as the coach of the team that had won the championship the year before," he continued. "Unfortunately, the experience for the kids was, in some cases, downright nasty. The way they were treated by fans from other towns was disgraceful. We followed the same track as the team the year before had. We were beat by Park City American and then came back to beat them for the District championship.

"The next day, when we went to practice for the States, we found that Unity Field [had been marred]. It got worse. When we played our first game in the States in Stamford, the fans were vile, screaming profanities at the kids who were on the field. This went on during the entire game, upsetting the kids so much that they came off the field crying. I was really put off by what had happened. So, it was a good time for us to go away.

"The following year, the kids who had won it all the year before were playing in a 13-year-old All-Star tournament in New Hampshire, so I followed them up there to watch them play. The same thing happened. The fans were vile, screaming obscenities, awful stuff, at the kids, 13-year old kids. I couldn't believe it was happening. It was disgusting what the fans were yelling at them. Carl Stotz would have been appalled at how the kids were treated by these adults," Baldwin said.

In 1990, 12 of the 1989 team kids played Babe Ruth League baseball, with 10 of them making All-Stars. Jason Hairston played soccer, and, of course, Dan McGrath moved back to Australia. That fall, Chris Drury headed for Fairfield Prep, while Cody Lee, Matt Basztura Todd Halky, and Matt Sewell attended Trumbull High School. Kenny Martin remained at St. Catherine of Siena School, Andy Paul went to Hopkins School, and everyone else, except Dan McGrath, took their classes at Hillcrest Junior High School.

The Trumbull Babe Ruth All-Stars came out of the District 2 loser's bracket to make it to the championship game, but lost to Wilton, 11-6.

A monument is built in Trumbull in tribute to their victory

The Trumbull Town Council authorized a $3,000 appropriation toward the acquisition of a monument commemorating the Trumbull National Little League world championship.

"I am very pleased," said Manager Tom Galla. "I think there should be a monument to the boys in honor of a feat that probably will never be equaled. It's something the town will remember forever."

League President John DelVecchio also expressed his support, "I know some people think the boys have had enough [glory] already, but these 15 young kids gave up their whole summer."

1994 – Five years later...

Five years after they became celebrated Little League champions, the 15 "boys" were now 17 or 18 years old and had grown into young adults.

Some still played baseball, while others had moved into other sports; many were multiple-sport high school athletes. Many captained a variety of high school teams in different sports. Most have remained residents of Trumbull, but a few moved out of state or even out of country.

Time had changed many things except that they remained friends, even when they sat in dugouts on different sides of a field or on benches on different sides of the scorer's table. Some had graduated from high school in June and would enter college in the fall, while the rest would enter their senior year of high school.

Besides being teammates on St. Joseph High School's baseball team, Ken Martin and Chris Kelly played American Legion ball together. Dave Galla and Chris Kelly remain best friends, and both played shortstop in high school, but for different schools. When summer American Legion baseball started, Dave, Trumbull High's shortstop, moved over to second base to match up as Chris Kelly's double-play partner, who played shortstop. Their American Legion team won the Zone IV championship title with a 25-7 record. Meanwhile, Chris Drury played baseball for Fairfield Prep. In a key high school baseball matchup, Drury's Prepsters took it on the chin, losing to Kelly and Martin's St. Joseph High School Cadets, 12-0, a loss that knocked Prep out of the state tournament.

UNLIKELY CHAMPIONS: A MIRACLE IN WILLIAMSPORT

Matt Sewell played on the Trumbull High School baseball squad as a relief pitcher who saw little action in his senior year. However, his Constitutional Law team did well in a national competition in Washington, DC, and Matt's First Amendment presentation received the grade of "best in the country." Jason Hairston had moved to Maryland, where he excelled in baseball and soccer, while Dan McGrath played several sports "down undah" in Australia.

On August 7, 1994, 10 of the guys met at the Galla's home in Trumbull for a reunion. Five couldn't attend. Understandably Dan McGrath didn't make the trip from Australia, and Chris Drury had a workout in Boston. Cody Lee and Matt Basztura had out-of-state prior commitments, and Dan Brown had obligations in New Jersey. A photographer from *Sports Illustrated* and reporters from three newspapers would attend.

The boys chatted, joked, played Wiffle ball and enjoyed each other's company. And, as teenagers usually do, they enjoyed some food. Then the talk turned to what had transpired five years earlier.

"No one knows what we'll face down the road," Jason Hairston said. "I fully appreciate how fortunate I was to play with this bunch of guys during that time of my life. Baseball has always been fun for me, but I know there're more important things out there."

So, five years later, Andy Paul recognized where their collective baseball careers stood when he said "It doesn't matter that we didn't turn out to be superstars. It wouldn't be right if we were all still playing baseball together. We can still be good at whatever we're doing. This experience helped us do that."

1999 – Ten years later…
It's July 1999, and the boys of the Summer of '89 are now nearing their college graduations, planning for life after college and starting their careers.

Once again, the 1989 Little League champions reunite. This year, the Bridgeport Bluefish, a minor league baseball team for which Andy Paul's dad works, hosts. Twelve of the guys join the celebration at The Ballpark at Harbor Yard in Bridgeport on Saturday evening, July 17 on "Trumbull Little League Night."

Todd Halky and Matt Basztura have out-of-state work commitments and cannot attend, while Chris Kelly plays first base for the St. Louis Cardinals' Class A team in Peoria, Illinois. As the announcer introduces each player in attendance to the crowd in a pre-game ceremony, a current Trumbull Little Leaguer escorts them onto the field. Ken Martin receives a special escort, his 10-year-old brother, Doug. The Bluefish presented each of the players with a T-shirt that said "1989 World Champions" on the front and "10-Year Reunion" on the back.

Later, they gathered at a local restaurant where their hosts treated them to videos of their wins over California and Taiwan during their meals. The next morning, they teed off for a round of golf at Tashua Knolls Golf Course in Trumbull.

2009 – Twenty years later...
Just as they had for the five-year and 10-year celebrations of their magical summer, most of the members of the team returned to their roots. They reprised most of their past gatherings – shared a meal, drank some beer, played some golf.

But this year they added a new event, for they realized as you get older, start your own family, and achieve success in your career, you grow thankful for who you are, for all you have achieved, and for your many blessings. It is time to give something back to your community, to say thank you, or perhaps enlighten the community to a new or an unrecognized need.

For their 20th reunion, Trumbull's champions, now in their early thirties, decide to do something for their community.

In 1989, Trumbull Little League started a Challenger Division of Little League Baseball in Trumbull, which allows boys and girls with physical and mental challenges to play baseball. Many players from the 1989 team had helped out when it started, so this proved a natural fit.

"The Challenger Program is kind of close to our hearts, and we just didn't want to come back and go to a bar, we wanted to do something that made sense for this event," Ken Martin said. "Helping the Challenger Program makes sense. We're real excited about doing this."

So, on Saturday afternoon, August 8, 2009, some 500 people showed up to watch a Home Run Derby at their old home field, Unity Park. Everyone from the 1989 team showed up, except Dan McGrath, who could not return from Australia, and Chris Fasano, working in Los Angeles. Players from the 1989 team faced a team of current Trumbull Little Leaguers. The organizers charged no admission, but in true Little League tradition – even in Williamsport – they passed the hat, and raised a few thousand dollars that afternoon.

In the first round, five of the "Old Guys" came up "goose eggs" trying to hit the flight-restricted baseballs over the short fence, but Ken Martin, Chris Kelly, Matt Basztura, and the "buffed-up" Jason Hairston, who whacked four over the fence, advanced to Round 2.

Martin, who hit six, moved into the quarter-finals against Jason Hairston, with two. In the semi-finals, Hairston knocked Ken Martin out with a 4-1 win and moved to the finals as the class of '89 representative against Kyle Bova of the 2009 Trumbull American's. In the finals, Bova defeated Hairston 3-1 to take the title.

UNLIKELY CHAMPIONS: A MIRACLE IN WILLIAMSPORT

Matt Basztura
  The son of Rudy and Cheryl Basztura, Matt played four years of baseball and football at Trumbull High, earning All-Conference honors in football his junior and senior years and All-Conference honors as a junior in baseball, and honorable mention All-Conference in baseball as a senior.
  After graduating from Hamilton College in 1998 with a degree in Spanish, where he played football (four years) and baseball (three years), Matt worked as a ticket agent for the New York Mets. In 1999, Matt entered the Federal Law Enforcement Training Center in Georgia, and worked as a federal border patrol agent in Arizona for several years. He currently works for the US Department of Homeland Security in New York.
  Though I sent Matt several emails, I never received a response, so I have none of his personal recollections to share, much to my disappointment. He had some wonderful moments that summer, moments that came at critical junctures. He hit .475 before Williamsport, with four home runs, scoring 21 runs and driving in 15. He was held hitless in just two games to that point. As the number 3 batter until the final game, he was a real table-setter for Trumbull while playing superb defense in center. He deserves as much credit as anyone for getting Trumbull to Williamsport.

Dan Brown
  Dan is the youngest of six children of Bill and Kathy Brown, and his family moved to Trumbull just before he entered kindergarten.
  After Dan's freshman year at Trumbull High School, his family moved to New Jersey. "I completely disappeared as far as they [the team] are concerned." Eventually, he did go back for several reunions/gatherings.
  At Plainsboro High in West Windsor, New Jersey, Dan played football, basketball, and baseball, captained the basketball team his senior year, and earned a spot on the Second Team, All-Mercer County in football. He also played American Legion baseball and made All-Stars. But as Dan put it, "My high school years weren't ones I remember fondly."
  After high school, Dan tried college, but soon dropped out.
  "I had some issues, got into drinking and drugs, wasn't a very good student, and [had] graduated from high school with extremely mediocre grades. I had no thoughts about going to college, though I tried the college thing, attending High Point University, but after two weeks, I gave it up. I wasn't ready for that whole experience."
  He actually spent time working "...lots of crappy jobs after high school, and struggled for a while into my twenties." When asked if his Little League experiences had any impact on this phase of his life, Dan made it clear - "Absolutely not. I just hung around with the wrong crowd."
  "One of my jobs was pumping gas on the New Jersey Turnpike. While working there, a manager let me work inside the office doing paperwork, which is when I realized I was decent with numbers. This was

much better than working some crappy gas-pumping job. Eventually, I got a bookkeeping job at a pool company. The woman who I worked for was a CPA, and taught accounting classes at night at a local community college, [and she] encouraged me to take some classes. So I took some night classes part time, and got the general requirements so that I was eventually able to transfer to Rutgers."

A few years later, Dan received his degree in Accounting from Rutgers University in New Jersey.

Eventually, Dan and his wife moved to Vermont where the University of Vermont accepted him into its graduate school to study Applied Mathematics.

But first, he took an accounting position at the Vermont Refugee Resettlement Program, which he considers "...one of the best experiences of my life." The organization helps refugees from war-torn countries, mostly in Africa, get settled in the US through the United Nations' High Commission on Refugees. While attending Vermont, he taught his own undergraduate course in Calculus, "...which was quite an experience. I wasn't a teaching assistant. I did everything myself, designed the tests, did all the grading."

He currently lives in New Jersey almost exactly where George Washington crossed the Delaware River on Christmas Night in 1776. Dan married his high school sweetheart, Jessica, whom he met in his sophomore year. They have two young children, a daughter named Maya, and a son, Luke.

"Most of my memorabilia from the Little League World Series I've put away," Brown related. "But I do have one interesting item that I've kept; it's a team picture from Williamsport that came from a McDonald's restaurant in Williamsport that was being renovated. Anyway, the manager of the place contacted Trumbull Little League and eventually the picture got to my brother, who gave it to me. It hangs in my office today. So, now, everyone in my office knows about it. I also put the Little League thing on my resume now, which is good; it serves as an icebreaker.

"I still have my uniform and a ball that we all signed, and a ball signed by the Taiwan team, and the glove I wore in that game, all set up in a big display case.

"I don't really follow sports all that much since we don't have TV in our home. Sometimes I'll watch something on the Internet. I run now, that's my hobby. But I do take my kids to different sporting events nearby.

Paul Coniglio

The son of John "Bugle Boy" and Kathy Coniglio, Paul stopped playing baseball after his sophomore year at Trumbull High to focus on soccer, where he earned recognition as an All-State goalkeeper. After graduating from Trumbull High School in 1995, Paul attended Trinity

UNLIKELY CHAMPIONS: A MIRACLE IN WILLIAMSPORT

College in Hartford, where he played four years as goalkeeper.
After graduating from Trinity in May 1999 with a degree in Economics and Political Science, Coniglio joined Conning & Company in Hartford as a stock analyst. Since then, he has worked for several companies in business development, business and strategic planning, and mergers and acquisitions. Paul co-founded Colony Grill Development LLC, the parent company of pizzeria Colony Grill, famous for its hot-oil pie, drizzled with jalapeño-infused oil. Besides that great pizza, [Author's Note: I've been there many times; the pizza is *terrific*!] the restaurant's décor features memorabilia from the 1989 Little League World Series championship.
 Paul never responded to any of my emails, and thus, this short profile.

Chris Drury
 If you really want to know what drives Chris Drury, just think about what he once told a reporter regarding what he and his teammates did in 1989: "My biggest memory is how much of an underdog we were. No one thought we'd do much once we got out of our district, and certainly no one dreamed we could win the whole thing. It's hard to get respect coming from the northeast in baseball. But doing something as a team that people say you won't be able to do has always been exciting for me. You look at the statistical chance of a team from our town...half of our town...winning it all, it's pretty amazing stuff."
 In an interview with *Connecticut Post*'s Chris Elsberry in 1994, Drury said, "The best thing was right when the game ended. It was like...30...40 seconds. The team and the coaches all piled on each other. There was no media, no families, just us. It was our celebration."
 Of course, who could tell that winning and success would become as much a part of Chris's life as they have? Success often follows when an individual's talent and hard work are supported by a cast of skilled teammates who accept the premise that hard work can overcome deficiencies in talent. Add in a measure of luck and good timing, and, voila, you have a winner.
 As Drury's best friend Ken Martin once said, "He's just a tough, quiet, humble kid who loves to compete and hates to lose. Then again, Chris doesn't lose too often."
 Imagine winning two national youth sports championships barely before you enter your teens, and within months of each other.
 Chris Drury did it.
 In April 1989, Chris led his Greater Bridgeport Pee Wee hockey team to the US Amateur American Hockey Championship in Chicago with a record of 64-2-1.
 Less than five months later, his Trumbull National Little League

team defeated Taiwan for the Little League World Series Championship. Imagine winning a high school state championship in hockey. Chris Drury did it.

As a freshman at Fairfield College Preparatory School (Fairfield Prep) in Fairfield, Connecticut, the Jesuits' hockey team won the Division I State Championship. In his four-year hockey career at Fairfield Prep, Chris scored 95 goals and provided 93 assists while leading the team as captain during his senior year.

In addition to his excellence on the ice, Chris also played and caught a good game of baseball at Fairfield Prep, mixing in some mound time as well as a few games at the hot corner. His baseball coach at Prep, Ed Rowe, called Chris "...a fierce competitor. I wish I had 18 kids like Chris on my team. He was a quiet leader...led his team by example...a smart player. When he entered Prep, he was part of the best freshman baseball team ever at Fairfield Prep."

Unfortunately, his baseball career took a turn when he broke his wrist before the start of the season his junior year at Fairfield Prep. Because he could not play baseball, Division I college teams didn't get the chance to properly evaluate his talent and recruit him during that most important period.

Years later, Fairfield Prep retired his hockey jersey number, 18, which his older brother Ted also wore at Prep – the only number retired in Fairfield Prep's hockey history. It hangs above the school's home rink, the Wonderland of Ice, in Bridgeport.

In 1994, *Connecticut Post* selected Chris as its "Athlete of the Year."

After graduating from Fairfield Prep in 1994, the Quebec Nordiques drafted Chris in the third round (72nd overall), the *second* high school player chosen in the draft that year. That fall, he headed to Boston to play hockey on a full scholarship for national powerhouse Boston University and its coach, the legendary Jack Parker, who possessed one of the best winning percentages of all time.

Imagine winning a national collegiate ice hockey championship. Chris did it.

In his freshman season, BU won the NCAA Division I Ice Hockey Championship. The Terriers also won four of four Beanpot Crowns [an annual tournament among Boston's four largest universities] during his four years.

Chris's 113 career goals top the list of all-time goal scorers at Boston University, while his 214 points place him third all-time. He is the first and only BU player to eclipse 100 goals and assists in a career. In both 1997 and 1998, Chris was named Hockey East's Player of the Year and a First Team All-American. He capped his collegiate career in 1998 when he earned the Hobey Baker Memorial Award, the recognition as the best college hockey player in the country.

Imagine winning the Stanley Cup in the National Hockey League. Chris Drury did it.

A few months after graduating from BU in 1998, Chris began his professional hockey career with the Colorado Avalanche [the Nordiques had relocated from Quebec to Colorado in 1995]. In his inaugural season, Chris earned the Calder Memorial Trophy as Rookie of the Year, and in 2001, the Stanley Cup included the etching of his name as a member of the NHL-champion Colorado Avalanche.

As of 2014, Chris stands as the only hockey player to have won both the Hobey Baker Memorial Award and the Calder Memorial Trophy.

His NHL career also included stints with the Atlanta Flames, Buffalo Sabres, and New York Rangers. After captaining BU as a senior, Chris also wore the captain's "C" for both the Buffalo Sabres (2005-2007) and the New York Rangers (2008-2011). When he signed as a free agent with the New York Rangers in 2007, he chose to wear No. 23 in honor of his childhood hero, former New York Yankees first baseman, Don Mattingly.

Chris played professionally for 12 years in the National Hockey League, ending his NHL career ranked 30th among American scorers, with 615 points, and fifth all-time in playoff-game-winning goals with 17.

After an injury-filled 2011 season, he hung up his skates one day before his 35th birthday on August 19, 2011 to spend more time with his wife, Rory, and their three children, and to focus more time on a business venture, the Colony Grill in Fairfield, which he co-owns with three of his Trumbull National teammates – Ken Martin, Cody Lee, and Paul Coniglio.

Playing for the United States Olympic Hockey team, Chris also earned accolades, winning a pair of silver medals – the first at the 2002 Winter Olympics in Salt Lake City, and the second in Vancouver at the 2010 Winter Games. Drury also earned a bronze medal at the 2004 World Championships in Prague.

The Peter J. McGovern Little League Museum Hall of Excellence in Williamsport enshrined Drury during the 2009 Little League World Series.

Matt Lindner, a writer for baseball fan website *The Outside Corner*, paid tribute to Drury's career in his August 19, 2011 perspective entitled "*Little League Legend Chris Drury Retires from the NHL*"... calling Drury "One of the greatest players in Little League..." and added, "There's a generation of baseball fans who will always remember him for that summer of 1989 as we crowded around the television sets in our parents' living rooms, watching Drury and his mates live out our childhood dreams."

Finally, Lynn Zinser, writing in *The New York Times*, described how life would be different for Chris in retirement, in a story entitled, "*A Reluctant Sports Star Discreetly Takes His Leave*"...

Retirement will finally allow Chris Drury to slide out of a spotlight that he never wanted but that he could never shake - one that found him when he was 12 years old. [He] once told me he learned his aversion to the spotlight when his Little League team returned home from Williamsport as champions. He was singled out as the star, but to him, he was just one of 15 boys who loved to play baseball. He learned to skirt attention by clamming up.

For reporters, Drury's reticence was maddening, because Drury was the ultimate clutch player. Of his 47 career playoff goals, 17 were game-winners. And he followed every one of them with at least one shrug and by foisting credit off on whoever passed him the puck.

'Chris is always in the right place at the right time, and that's not a luck thing,' Dave Galla, one of Drury's Trumbull teammates, told me when I wrote an article about them. 'But what he's done is nothing short of amazing. The greatest thing about him is his ability to remain a real person. He never lost touch with reality.'

Alas, the first time this author met Chris, he politely refused to grant me an interview. So, while I had hoped he would reflect on his Little League experience, and how it affected him, the life lessons he learned, and what advice he might provide to a 12-year-old about to take the field in Williamsport, that will not happen here. Maybe some other time…

While I am certainly disappointed we never had a chance to talk, I have chosen to honor his modest request for privacy. I had waited a long time to meet this special young man who had done so much in his 37 years, and had hoped to gain some insight into what makes someone who seemed to enjoy the pressure of a high-stress situation so much, so reticent.

Chris Fasano

The son of John and Mariann Fasano, Chris played soccer and hockey at Trumbull High School and went to Villanova University, where he earned his degree in accounting. He is a vice president with Lions Gate Entertainment Corp. (Lionsgate), a leading global entertainment company based in Santa Monica, California.

Chris also never responded to any of my email attempts to contact him. I had hoped to speak with this young man who has made accounting his career, as I have.

David Galla

David Galla, the son of Tom and Sandy Galla, is Vice President and Regional Manager for People's United Bank. He runs several of the bank's retail branch operations in Trumbull.

I met Dave quite unexpectedly early one morning at a breakfast fundraiser event at the Holiday Inn in Bridgeport. I immediately recognized him, having seen David in so many photos from clippings his dad had given to me. He looked much like he had in his youth, a great smile, athletic, but a lot taller. His People's United Bank logoed name tag confirmed my appraisal.

Dave remembered some moments from his post-Little League career...

"The next spring, you're no longer the underdog. Everybody wants to beat the kids from Trumbull. That carried through until I stopped playing baseball at 31. [Author's note: David returned to the diamond in 2014, once again playing in Bridgeport's Senior City League.] The adjustment for a kid from the Little League field to a big field is hard enough, but when you're adjusting and you've won a major championship the year before, it is even more difficult. There are expectations that you are going to be able to perform better than anybody else. Lucky for me, I played second base, so the transition was easier for me.

"I remember one game when I was a senior at New Haven where we played at Merrimack College. I was playing centerfield. There was a group of guys at Merrimack who would sit in centerfield with a cooler, and they would just harass anyone who played out there. So that day, I was their target. But I won that day. A friend of mine, who played for Merrimack, told everyone how I had played on the Little League World Series team, and I was abused all day. And it was great because I had a really good game. They just jawed at me about how this wasn't Little League anymore; they were just having fun. It wasn't a big deal. I had learned you just have to tuck your ears in, stay focused on the game. It happens everywhere in sports. I remember it happening all through high school and even in Senior City Baseball when I was 30. I mean, at what point does it go away? This happened when I was 12. What are we talking about here?

"I also played soccer, ran track, some basketball, but baseball is what I always gravitated to.

"I played shortstop my junior and senior years at Trumbull High for Jerry McDougall, who was a great coach, and filled in at second base and shortstop my freshman and sophomore years. I made All-State my senior year and played in the Connecticut All-Star game against Massachusetts at Fenway Park; we got crushed. I got to turn a double play in the game and scored our only run in the game. It was an awesome experience.

"I went to Marietta College in Ohio where I played freshman, JV, and varsity ball my freshman year, and started in the Division III College

World Series that year. I played third base, a position I had never played before, for the first time in the semi-finals of the Midwest Regional. I went into the game in the third inning, having never stood at the spot on a baseball field in my entire life. Luckily the first ball hit at me was hit so hard that it hit me square in the chest, I picked it up and threw it to first base. I played for Don Schaly like my father.

"I got a little burned out that year having played in over 100 games that spring, and I was far away from home. I had planned to transfer out of Marietta to the University of Connecticut. I was going to stop playing baseball, which would have been a bad idea. That summer I ended up played for Fedell's [in the Senior City League in Bridgeport] because my buddies were playing. Frank "Porky" Vieira [baseball coach at University of New Haven] came to a couple of the games, so I ended up transferring to the University of New Haven, which was a great decision. My junior year at UNH, we played in the Division II College World Series. Later, my buddies joked that I should transfer to a Division I powerhouse so I could say that I played in the Division III, II and I College World Series.

"I'm a Yankee fan, but now I'm a Red Sox fan between the sixth and eighth innings, because my buddy, Craig Breslow, pitches for the Red Sox. I missed hitting against him by one pitch in college, during the City Series [in New Haven] my senior year when Craig was a sophomore at Yale. We were playing Yale for the championship, and I had hit two home runs that day off their pitcher. It was the bottom of the seventh. As our leadoff batter stepped to the plate, Craig went down to the bullpen to warm up. I knew they were getting him ready for me, to set up a lefty-against-lefty matchup. I figured I was going to face Craig and he's going to make me look dumb. But our leadoff guy hit the first pitch for a single, and because Craig wasn't warmed up yet, I didn't face him. The next pitch I hit over the trees in right-centerfield for a home run. Then they brought Craig in. So I had three home runs and missed seeing Craig by one pitch. I caught Craig in Senior City ball for a while. He was awesome."

In 2007, the University of New Haven inducted Dave into its Baseball Hall of Fame. Highlights of his storied career include:

- David starred for the Chargers for three seasons, helping lead UNH to the NCAA Division II College World Series in 1998 and two City Series Championships.
- In his first season at UNH in 1997, Galla hit .426 in 25 games to earn First Team All-Conference and First Team All-Region honors. He would go on to earn two more All-Conference awards at UNH while playing different defensive positions each season.
- In 1998, he hit .389 with 10 doubles, two triples, 10 home runs and 46 RBIs as the team went 29-11-1 and made a run to the College World Series for the final time under Coach Vieira.

In 38 games as a senior, he drove in 61 runs – a school record that still stands as of his induction (2007) – mashing 13 doubles and 13 home runs.
- Galla finished his three-year career with a .373 batting average in 100 games, logging 126 RBIs, 31 doubles, five triples and 26 home runs. Galla ranks among UNH's all-time top 10 in career batting average, home runs, and RBIs, and was tied for second on the single-season home runs list with 13 in 1999.
- He was instrumental in the implementation of the Student-Athlete Advisory Committee, serving as its President for the first two years.

David serves on the Board of Directors of University of New Haven Alumni, as well as the Bridgeport Regional Business Council. He and his wife Traci have two boys, Cole and Sean, who, of course, love to play baseball.

Jason Hairston

Jason is the son of George and Indira Hairston.

"We moved to Rockville, Maryland the day before I started high school," Jason related. "I played high school ball at Good Counsel High School in Silver Springs, Maryland. I remember playing in a tournament [in Connecticut] the day before school was to start in Maryland, [I] hopped on a train, got in at one in the morning, and was in school the next morning at 7:00 AM. It was very, very tough, especially my first year. The only reason I was able to transition was sports. I played soccer at a high level, so I was able to transition quickly. I also played varsity baseball in high school for three years.

"I had a good baseball career in high school; we got to play in some championship games," Hairston commented. He was selected to the Second Team All-Montgomery County his junior year.

I went to Providence College [PC]. Kenny Martin was there, he recruited me. I started college a year later than the other guys since I took a year at West Point Prep Academy because I got an appointment to the Naval Academy and also to West Point.

While Jason may have been a better soccer player [he was recruited by several major colleges], his love of baseball, the atmosphere and location of Providence, as well as the reputation of its baseball program, attracted Jason to Providence College.

"At Providence College, we had a good team and won the Big East Championship in 1999, the last year Providence had a baseball team. The program was terminated due to Title IX, so I finished my college baseball career at Bryant College." [Author's note: The full story of how and why the Providence College baseball program was terminated is chronicled in Paul Lonardo's book, *Strike IX*.]

An interesting sidebar to this story is that Jason's Trumbull Little League teammate, Ken Martin, who played baseball at Providence for two years, helped break the story that told of the impending demise of the baseball program, when Ken was sports editor of the school's student newspaper, *The Cowl*.

The Friars' baseball website described Jason as a "speedy defender...a contact hitter who turns infield ground balls into hits...has the green light to run...makes things happen when he gets on base." As a sophomore, Hairston, the cousin of a family of major leaguers with the same surname, worked his way into PC's starting line up with a .339 batting average, while stealing 19 bases in 21 tries. He was also an excellent bunter, leading the team with eight sacrifices that year. Career-wise at PC, Jason batted an even .300, scored 80 runs in 120 games, and stole 30 bases in 35 attempts.

"Most of my memorabilia is at my parent's home in Maryland. There is lots of stuff, coats, shirts, jerseys, even a ring that they gave us, most of it stored under my bed..."

Jason has worked as an information technology and business solutions consultant with several major organizations over the past 15 years.

He currently coaches varsity baseball at Washington-Lee High School in Arlington, Virginia, and is a volunteer coach for the McLean, Virginia, American Legion. He maintains his connection with soccer by coaching a youth soccer team for six-to-nine-year-old boys and girls.

Jason, married, recently became a father. Even before the birth of his son, Jason wanted to show his new son how much his dad loved baseball. "I'm already starting to put baseballs in his crib, and getting him uniforms to wear," Jason laughed.

Todd Halky

Todd, the son of Bob and Betty Halky, played four years of baseball and wrestled while attending Trumbull High School. Todd threw out 10 runners in the 20 games he started as catcher his senior year.

He graduated from the University of Richmond, where he double-majored in Finance and International Business. His sister had gone to Richmond..."She paved the way. Also it was the best academic school I got into. I was picking academics above everything else. I knew since I was very young that I wanted to work on Wall Street. I got my first briefcase when I was 12. My dad and I had a baseball card business. I liked the money." Todd graduated cum laude in 1998.

"After college I knew I wanted to get back here [the northeast] to work in investment banking."

Todd's career played out much as he had planned since his youth, starting in corporate finance and internal financial reporting, as he eventually moved into a senior research analyst role with various hedge funds. He is currently starting his own hedge fund.

Todd is married with three children. He met his wife, who also attended Richmond, in New York City through a mutual friend. Their first date came about as the result of a bet they made based on baseball, the Yankees vs. Mariners playoff series in 2001. Todd would take *her* out if the Yankees lost and she would take *him* out if the Yankees won. "All I wanted was for her to go out on a date with me," Todd laughed. "It was a win-win either way."

Todd coaches his daughter in a softball league, and his four-year-old son plays T-ball. Their toddler is just getting warmed up...

Chris Kelly

The son of Michael and Kathy Kelly, Chris played shortstop at St. Joseph High School [Trumbull] and also on Trumbull's American Legion team. He captained the team his senior year. Chris then went to Catawba College in Salisbury, North Carolina, where the St. Louis Cardinals selected him in the 20th round of the Major League Baseball draft in June 1998, making Chris the only member of the 1989 Trumbull Little League champions to play professional baseball. From his diminutive 5-foot, 1-inch stature as a 12-year-old, Chris grew into a towering 6-foot, 3-inch, 210 lbs. professional baseball player.

Injuries limited Chris's career to 45 games and 156 plate appearances over three years with the New Jersey Cardinals of the New York-Penn League (1998) and the Peoria Chiefs of the Midwest League (1999 and 2000).

Chris owns Newtown Kitchen and Bath, a full-service kitchen and bath design and remodeling business in Newtown, Connecticut.

Unfortunately, Chris chose not to meet with me to talk about his experiences. He gave no specific reason other than that contained in his email response to my invitation: "Thank you for contacting me to discuss the Little League team. Although I do appreciate the offer, I really don't feel like I have anything to talk about. It was a great experience, but beyond that I don't have any stories to share or discuss. Sorry I could not be more help to you. Best of luck with the book."

Once again, I respect his choice and hope to someday sit down and chat with him. As a self-proclaimed baseball nut, I had so looked forward to meeting Chris. Maybe it will happen someday...

Cody Lee

Cody Lee, the son of Henry and Lory Lee, played hockey while at Trumbull High School, then attended Norwalk Community College upon graduation. He is a co-owner of Colony Grill and owns Cody Lee Masonry in Westport, Connecticut. I met Cody briefly at a golf tournament he played in with his brother. I do know that he is an excellent golfer and plays to a single-digit handicap. Cody and his wife Amie have one daughter. Unfortunately, Cody never responded to my emails. As the team's jokester, I had hoped to enjoy an afternoon with him reminiscing about the many pranks he pulled during the summer of 1989, as well as the remarkable game-saving play he made at the plate against Taiwan.

Harlen Marks
The son of Dave and Alice Marks, Harlen played tennis while at Trumbull High School, serving as team captain his senior year, playing as the team's No. 1. Harlen studied criminal justice at Sacred Heart University. He is the manager and a part-owner of Learning Express Toys in Darien, Connecticut, a specialty toy store. Harlen is married, and he and his wife Christine have two children.

I sent Harlen a couple of emails inviting him to share his memories, but never received a response. As a result I have little information about what he has done since 1989 or about what life lessons he may want to share about his experience.

Ken Martin
I met Ken Martin one afternoon when I stopped in at Colony Grill, a pizza restaurant-bar located on the Post Road in downtown Fairfield [about 10 miles south of Trumbull] that he manages and co-owns with three of his Trumbull buddies.

I spotted Ken quite easily, a lanky 6-foot, 3-inches-or-so, a tall, dark and handsome 30-something. Even as a 12-year-old in 1989, he stood the tallest kid on the team, so I knew it had to be him. The smile was the same one I had come to know in all those clippings the Galla's had collected. He hadn't changed much; he just stood a bigger version of the 12-year-old slugger. I walked up to him and introduced myself.

"Hi Ken, we've never met. I'm Chris Gallo." He smiled back at me quietly yet warmly, saying, "You're the one writing the book." I immediately knew I would like him.

Ken proved another of the guys who did not want to talk. In an email, he said, "I know you have spoken to many of the guys from the Trumbull team, and I wish you success with your book. But I would prefer not to speak further on- or off-the-record about my experience and memories from that time, which I certainly hold dear. All the best and thank you again for your email."

Nevertheless, I have found some of Ken's reflections about 1989 in other sources.

At the team's five-year gathering, Ken told a local reporter, "There was so much attention that it started to be a little too much after four, five months. But I think I appreciate it now even more than before. It's something I'll always have."

UNLIKELY CHAMPIONS: A MIRACLE IN WILLIAMSPORT

Ken Martin played baseball and basketball at St. Joseph High School and led the baseball team as its captain as a senior. He then enrolled in Providence College where he played baseball. Ken said, "I stopped playing baseball after two years at Providence College because I couldn't hit the slider. I realized there were players a lot better than me. I wasn't fooling myself."

After Ken graduated from Providence, he worked for NBC Sports and then he ran the online sports page for *The New York Times*, conducting interviews for the Olympics.

If I had known of his talents, I might have asked Ken to co-author this book. He is a terrific writer.

A January 2012 story in *Trumbull Patch* provided more details about Ken: "He's always wanted to be an entrepreneur. He said, 'I thought I would own and operate a business one day.' Martin started the Colony Grill with three friends from his Trumbull Little League days: Chris Drury, Paul Coniglio, and Cody Lee. Colony Grill serves pizza and refreshments."

Ken is the son of Kenneth and Donna Martin. Ken and his wife, Ailis, have five children.

Danny McGrath

The blond-haired, freckled leftfielder from Australia, the son of Daniel and Susan McGrath, almost didn't get to play in the 1989 Little League World Series. "I was born in Melbourne, Australia in '77. My father worked for the Australian Navy, overseeing the manufacture of helicopters at Sikorsky Aircraft in nearby Stratford. We spent a four-year stint in Washington, DC and then in the mid- to late-80's spent time in Connecticut...we stayed that summer of '89 purely because of the [All-Star] baseball team."

"This lot of kids, they kind of knew they could go somewhere," Danny's father told *Bridgeport Post-Telegram* writer Carole Burns. "I tried to hang around as long as possible so my kid could play on the all-stars. I don't think my son will participate in something as big as this again, not in Australia, and certainly not in baseball." Danny's mom, Sue said, "We wanted him to have the opportunity to play again."

Four months after Trumbull's win, the McGrath family did move back to Melbourne.

"I've got to take him home for speech therapy because he doesn't talk like me anymore," Danny's father said in his own Aussie-talk. As for his returning to Australia, Danny had mixed feelings, "I like it and I don't like it. I like it because I get to see my grandmother and my cousins, and I don't like it because I won't get to see my [American] friends."

"I left the country only a couple months after we won and so it was very easy for me to assume the life of a normal kid – moving to Australia meant that only a few people had even heard of the Little League World

Series. So I came here, went to high school at De LaSalle and played Aussie rules, basketball and baseball. I lived in Melbourne until I returned [to the US] at 18 to go to college. I stayed almost 13 years and got married."

Dan was named the best left-handed pitcher under 18 in Australia and played on the national U19 team that toured the world for six weeks and competed in the world championships in Canada. Dan also captained De La Salle's Australian Rules football and baseball teams.

"I played ball here in Australia and enjoyed it. I was fortunate enough to have a decent growth spurt by 15 and coordination came soon after. I represented my state every year in our national championships for six years straight and travelled the world on three occasions as a representative for our Junior National team...even caught up with some of the coaches when I played in an international tournament on the East Coast in the early- to mid-1990s.

"I played state-level baseball all my junior years and represented my country on four occasions, then played semi-pro ball as a teenager but as an amateur to maintain my status in our national league here called the ABL.

"I pitched at Fenway Park against Korea, caught up with a few guys in Cape Cod, so, Little League was my platform to start...and the next decade was pretty cool for me as I eventually earned an academic scholarship to play and pitch for the University of Minnesota Gophers, where I met my wife [Susan played volleyball at Minnesota for four years] and have been pretty much living my dream ever since...so you could say that the enjoyment that started in '89 has continued!"

Danny did a little more than simply play and pitch for Minnesota; he was selected Second Team Big Ten in 1998 and 1999 as a starting pitcher. The 1998 Gophers won the Big Ten tournament, compiling a 45-15 record, with Dan contributing six wins. He earned the "George Thomas Most Improved Player" award that year. In 1999, Minnesota was 46-17, while Dan went 6-0 and won the "David Chelesnik Scholarship Award."

"I was not drafted but offered a contract with a Minnesota independent league team in Duluth but passed as my interest in slugging it out was low and I wanted to move on with my life a bit. The goal to play professional ball had left me but I was very much interested in coaching, had been since I was 15; coached an U12 team.

"I moved back to Australia six years ago with my wife and eldest son, Caleb. We now have two more additions – Ethan (four), Kyle (two), and boy do they love their baseball. All three boys take part in the game at my local club, Sandringham Royals. I was the head coach for four senior men's teams before stepping down for family reasons...I now coach a men's team but I enjoy spending my Saturday morning running a T-ball program for four-to-seven-year-olds with over 60 participants from our area! My oldest, Caleb (eight), eats and sleeps the game – he and his brothers are with me almost every minute of a game, in their uniforms and we spend hours playing catch, hitting and enjoying the game."

Danny earned a degree in Psychology at Minnesota and later attained his Master's in Education. He teaches elementary school, grades 5 and 6 in Melbourne, going on 10 years.

"Love Aussie Rules Football – big fans over here of the game and my kids and wife, Susan, enjoy it, too. Our favorite team is the St. Kilda Saints and we are very passionate supporters...one of the best games invented and a true test of a man's skills and capacity to be athletic. We support the game at many levels (grassroots, local, and pro). Fishing, camping, off road dirt bike riding (only recent)...and just playing with my kids! I also played soccer for a couple years, basketball until 16, and Aussie rules footy!

"My trophies are still displayed in my childhood (parents') home...my kids get to see them when they visit. The ring – well, I keep that with me and only bring it out on special occasions – usually when I am asked to be a speaker at a local baseball function...Saving the ring for my boys to have when they get older.

"I met the love of my life in college...but we didn't go out until our junior year. Susan was a setter for the Gophers [volleyball team] from 1996 – 2000, playing alongside one of her sisters. Her two oldest sisters played basketball for the Gophers.

"Susan is a successful nurse in the largest and busiest hospital in our state here (Victoria) called the Alfred Hospital. She retired from volleyball and has joined our club's women's baseball team for a bit of fun and exercise. Plus it allows her to show off her own skills to her three baseball-mad boys!

"Simply put, my Little League experience has been part of my shaping as a person both with baseball and outside of it. While baseball does not define me as a person, it certainly has had a profound impact on who I am today...the people, the experiences, and things I have achieved because of baseball have been a positive and will be held dear to my heart. I only wish my boys will one day enjoy baseball and its simplicity the way I have – with respect and utter joy."

As summer approached in 2014, Dan and Susan, along with the boys, were packing for a move to Minnesota. Dan's email said, "Moving back to Minnesota...where my wife's family is...going to see if it is where we want to live permanently...time will tell."

While Little League officials could not confirm it, many believe Danny McGrath the first Australian to play in the Little League World Series, because no team from Australia played in Williamsport until 2013. [Author's note: The 2013 team from Perth Metro Central Little League in Australia finished 0-3 in their first appearance in Williamsport, losing to Mexico, Puerto Rico, and Corpus Christi, Texas.]

Andy Paul

The year following their championship, Andy played on a team for 13-year-olds coached by Tom Galla, but admitted "I really struggled with a shoulder injury and probably should have taken some time off from the game. I know Coach Galla was pretty frustrated with my play, as was I. It was really tough trying to follow up the dream year, especially playing on a regulation size field at 13 years old. Those bases are far apart and the mound is far from the plate at that age!"

Andy, the son of Kenneth and Holly Paul, played football, basketball, and baseball in high school, The Hopkins School in New Haven, but eventually hung up his spikes in college [Trinity College in Hartford] due to the bad shoulder that plagued him through middle school and high school. A few years after Bartlett Giamatti had passed away, his wife taught Andy 12th grade English at Hopkins.

"I was a good high school player and played with Ken Martin, Chris Kelly, Dave Galla, and a few other guys during the summer on the Trumbull American Legion team. It was a lot of fun to keep playing with some of the guys from when I was 10 and 11 all the way up to 18 years old."

Andy Paul played varsity football, basketball and baseball at The Hopkins School, hitting .392 with 18 RBI and had a 6-2 record with a 2.44 ERA and 37 strikeouts in 47 innings as a pitcher his senior year.

An American Studies major with an English concentration at Trinity, Andy graduated with Paul Coniglio. After college, Andy moved to Jackson Hole, Wyoming, for one year. He then moved back east and worked in the Philadelphia area for a minor league baseball team in sales and marketing as well as food and beverage, before moving back to Connecticut to work in baseball and sports marketing.

In 2005, Andy moved to South Carolina, his wife's point of origin, to work for the Greenville Drive, the Class A team for the Boston Red Sox. Andy met his wife, Beth, in Connecticut when she worked at the Arena at Harbor Yard in Bridgeport, Connecticut. After five years, ARAMARK offered Andy a position at Clemson University, helping manage the campus food/beverage operation, which handles the concessions for campus dining halls, retail, catering and vending, and athletic events at Clemson. "I love it and have been there ever since," Andy commented.

"My wife is the assistant general manager for a 15,000-seat arena in Greenville, South Carolina," Andy continued. They have two children, a daughter, Birdie, and a son, Marshall, so while he loves to play golf, Andy probably doesn't get much free time to do so. Both children "...played T-ball this past spring on the same team and will continue to play that, soccer and other youth sports."

Andy is a Phillies fan, and "...loves Clemson football and UConn basketball."

Matt Sewell

Matt Sewell, the son of Ed and Nancy Sewell, played four years of baseball at Trumbull High School and graduated with a 4.05 GPA, then went to Washington and Lee College in Virginia, and ultimately medical school. He is a cardiologist in suburban Philadelphia.

Coach Tom Galla

"In thinking back, most of what went on that summer did not involve great strategy or advice," Tom reminisced, "except when I had to go out to talk to Andy during the San Pedro game after they had hit all those home runs. I told him that '…it was no big deal' because I knew we could come back and score plenty of runs for him. I was trying to get him to look forward rather than dwell on the home runs he had just given up. Once he realized he started having some success with the dart pitch, he settled down and gained confidence. It was a big moment for him and the team. As coaches, we got them ready then let them play the game."

In a story in *The Marietta Times* the day before the championship game, Tom's college baseball coach, Don Schaly, remembered Tom Galla as "…a great hitter. He batted in the No. 3 slot here and drove the ball on a line. He was a great competitor and a great guy." From 1968 to 1970 Galla played second base, third base, and even caught occasionally for the Pioneers. According to Schaly, he even caught former major league reliever Kent Tekulve "a little bit."

Coach Galla made second team All-Ohio Conference as a second baseman in 1968 when he batted .415, and first team All-Ohio Conference in 1970 as a third baseman when he hit .393.

In the story, Schaly also said he was "…proud of Galla's Little League success but even prouder of his success in the business world."

When asked how he found all the time to run team practices and coach games that summer, Tom simply acknowledged the patience of his business partners and staff at Curtiss, Crandon & Moffette, Inc., who covered for him, thus allowing him to spend as much time as needed getting the Trumbull Nationals ready to take a trip to Williamsport.

EPILOGUE TWO

THE END OF THE TAIWAN DYNASTY

So what happened when the Taiwanese kids and their coaches returned to their island nation without the championship trophy?
 Did everyone celebrate them for having a successful season that saw them lose just one game? Did they get college scholarships, rewards, or other honors for all they had accomplished... or did everyone treat them poorly, because expectations ran so high? After all, getting to the Little League championship game is a fete in itself. How did their family, friends, and their community respond? Did their lives change after this loss?
 Did Trumbull's win really end the dynasty that Taiwan had established in Williamsport over the previous 20 years? The record will show that after 1989, Taiwan returned to the winner's circle in 1990 and 1991, and then again in 1995 and 1996; four titles in seven years; a pretty good record. In fact, Kaohsiung Little League won the 1996 championship, and remains Taiwan's last champion. Their drought now extends to 17 years.
 In order to understand the importance of baseball to the Taiwanese people, the following material provides different perspectives from which the reader can draw his or her own conclusions.
 An article in the August 15, 2013 issue of *Asia Life* written by Samuel Chi asked this question: **What Happened to Taiwan's Little League Champs?**

> They were once the most dominant team in their sport. They won nine championships in an 11-year span. Their 17 overall titles more than double the total of the next-best team. They were so dominant that on the rare occasion when they lose, it's considered an upset for the ages.

So are we talking about the New York Yankees? Montreal Canadiens? Yomiuri Giants? No. This is about Taiwan's Little League baseball teams.

The 67th Little League World Series begins Thursday in Williamsport, Pennsylvania, and Taiwan will once again have a representative in the 16-team tournament. But the Taiwanese are not the prohibitive favorites they once were. In fact, the 12-year-olds from Taoyuan might be a long shot to end Taiwan's 16-year championship drought.

Just what happened to Taiwan's Little League teams? Those boys of summer once won 31 straight games at Williamsport – including the 1973 champions from Taiwan that won its three games with a cumulative score of 57-0 while not allowing a single hit in the entire tournament. But since winning the 1996 tournament, a team from Taiwan has reached only one final, losing to Chula Vista, California, 6-3, in 2009.

Forget the oft-cited and baseless accusation that Taiwan once used overage players to achieve its feat. That was never the case. Full disclosure: This author played Little League ball in Taiwan in the golden age of the 1970's. The competition was so fierce that player eligibility was checked scrupulously in tournaments throughout the island. Little League Inc., did its own investigation in the '70s and found not one shred of irregularities.

Taiwan's one-time dominance can be best explained this way: Winning meant much more than just fun and games.

Taiwan's Little League success not coincidentally came at a time when the island was faced with a mounting diplomatic crisis. As Taiwan won its first Little League title in 1969, it was in the process of being kicked out of the UN, which preceded Nixon's landmark 1972 visit to China to normalize relations with the Communist mainland. When the US officially severed ties with Taipei to recognize Beijing in 1979, Taiwan's international isolation was complete.

In this crucible Taiwan's youth baseball dominance stood as a beacon in the island's uncertain future. Not just at the Little League level, Taiwanese teams also hoarded Senior and Big

League titles – with 17 championships apiece, the last also came in 1996. These teams' tournament games in America were broadcast live on state television in the island's wee hours. In the darkness you could hear wild cheering throughout the neighborhood with the blasting of firecrackers greeting each victory.

Taiwan was never known for athletic prowess other than the decathlon silver medal won by C.K. Yang in the 1960 Rome Games. Its Olympic profile is about as impressive as India's, with a few medals here and there in minor sports. But the success of the youth teams cemented baseball as the island's undisputed favorite pastime. Many of the Little Leaguers would go on to play professionally in Japan and Korea and later Taiwan's own pro baseball league, the Chinese Professional Baseball League (CPBL), founded in 1989. In the past decade or so, Taiwanese sluggers have started showing up in the US Major Leagues.

The island's passion for adult baseball, however, never matched its fervor for the kids in the 1970s and 80s, and it's easy to see why. The young boys were playing for much more than a sponsor and a paycheck; national pride was at stake. At the Little League World Series, they weren't playing for Taipei or Kaohsiung or 7-Eleven or Brother Hotel. They were playing for Taiwan.

With the advent of the "Chinese Taipei" moniker and the ban on the use of Taiwan's national flag at most international sporting events, Williamsport is one of the last places on earth where an ROC flag may be proudly unfurled and waved.

In the past, hundreds of Taiwanese expats and international students would regularly pack Lamade Stadium whenever their team was playing. For every ball-playing little boy in Taiwan, Williamsport was Shangri-La. But times have changed.

While Taiwan is still diplomatically isolated, its residents no longer feel a sense of impending doom, thanks to the rapid rapprochement with the mainland in recent years. The island's economy, booming since the late 1970s, has raised living standards to the point where Taiwan's per capita income (purchasing power parity) now exceeds that of the UK and

France.

With most of the island's population enjoying a comfortable life, the hunger for baseball glory waned. A dispute with Little League Inc., over the size of districts didn't help matters, as Taiwan withdrew from competition from 1997 to 2002.

During its absence, Taiwan's old rival Japan was once again ascendant. Japanese teams have appeared in 10 of the last 15 finals, winning five titles. Since their return in 2003, Taiwanese teams' inability to defeat Japan in Williamsport (as both teams are always in the same bracket) has been the chief reason for the prolonged championship drought.

This year's team from Taoyuan easily won the Asia-Pacific regional, going 7-0, though its recent predecessors have all done that, with little success once reaching Williamsport. Maybe this group of kids will finally end the 16-year drought. Maybe they won't. But win or lose, it's now just a game. And that's the way it should be.

Joseph Yeh, writing for *culture.tw* in July 21, 2009, put a historical perspective on Taiwan's changing Little League baseball legacy in an article entitled ***Age of Glory: Taiwan's Little League Hegemony of the '70s***. Yeh called it "The dawn of the Taiwan dynasty in Little League Baseball."

Taiwan joined Little League Baseball in 1969, when Taiwan's Chinese Baseball Association was convinced that the local baseballers were good enough to compete at an international level.

The purpose for dispatching local teams abroad, however, was not entirely to promote physical exercise; it was also for political reasons.

As pointed out by Junwei Yu, a National Taiwan Sports University professor, in his English-language book on Taiwan baseball history *Playing in Isolation: A History of Baseball in Taiwan* the then-ruling Kuomintang government realized that on the international stage baseball could become a 'powerful propaganda tool' to promote a state that was then being largely pushed aside by the resurgent People's Republic of China. As a result, baseball was given a mission: to use the sport to upgrade

Taiwan's international status.

Since the only mission of sending a team to compete in the Little League Baseball was to win, Taiwanese officials took the selection of players for the first-ever 1969 national team very seriously. The island authorities, whether intentionally or not, ignored the Little League Baseball regulation which stipulates that the teams representing an entire country must be formed on the basis of local communities.

The first-ever national squad, featuring nine players from the south, two each from the central and the east part of Taiwan and one from the north, was called Taichung Chin Lung, or Taichung Gold Dragon.

So, when the 1969 team won the Little League championship, the people of Taiwan were overwhelmed with delirious joy.

When the Gold Dragon players finally returned from Williamsport, they were greeted with an unprecedented eight-hour long parade on military Jeeps, sweeping across every major thoroughfare with more than half a million citizens filling the streets and lining the sides of pedestrian bridges just to witness the national heroes.

The celebration spread across the island.

The island-wide focus on the one hand made these student players national heroes and won them fame as well as fortune overnight. On the other hand, with all eyes upon these 10-year-olds as they were endowed with the sole mission to win the world championship, the children were all under unimaginable pressure.

A year later (1970) when the national championship team lost its opening game in Williamsport to Nicaragua, the whole nation was stunned.

The surprise later turned into fury, as many countrymen who watched TV or listened to the radio broadcast smashed their expensive televisions or radio to express their anger. Head Coach Wu Min-tien even offered an apology to the nation, saying 'how can we face the public after we go home?'

Taiwan returned in 1971 and 'promptly reclaimed the title that had been lost a year earlier, largely thanks to the superhuman performance of ace pitcher Hsu Chin-mu, who, despite facing another brilliant young hurler and later manager of the Pittsburgh Pirates, Lloyd McClendon, notched an amazing 21 strikeouts over nine innings.'

This championship 'was only the beginning of Taiwan's later hegemony over the Little League: over an 11-year period, Taiwanese boys were unstoppable, winning 31 straight at Williamsport.'

As Yu noted in his baseball history book, the Little League Baseball championships "completely altered baseball, which children, parents, schools, the public, and the government now perceived as a means to an end, not an end in itself. Fueled by world championship mania and state support, Taiwan reached a point at which players became playing robots."

Still, one cannot deny that it was the strong base that Taiwan built during that period that resulted in the transformation of the small island nation into one of the top baseball strongholds in the world.

With this solid foundation, the seed of baseball continued to flourish in the land, finally giving birth to Taiwan's own professional baseball league in 1990.

EPILOGUE THREE

CONGRATULATORY LETTERS

In the weeks following their triumph in Williamsport, congratulatory letters arrived at the Galla home from *everywhere*. A sampling follows...
"...it took the *Boys of Trumbull* to show and remind America of the essence and beauty of the Great American Game...baseball." – Tom Sepio, Meriden, Connecticut
"Their courage and class in the face of enormous odds is an inspiration to us all. Their efforts not only brought them the joy of achieving their goal but also brought together the entire town." – Jim Hoffman, Chairman of the Trumbull Community Prevention Council
President George H. W. Bush, who would host the team at a Rose Garden reception in November, wrote:

> It gives me great pleasure to offer my warmest greetings and heartfelt congratulations to the players, coaches, and supporters of the Trumbull, Connecticut, Little League Team, for winning the Little League World Series.
>
> All of you can be justifiably proud of an accomplishment that has brought such acclaim to your team, your town, and your country. Hours of practice, teamwork, and good sportsmanship are directly responsible for bringing you to the Little League World Series.
>
> The team from the Far East was a formidable opponent and a worthy title holder, but it's great to have the trophy back in America. I proudly join all my fellow citizens in saluting you for representing our nation and our young people in such an exceptional manner.
>
> Mrs. Bush joins me in sending best wishes for every future

UNLIKELY CHAMPIONS: A MIRACLE IN WILLIAMSPORT

success, both on and off the baseball diamond. God bless you.

A Western Union Mailgram from Connecticut's Governor William O'Neill said, "On behalf of the State of Connecticut I want to congratulate the entire Trumbull Little League team on your outstanding achievements. Everyone is thrilled."

US Senator Joseph Lieberman sent a congratulatory letter when they won the US title, "I want to extend my sincere congratulations on winning the United States Championship. Your 6-3 win over San Pedro, California was most impressive. All of Connecticut's good wishes go with you as you face Kaohsiung, Taiwan. Remember, hard work and determination are the tools of victory!"

A few days before his untimely passing, Commissioner of Baseball, A. Bartlett Giamatti sent this telegram:

> Dear team
>
> As your neighbor, I would like to congratulate each of you and your community on the occasion of your wonderful win in the Little League World Series.

Bobby Valentine, Manager of the Texas Rangers, and a native of Stamford, Connecticut, wrote:

> Dear Coach Galla and the Boys of Summer:
>
> Congratulations on an outstanding year! Yesterday, you inspired and enabled your town, state and this great country to share in your field of dreams. Thank you.
> (P.S., Where did you guys learn to spit like that?)

Bob Schaefer, a Norwich, Connecticut, native and a coach with the Kansas City Royals, sent this letter:

> Dear Players, Coaches, and Parents,
>
> Congratulations on winning the Little League World Series. You have accomplished a tremendous feat and have brought a great deal of pride to the United States and the state of Connecticut.
>
> We watched the last three innings of the championship game here in the clubhouse in Kansas City. George Brett, Bo Jackson, Bret Saberhagen and most of the other players and coaches were cheering every move you made.
>
> It gave me a great deal of pleasure knowing a team from my home state was playing as well as you did. I know it had to be a great thrill for all of you involved as I

remember my Little League days in Fairfield, although we were not nearly as successful as you.

Best of luck to each and every one of you and hopefully, some day some of you will watch a Little League World Series in a Major League clubhouse.

Another example of how the Trumbull Little Leaguers captured the hearts and attention of fans everywhere took the form of a letter that Tom Galla received, a few days after returning home, from Mrs. Scottie Parrish of Lancaster, PA. She wrote:

Dear Mr. Galla:

CONGRATULATIONS!

What a game! What a great team! What a triumph! I do believe the entire country was rooting for you. Thought you and your players would enjoy adding the enclosed story to your scrapbook. The sidebar story on the reverse side tells you the "big boys" were rooting for you also.

Enclosed with Mrs. Parrish's letter was an article from her local newspaper highlighting the previous day's Major League Baseball action...

Somehow, the underdogs always stick together. So was it any surprise the Baltimore Orioles celebrated their latest victory by cheering for an upset in the Little League World Series? The improbable Orioles got both their wishes on Saturday. They beat the New York Yankees 6-4 on two solo home runs by unlikely cleanup hitter Joe Orsulak (14 career homers in over 1,500 major-league at-bats) and then gathered around the television set and loudly rooted as the Trumbull, Conn. kids stunned Chinese Taipei.

Until that game, no Orioles cleanup hitter had gone yard in over three weeks.

Another note that Tom Galla received came from Milton Goldsmith of Scottsdale, Arizona:

Dear coaches and managers:

I had never heard of Trumbull and I didn't know where they were. But I do <u>now</u> – Right on top of the world! Congratulations to you, your staff, and a well-coached bunch of kids!

UNLIKELY CHAMPIONS: A MIRACLE IN WILLIAMSPORT

From Marblehead, Massachusetts, Joe Ryan, "former Coach, Manager & President" wrote, in part:

Dear Tom,

Congratulations to you, your staff, your team, your town. I started writing this in the fifth inning and am so glad I am able to mail it.

I have felt so sorry for these American kids playing their hearts out, only to lose by a 21-0, etc.

These kids have only a couple of months to prepare for the L.L World Series, where the kids from the Far East, when recruited, move, their parents offered jobs, housing, etc., anything to get the child near the action and it is so totally unfair to our kids.

Pass my best wishes to Kenny Martin, shades of 1951 and Bobby Thompson of the N.Y. Giants and to Chris Drury, hope he keeps that tooth separation that allows him to effect that spit and to all the other players on your great team.

You and they are right up there with the 1951 N.Y. Giants, the 1980 Olympic Hockey Team and the 1969 Mets...the Lone Ranger, Superman, Batman and Hopalong Cassidy.

Chris Drury's future baseball coach at Fairfield Prep, Edward Rowe, wrote,

Dear Tom,

I would imagine that, by now, you and your players have been congratulated in more ways than any of us ever dreamed of, but I wanted to extend my personal sentiments of admiration, praise, and gratitude for all that you have accomplished.

After 25 years of experience I am convinced that only fellow members of the coaching fraternity (and their <u>wives</u>, of course) can fully understand and appreciate the emotions that a wonderful group of youngsters can engender by their effort and friendship.

Your leadership, example, and inspiration were certainly vital elements on the road to your team's success. You demonstrated to the world what <u>real</u> coaching is all about!

CHRISTOPHER GALLO

I guess you don't have to be told this but here it goes anyway – Take a deep breath, relax, and enjoy it – Carpe Diem.

Thank you for all you've done for the kids. They <u>always</u> come first.

You really <u>are</u> #1!!!

P.S. Your son did a marvelous job in a difficult situation. (I know – my son, Eddy, played for me at the Prep.) Give him my best!

Another letter to Tom Galla from Clyde Collins, General Manager of Aetna's Commercial Insurance Division in Trumbull said, in part,
Dear Tom:

Congratulations to the Tommy Lasorda of Little League!

You and your guys were great, as watching the game on TV brought back memories of the US Hockey victory over Russia in the '80 Olympics.

Eleven year-old Adam Schupak of Willow Grove, Pennsylvania, wrote, in part

Dear Trumbull, CT Little League Champs,

Congratulations on winning the Little League World Series and bringing the title back to the USA. The game was great.

Did you enjoy your post game swim? Instead of saying "I'm going to Disney World" like Frank Viola and Joe Montana your team said, "We're going to the pool." Here are some of my game's best and funniest votes:

Player: Chris Drury and Ken Martin
Throw: Dan McGrath
Closest play: At 3rd base
Funniest play: When Dave Galla fell down (It was a tough play and I am not taking anything away from him)
You don't see it every day: When Chris Drury was stepped on at first and when Cody Lee was safe on two errors (Was that a record?)

How does it feel to win a title? Do you like all the publicity or are you thinking, "It was nice, but school starts in a week and I want to get on with my life?"

UNLIKELY CHAMPIONS: A MIRACLE IN WILLIAMSPORT

Joseph Bellman's note as President of the Ocean Springs, Mississippi National Little League was simple, "Good for You! Congratulations on a job well done. We are proud of you." The note was signed by the league's entire leadership team.

A fan from West Haven, Connecticut, Paul Edwards, composed his letter as the game progressed,

> I am watching, as the game is in progress, and I find myself drawn into the intensity of competition as never before. (Aside from when I played hockey.)
>
> I am compelled to... (excuse me Cody just got hurt) say to you how truly thrilling it has been to follow your team's progress to the final of the LLB WS.
>
> I have a son in LLBB. And will have two in it next year.
>
> It is, without a doubt, a most fulfilling... (Ken just hit a home run) experience to see young children have <u>fun</u> at what they do, and a notch higher to see Trumbull in the finals.
>
> My hat is off to you. My compliments and kudos. (Whether you win or not you have done a, or have had the opportunity to be a part of, a wonderful thing.)
>
> (Please excuse this hastily written note, but it is proper that it has been written on my lap on a piece of paper from my son's notebook.)
>
> It's the 6th...1 out...2 outs...THREE!
>
> You have succeeded and tears of joy are streaming. Congratulations!
>
> Please pass along very happy congratulations to all of the team members and coaches.
>
> (It's not just Trumbull that's proud of you.)

Henry Sacks of Camp Springs, Maryland, said, "Thank you – for the thrill your wonderful team gave me and millions of other Americans across the country last week. It's been a long time since anything on TV made me feel this good!"

Frank Marshall, Jr., of Pompton Lakes, New Jersey, wrote,
Dear Mr. Galla

> May I add my best wishes to the millions who already have on your team's victory over Kaohsiung, Taiwan.
>
> I guess you got the bats you needed as you stated in the pre-game interview. I applaud you on your composure

during the game, and the way you handled the team.

Again, great job! Thanks for bringing some more pride to America, and putting Trumbull on the map!

P.S. I was an alternate on the 1965 New Hyde Park, Long Island Little League team who lost to Windsor Locks.

Finally, Tom received this note from a former Marietta College teammate, Al Witmer, of Harrisburg, Pennsylvania:

> Congratulations on your managing the Trumbull Little Leaguers to the Little League World Series Championship!
>
> The kids you coached demonstrated a lot of the characteristics of the guy I remember from Marietta College's Baseball Program: lots of poise, character, hustle, and toughness, as well as a great sense of the way the game is supposed to be played. You and your assistants did a great job.
>
> It was funny how I saw your team beat Taiwan on Saturday. I had just come home from coaching and playing for a Fast-pitch Softball team...Four of us had pulled hamstrings, two others hurt their knees, but still, I was feeling pretty good. But then, to be able to turn on ESPN, crack open a nice cold beer and see an old teammate take those kids through the Taiwan Team; I was very, very happy for one of the nicest guys I ever met at Marietta.
>
> Tom, congratulations again!

EPILOGUE FOUR

THE SPORTS WRITING COMMUNITY CELEBRATES THE VICTORS

In the days and weeks following their upset of Taiwan, the team was recognized in newspapers across the country for what they had accomplished. Here are a few of the many:
Trumbull's weekly newspapers chimed in with their congratulatory editorials to welcome the boys back.
The *Trumbull Times* printed this editorial, with the title "*Keeping Perspective*":

> Do we congratulate our Little League champions or do we thank them? We suggest a little of both.
>
> The way those 15 youngsters and three coaches made a town feel is almost indescribable. Trumbull feels good, prideful. We don't have to know them personally to be part of it. Who knows why... or cares?
>
> Coach Tom Galla wants us to care beyond the game. Galla knows that for most, fame is fleeting. "I think we have to help them get back to their normal routine," he said. "This isn't going to pay their bills. This isn't going to put them in the major leagues."
>
> Galla's call to "be kind to them...help them get back down to earth," is not culled from something without precedent. Many sad stories have been relayed about kids who became stars and could not handle it...
>
> Early indications are that the champs will remain kids for the foreseeable future. Galla and his assistants, Ed Wheeler and Bob Zullo, special, yet regular people themselves have strived

to make that happen.

The return to school will be an acid test. Will the kids draw their fame like a loaded revolver to impress fellow students or to cut corners in the classroom? Will other students play up to them too much, leaving little room to breathe the oxygen below the clouds?

Galla's handling of the team was lauded by Henry Lee, father of catcher Cody Lee. "No one could have done a better job keeping level heads on these kids," declared Lee. "It was like he had been through all of this before."

So until we have reason to question whether this whole experience has been good, and we don't think we ever will – the appreciation of your home town, the state, the nation, and everyone who ever stepped out on a pockmarked, overgrown, and disfigured baseball field in the sweltering summer heat – is now given to you, Trumbull Nationals. Thanks, a lot. It sure has been great.

On the same day, the other local weekly newspaper, *The Trumbull Reporter*, printed a *"Viewpoint"* column written by Editor Alan Olenick, entitled *"**Trumbull restores our faith in baseball**."* Excerpts from that editorial follow:

Unbelievable.

That was the word on most people's lips on Sunday as Trumbull showed its spirit in recognition of the Trumbull National Little League team which just captured the LLWS.

As most people, I watched the game on ABC-TV on Saturday afternoon. I cringed when I heard the announcers say these kids were the underdogs.

I had, on good word from Sports Editor Jim Fuller, that this team not only had a chance to win, but that there weren't many teams that they couldn't beat. He should have known, he was with the team in the Eastern Regionals in Bristol and in Williamsport, Pa., since their first game Tuesday.

His prognostication came on Tuesday – long before any other media started to believe in this dream team.

What made this win special went far beyond the fact that these young men ended a string of losses for America in the Little League World Series.

These kids were the ones who made the win special.

UNLIKELY CHAMPIONS: A MIRACLE IN WILLIAMSPORT

They were classy, good sports, gentlemen, gutsy, determined, and, most of all, excited for the nature of the sport.

Trumbull also has to be credited with getting involved with the same type of excitement in rooting on the team.

On Sunday, the streets of Trumbull were lined with people as the two buses which carried the team made their way through town.

Team Manager Tom Galla also deserves much credit for the way the team handled the pressure both on and off the field.

Galla wanted the team to enjoy the time they had but he wanted them to lead healthy, normal lives.

In one aspect that has to be noted, the game and festivities came on the heels of one of the biggest blots in the game of baseball in the fact that Pete Rose was suspended from baseball last week.

There used to be a time that we could tell these kids that we hoped they grew up just like Rose.

Now we'll have to clarify it by telling them that they could emulate his talents as a player, but certainly not the other aspects of his career.

The boys of Trumbull certainly restored our faith in the game and in youth in general.

Their triumph is something we all can share in. These young men certainly made all of our lives a little more special.

Norm Frauenheim of *The Arizona Republic* wrote a column entitled *"Remembering what baseball is all about,"* excerpts of which follow:

Scandal is not the American pastime. A bunch of kids proved it Saturday. They provided a reason to cheer. Actually, they did much more. A Little League team from Connecticut scored a huge victory for everybody sick of Pete Rose.

Baseball took a huge beating last week. The lousy flap, Rosegate, was enough to chase a lot of people out of the ballpark into a bomb shelter.

Then, a team of 11- and 12-year-old boys from Trumbull, Conn., arrived. Their victory in the Little League World Series was a welcome reminder that our field of dreams has not turned into a nightmare.

Trumbull beat Taiwan.

The Trumbull gloves might have been made in Taiwan. The uniforms could have come from Hong Kong. Those shoes might have been Japanese. The shin guards might have come from Seoul and the scoreboard from Singapore.

I don't want to know where those aluminum bats were produced. The sport would be better served if all that aluminum was turned into foil.

For once, only the score mattered. USA 5, Taiwan 2.

Most Americans either have played Little League, or have somebody in the family who has. It's our game as no other is. But for some reason, Taiwan has dominated [in recent years]. For me, the long string of defeats had become intolerable. I just couldn't figure it.

But Trumbull's victory made an important difference at the end of a week full of bad news.

Baseball is the picture of Trumbull pitcher Chris Drury leaping in celebration.

Hubert Mizell, a sports columnist in St. Petersburg, Florida, expressed his thoughts in a wonderful, tongue-in-cheek column for the *St. Petersburg Times* the morning after the win, entitled "***Little League win was wet and wonderful.***" Here's some of what he wrote:

> At last, in baseball, the 'spitter' is legal. But instead of 'loading up', Chris Drury kept 'unloading' before every pitch. His mom cringed, but I loved the kid. Heroic, crew-cut, expectorating Chris was a young'un straight off a Norman Rockwell canvas. Disgustingly adorable...
>
> For years, Far East teams had been too strong, too experienced, and too skilled. But, for a change, the Far East representative had no gangling, overpowering, 75-mile-an-hour fastballer to torch whatever Yankee opposition. The minute you saw Taiwan's 86-pound Chien-Chih Lee, and his submarine pitches not so unhittable, it was clear the kids from Trumbull, Conn., had a real chance...
>
> Inning after inning, Chris would stand on the mound, look to his catcher for a sign, then send two or three salivary missiles flying before delivering an effective pitch...
>
> Somehow in a moment so extraordinary, in a setting so angelic, not even the most fastidious parent could fuss. Chris Drury's nervous habit, at age 12, was no more objectionable than such juvenile properties as smelly sneakers, messy bedrooms, and

undone homework...

What's important is that Christopher and his buddies from Trumbull, an idyllic town of 34,000 characterized by $300,000 homes and $100,000 family incomes, were shattering the iron jaw of an almost-undefeated world champion. And enjoying the fruits of athletic competition as we too seldom see...

The reward for Chris Drury, and his huggable co-conspirators, is to stride proudly into sixth- and seventh-grade classes. To be heroes before peers...

It was good, for a summertime Saturday, to be away from Jose Canseco, Ozzie Smith, Wade Boggs, Dwight Gooden and their ultra-rich kind. To be instead looking over the right shoulder of Chris Drury. Williamsport was his Fenway, his Shea. A field of dreams, slightly moistened and terribly heroic...

The Chicago Tribune acknowledged the win with an editorial a few days later entitled "***In a matter of honor, Trumbull wins.***"

The good thing about the Little League World Series is that they take the 'world' part semi-seriously – unlike the Big League World Series, which presumes that the world ends after Toronto and Montreal.

The bad thing is that the United States doesn't win nearly as many Little League World Series these days as it does the Big League World Series. In fact, up until last Saturday, the Americas – whose ancestors not only invented baseball but also made a religion of it – had not vanquished foreign pretenders to the cherished crown since 1983.

And that continuing humiliation was imposed in spite of our having the good sense to give ourselves an edge by putting four U.S. teams in the eight-team annual tournament at Williamsport, Pa. Some edge. The last decade has been dominated by an assiduously cultivated baseball dynasty in Taiwan, which has produced a run of teams that have looked capable of at least holding their own in the American League East.

But a 5-foot, 1½-inch, 126-pound right-handed pitcher named Chris Drury, who throws junk – a curve, change-up and knuckleball – and his bunch of Little League All-Stars from Trumbull, a Connecticut city of 35,000, have put an end to that.

After knocking off Davenport, Iowa, and San Pedro, California, the Trumbull kids went into the final game of the 43rd Little

League World Series against Taiwan, which was after its fourth straight championship. But Trumbull wanted it bad. And they won, 5-2.

'These guys don't know how to lose,' their manager said. 'They didn't care who they were playing.' Sound familiar Cubs?

The morning after their victory, a *Bridgeport Post-Telegram* editorial page commentary entitled *"Trumbull's Little League and its triumph of 'heart'"* congratulated the team with these words:

> The so-called experts said it couldn't be done...the Trumbull National All-Stars [were] underdogs. But [they] did more than perplex the pundits. They shined."
>
> We take this opportunity to congratulate each and every one of the Trumbull players for their impressive accomplishments and for reminding us all that – no matter what the pundits say – you've got to have heart."

A week later, on Friday, September 1, 1989, *Bridgeport Post-Telegram* printed a 56 page Special Section, boldly titled "**CHAMPS!**" The pages included congratulatory ads from local merchants and businesses, numerous stories about the players and what they had done, and so many great photographs [including the cover photo which I have used with permission on the cover of this book] that it will forever evoke wonderful memories of an event witnessed by so many.

Fairpress (Fairfield, Connecticut) posted an editorial "*World-class kids do Trumbull proud*" that said (in part):

> What a terrific story.
>
> Fifteen kids defy the odds and all the predictions to triumph in a world-class event. They were told they could be giant killers, and they came through.
>
> Overcoming team after team...the Trumbull ballplayers took the world championship from a team of Taiwanese youngsters who had outplayed their other rivals by commanding margins.
>
> Through it all, team manager Thomas J. Galla and coaches Edward Wheeler and Robert Zullo displayed poise and confidence that obviously influenced the kids they led. What a great contrast to the mad-dog Little League parents who goad and drive their players, ruining the joy of competition and the self-esteem of the child athletes in their charge.
>
> Watching the Trumbull kids batting, fielding, pitching, it was

evident they were *enjoying* themselves. Wiggling the bat as they awaited a pitch, working hard on a wad of chewing gum or settling easily under a fly ball, the all-stars played a solid, cool game of baseball and brought home the World Championship.

The adulation of their hometown and the attention of national and local news reporters have been calmly and graciously accepted and enjoyed.

Because Galla recognizes that the all-stars will return…to a more mundane world, he came up front very early to ask his town's help bringing the boys back down to earth. This attention to the kids' sense of self – and the lasting values of discipline, commitment and modesty – is so important.

And it's part of the joy of Trumbull's experience that its children are learning these lessons.

Congratulations Trumbull.

APPENDIX

UNLIKELY CHAMPIONS: A MIRACLE IN WILLIAMSPORT

1989 Trumbull National Little League All-Stars
Starting line ups

Date	Game vs.	#1	#2	#3	#4	#5	#6	#7	#8	#9
July 15, 1989	Stratford National	Drury	Hairston	Basztura	Martin	Paul	Brown	Sewell	McGrath	Galla
July 17, 1989	Stratford American	Drury	Galla	Basztura	Martin	Paul	Brown	Sewell	Halky	Hairston
July 22, 1989	North End East	Drury	Galla	Basztura	Martin	Paul	Brown	Kelly	Sewell	Hairston
July 25, 1989	Fairfield American	Drury	Galla	Basztura	Martin	Paul	McGrath	Halky	Sewell	Hairston
August 1, 1989	Park City American	Drury	Hairston	Basztura	Martin	Paul	Marks	Brown	Sewell	Galla
August 3, 1989	Park City American	Drury	McGrath	Basztura	Martin	Paul	Brown	Halky	Kelly	Sewell
August 6, 1989	Forestville	Drury	McGrath	Basztura	Martin	Paul	Brown	Lee	Sewell	Kelly
August 8, 1989	Hamden	Drury	Halky	Basztura	Martin	Paul	McGrath	Brown	Sewell	Hairston
August 13, 1989	Forestville	Drury	McGrath	Basztura	Martin	Paul	Brown	Galla	Kelly	Hairston
August 15, 1989	Swanton, Vermont	Drury	Halky	Basztura	Martin	Paul	Brown	McGrath	Galla	Hairston
August 16, 1989	Manchester, New Hampshire	Drury	Galla	Basztura	Martin	Paul	Brown	McGrath	Lee	Hairston
August 17, 1989	Cherry Hill, New Jersey	Drury	Halky	Basztura	Martin	Paul	Brown	Kelly	Galla	Hairston
August 19, 1989	Brandywine, Delaware	Drury	McGrath	Basztura	Martin	Paul	Brown	Kelly	Galla	Hairston
August 22, 1989	Davenport, Iowa	Drury	Halky	Basztura	Martin	Paul	Brown	McGrath	Galla	Hairston
August 24, 1989	San Pedro, California	Drury	Hairston	Basztura	Martin	Paul	Brown	McGrath	Lee	Galla
August 26, 1989	Kaohsiung, Taiwan	Drury	Basztura	Martin	Paul	Brown	McGrath	Galla	Lee	Hairston

1989 Trumbull National Little League All-Stars
Final Statistics

Batting Statistics

Player Name	AB	R	H	RBI	AVG	2B	HR	BB	K	OBP
Chris Drury	54	26	29	19	0.537	10	6	8	2	0.597
Dan McGrath	28	12	10	8	0.357	4	0	12	6	0.550
Matt Basztura	48	22	20	15	0.417	5	4	9	16	0.509
Ken Martin	48	27	27	36	0.563	3	11	13	6	0.656
Andy Paul	42	17	20	24	0.476	1	9	10	10	0.577
Dan Brown	43	7	11	16	0.256	2	2	7	6	0.360
Cody Lee	20	8	6	4	0.300	1	0	4	8	0.417
Todd Halky	25	8	10	7	0.400	1	0	4	1	0.483
David Galla	29	8	10	4	0.345	0	0	3	8	0.406
Chris Kelly	21	7	8	5	0.381	2	0	6	5	0.519
Harlen Marks	15	5	2	1	0.133	0	0	4	4	0.316
Jason Hairston	26	9	8	8	0.308	1	1	8	3	0.471
Paul Coniglio	8	4	3	2	0.375	0	0	2	4	0.500
Chris Fasano	2	1	1	0	0.500	0	0	1	1	0.667
Matt Sewell (a)	16	9	8	3	0.500	0	0	9	2	0.680
Team totals	425	170	173	152	0.407	30	33	100	82	0.520

Pitching Statistics

Pitchers	IP	H	R	ER	ERA	K	BB	Record
Andy Paul	46.7	42	16	13	1.67	56	10	7-1
Chris Drury	42.7	34	19	16	2.25	54	27	8-0
Matt Basztura	3.3	0	2	0	0.00	4	3	0-0
Matt Sewell (a)	1.0	0	0	0	0.00	3	1	0-0
Dan McGrath	1.3	5	1	1	4.51	1	0	0-0
Chris Kelly	1.0	1	2	0	0.00	0	2	0-0
	96.0	82	40	30	1.88	118	43	15-1

(a) Matt Sewell replaced by Chris Fasano on August 9, 1989 due to injury.

ACKNOWLEDGMENTS

It's crazy how ideas can hit you right between the eyes, like the evening I came up with the idea for this book. It was a beautiful summer evening a few years ago. Several of us were enjoying a drink and dinner after a round of golf at Brownson Country Club in Shelton, Connecticut, when I invited Tom Galla to join us at the table. After introducing him to the other guys, I mentioned that he had been the coach of the 1989 Trumbull Little League team. Eventually, the conversation turned to what a great baseball story it was, when I asked Tom why he had not written a book about what this team had done. He shrugged, and then I asked, "Would you mind...?" So, that's how the idea for this book started.

Tom, you have been terrific to work with. You are patient, thoughtful, courteous, energetic, emotional, and so proud to share this story.

Without access to Tom's extensive file of newspaper and magazine clippings and his videos from the Brandywine, San Pedro and Taiwan games, this story may never have been told. He has some amazing stuff in those boxes in his basement. Thanks Tom!

The material I found in those boxes of clippings was the basis for this book and included articles from newspapers, big and small, throughout Connecticut and around the US, including *Bridgeport-Post Telegram, The Hartford Courant, Bristol Press, The Waterbury Republic-American, The Trumbull Times, The Trumbull Reporter, The Boston Globe, Daily News* and *The Williamsport Sun-Gazette*. I had found Blackbeard's treasure.

And thank you Sandy Galla for allowing me to intrude on your life as well. How often did I stop in to ask questions, share stories or just enjoy those great photographs you took 25 years ago? I bet you never thought they would be published. Thank you for sharing your memories as well.

Likewise, their son David, who is a real "chip off the old block," has been just as ready, willing and able to help every time I called. There is no doubt it would have been more difficult to find everyone without your help, David. Maybe it's your role as the coach's son, but you have done a remarkable job of keeping in touch with all your former Little League teammates.

David was also very generous with his time, sitting down to tell his story, or at least what he could remember about that summer and the years that have transpired. David, I know you doubted your memory, but it's still working well. Thanks! You have made a real difference!

I am also so grateful to the other members of the 1989 champions who have blessed me with their time either by sitting down to speak with me about what happened during that summer and the years since, or by

UNLIKELY CHAMPIONS: A MIRACLE IN WILLIAMSPORT

responding via emails to my list of questions, and then to many follow up questions. I have learned so much about what it takes to be a champion, how to handle all the stuff that happens afterwards, and continues to this day, and about how their lives were impacted. I thank Todd Halky, Andy Paul, Dan Brown, Jason Hairston, Matt Sewell and Dan McGrath, as well as David Galla, for opening my eyes to what this story was really all about. You have made it clear that this story, *your* story, is probably the biggest story to hit Trumbull in years. And it is one of the most inspirational stories in youth sports, ever.

    Ed Wheeler, who I consider the forgotten man, thank you for your time! Your memories helped me more than you probably thought they would. I call you the forgotten man because you were not allowed to stay with the team, travel with the team or sit in the dugout during the games. After all your hard work, it must still hurt that you missed out on the best thing about that summer – being part of a team…a *winning* team.

    And a special shout-out to Todd Halky for loaning me the videos that his father Bob filmed during the Eastern Regional tournament, as well as the Forestville game, that summer. You will never know how important those videos were in finishing this book. Thanks Todd! Thanks Bob!

    I met Chris Berman many years ago when we were both undergraduates at Brown University. He broadcast men's basketball games; I was the student-manager of the team. Over the intervening years, we would occasionally "bump into" each other, either at a business function or at some Brown sporting event, usually a football or basketball game against Yale. Our conversations always turn to reminiscing about our Brown experience. The last time we did so was at a Brown Alumni event in Rye, New York, in May. I asked if he would write the foreword to this book and he quickly agreed. Chris, I am so honored that you took time from your crazy schedule to write the foreword. Thank you, my friend!

    As a baseball rules expert and consultant, Rich Marazzi lives the life any baseball fan would love to live - every day is a baseball day. He has written several books about baseball, hosts a weekly radio show "Inside Yankee Baseball," and hosts a group of baseball fans called "Silver Sluggers," who meet weekly at the Derby (CT) Public Library to talk about baseball. It was his idea to add - *A Miracle in Williamsport* - to the title of my book. Thanks for the inspiration, Rich!

    Jim Carpenter, who covered the 1989 Little League tournament for the *Williamsport Sun-Gazette*, was so generous with his time, loaning me material from his personal files, sending me so much incredibly useful information, and sharing some of his personal recollections from 1989. He is now the Religious Editor for that paper. Thank goodness for people like you, Jim. The first time we spoke, I knew I was on the right track with this book. Thank you!

    To my friend and mentor, Mike Bielawa, thank you for pushing me forward. You have been so important, guiding me to complete this book. As the successful author of several fun books about baseball, I agree - "Let's write 2."

I remember the day I met Matt Rudy, a new golf buddy, and learned he was a senior writer for *Golf Digest*. I almost couldn't believe my good fortune to meet someone with his talents...Matt has co-authored many books about golf...and his willingness to guide me through the self-publishing process. Who knows if this book would have ever made it into print without his help? Matt, you have been so generous sharing your time, your talents and your ideas. Thank you!

So many others stepped up at crucial moments while writing this book, such as Mickey Herbert, whose story about his trip to the World Series in Oakland with the team I have included [Mickey, it must have been one of the best trips you ever took!], John DelVecchio, Ken Paul, Ray Baldwin Morag Vance, Rick O'Brien, Mike Riccio, and Bill Bloxsom of *The Trumbull Times*.

Every successful business venture needs a good attorney to provide advice at critical moments. Alan Neigher joined my team as the perfect man at the perfect time in the process. Thank you for your help, Alan!

Every book needs a cover, and one that really works with the subject matter. I am not sure what I would have done without my daughter Jennifer's talents in graphic design. Jenn, I know how hard you worked on it. Your *first* book cover – it's *beautiful*.

You also need a good book design. Once again, Jennifer did much of the initial layout, and then the talented Chris Poston stepped in to finish the task. The two of you worked well as a team. Thank you both for the long hours you devoted. I truly appreciate your time and effort.

While this may be my first book, I knew the importance of having a strong public relations team in place. Thank you to Ed Katz and Steve Gaynes of Katnip Marketing for joining my team as well. Let's have some fun!

My final shout-out and thanks goes to Mark Zampino, the Z-man, for his editorial expertise and guidance. Not only is Z-man a great writer, but he is a huge baseball fan, even if he loves the Cleveland Indians. Mark, you have been so patient with me and helpful. If I have missed anything it is clearly my fault. Z-man did yeoman's work on this book. Thank you, Mark!

Oh, did I just say *final shout-out and thanks*? Well...obviously, I cannot finish without recognizing and thanking my wife, Debbie, who has been incredibly patient with me as I worked to finish this book. Every morning and every night, I locked myself in my office...I needed to focus on the book; she quietly understood. Thank you!

And our children...Jennifer (and her husband Jeffrey), Christopher and Jessica (and her fiancé Sam)...I love you all. Never stop reaching for your dreams…

   And to everyone in my family who believed in me when I was not sure I could actually write a book. Thank you for your support as well.

   So…now you know the story. Thank you for allowing me to tell it. And remember…the fabric of baseball is based on sharing stories of historical moments and games you have experienced with others. Pass this story on…let it inspire those who are willing to listen to it. Have a wonderful day!

Shelton, Connecticut

August 2, 2014

ABOUT THE AUTHOR

I loved playing baseball when I was a kid, starting with Wiffle ball with my neighborhood friends, pretending that we were playing either at Yankee Stadium or the Polo Grounds in New York. Later, I played Little League and then high school baseball at Fairfield Prep. Unfortunately, I was never blessed with the skills to play baseball at Brown University. Years later, I finally finished my on-field career on a slow-pitch softball diamond in Trumbull.

Now I am absolutely certain you are asking yourself - just because I am passionate about baseball does not mean I have to write a book about the game. Good question! Let me answer that. While in college, I wrote game summaries of American Legion baseball games for a local weekly and called in game reports for Brown's baseball games as the team's statistician/ student manager. I really loved doing that. After graduating from Brown, I explored going into the business side of baseball but chose to obtain a graduate degree in accounting instead.

It wasn't long before I realized being a CPA involved lots of writing - writing financial statement footnotes and reports, writing reports on special projects and assignments, and writing letters to clients explaining oftentimes complex subjects. I also wrote lots of business articles to promote our firm's business. And I knew that I loved everything about the process of writing. So as I approached retirement, I created a personal *bucket list* and right near the top was – *write a book*.

Going to my first big league game, a World Series game no less, was incredible. It doesn't get any better than that. But it did. Who hasn't gone to a game with their glove, hoping against hope to catch a foul ball during batting practice or a homer in the bleachers at Fenway? I've been blessed. One of the first times I went to Fenway Park while living in Boston during my graduate school year at Northeastern University, I caught a foul ball off the bat of Cleveland's Johnny Ellis. Moments later, in fact…it was the next pitch…Ellis knocked another foul ball into the seats down the first base line, right at me, again. Got it! Oh my God! Do believe that? It happened, believe it!

The following spring, I went back to visit my alma mater, Brown University, to watch some baseball. Brown was hosting Princeton. My coach, Woody Woodworth, asked me to keep the scorebook that day. I've only seen one no-hitter pitched in person. And guess what? It happened that afternoon. And I was the official scorer. Can you believe that? The only no-hitter I ever saw and I was the official scorer.

That summer (1975) was also a magical season for Red Sox fans as they won the pennant, led by two of the best rookies Red Sox fans ever saw, Hall of Famer Jim Rice and Rookie of the Year and MVP Fred Lynn. And who could forget Game 6 of the 1975 World Series, "the greatest World Series game ever played?" Bernie Carbo's shot off the Green Monster to tie the game topped by Carlton Fisk's dramatic homer off the left field foul pole to win it in twelfth. There were more heroics in that game than any fan should expect to see in one game. Did you see it? Though the Series ended the next night when the Cincinnati Reds finally burst the Red Sox bubble in Game 7, 1975 was the best summer of my life. I went to more than 60 games at Fenway that year, caught a "Yaz" homer (his 309th) in a 9-3 win over the hated Yankees that July, a game that was televised nationally by NBC as its "Game of the Week", and witnessed so many exciting victories that year that my voice was never the same from all the cheering. When it was over, I went back home to Connecticut and got married. *What a year!*

The passion has never left. If I pass a group of kids playing, I stop to watch. I love to talk to other baseball fans about baseball, no matter where I am. I prefer sitting in the bleachers at Fenway Park to a front row seat next to the dugout at Yankee Stadium because the real fans hang out in the bleachers. When the National Anthem is sung, I always say "Play Ball" when it's over. What else can you say? Then of course, "Take Me Out to the Ball Game" was the first song our first child, Jennifer, learned to sing. And she hadn't even been born yet.

As to my baseball skills, I never had much talent, though I would play whenever I could. In high school I mostly rode the pines, but that's how I met the girl I would eventually marry – Debbie, my best friend and wife of 39 years.

Though I'm not talented at playing the game, I love to tell stories. And telling stories is how we pass on the legacy of the game from father to sons and daughters, grandfathers to grandsons and granddaughters, one generation of fans to the next. It's why a game is broadcast with a play-by-play announcer and a "color commentator", whose purpose is to explain the game and tell stories about it. The late Bart Giamatti often claimed that "baseball stories were at the heart of the appeal of our game. The history of baseball is an oral one."

I love to write, and love what I do. Writing a book about baseball means I get to check another item off my bucket list. Did I tell you I love baseball?